Jerome and the Jews

Jerome and the Jews

Innovative Supersessionism

WILLIAM L. KREWSON

WIPF & STOCK · Eugene, Oregon

JEROME AND THE JEWS
Innovative Supersessionism

Copyright © 2017 William L. Krewson. All rights reserved. Except for brief quotations in critical publications or reviews, no part of this book may be reproduced in any manner without prior written permission from the publisher. Write: Permissions, Wipf and Stock Publishers, 199 W. 8th Ave., Suite 3, Eugene, OR 97401.

Wipf & Stock
An Imprint of Wipf and Stock Publishers
199 W. 8th Ave., Suite 3
Eugene, OR 97401

www.wipfandstock.com

PAPERBACK ISBN: 978-1-4982-1822-1
HARDCOVER ISBN: 978-1-4982-1824-5
EBOOK ISBN: 978-1-4982-1823-8

Manufactured in the U.S.A.   MARCH 30, 2017

All Scripture quotations, unless otherwise indicated, are taken from the Holy Bible, New International Version®, NIV®, copyright © 1973, 1978, 1984, 2011 by Biblica, Inc.™ Used by permission of Zondervan. All rights reserved worldwide. www.zondervan.com.

To my loving wife, Bj,
and to my daughters, Char and Abby

Contents

Acknowledgments | ix

Abbreviations | x

Introduction: Jerome's Place in Christian Supersessionism | 1

1   A Survey of Recent Scholarship | 9

2   "Return to the Source": Jerome's Ambivalent Pursuit of Jewish Scripture | 30

3   "Back to the Hebrew Truth": Jerome's Ambivalent Quest for Jewish Truth | 70

4   "Bethlehem . . . Now Ours": Jerome's Ambivalent Remapping of Jewish Land | 99

5   "Ask the Jews!": Transforming Jerome's Supersessionism into a Basis for Christian-Jewish Dialogue | 138

Bibliography | 177

Subject Index | 193

Scripture Index | 205

Acknowledgments

I CANNOT FAIL TO acknowledge those whose investment in my life has made this book a reality. My thanks to my pastoral mentor and scholar, Dr. William C. Varner, who awakened my interest in the Jewish roots of the Christian faith and opened the door to academia for me. I am also grateful for the generous support of Cairn University's administration, which encouraged me to pursue doctoral work.

My advisor at Drew University, Dr. James Pain, helped to develop my interest in the early church. My doctoral supervisor, Dr. Virginia Burrus, further refined my concentration on the intersection of early Christian writers with Jewish ideas. Dr. Melanie Johnson-Debaufre also provided helpful guidance with my dissertation.

Finally, my deepest love and admiration goes to my wife, Bj, who listened to the ideas presented here, helped me to refine them, and encouraged me to pursue this work. "Omnia in gloriam Dei" (1 Cor 10:31).

Abbreviations

CCSL   Corpus Christianorum, Series Latina

CSEL   Corpus Scriptorum Ecclesiasticorum Latinorum

Ep.   *Epistle*

PL   Patrologiae Latina

Introduction

Jerome's Place in Christian Supersessionism

WHEN ASKED ABOUT THE Jewish people's aspirations for regaining the holy land in fourth-century Palestine, Jerome, the late ancient Christian ascetic and exegete, responds by casting perpetual blame on the Jews and redirecting divine blessing to himself: "Because you gave preference to these [forbidden] gods rather than the true God, you lost all that had been promised to you. In the gospel, the kingdom of heaven is promised to me."[1] The notion of the Christians as the only rightful heirs to "the kingdom of heaven" had been developing for almost three centuries before Jerome (Eusebius Hieronymus) was born of Christian parents. His birthplace was Stridon, in the northern part of the Roman Empire (in the western Balkans). He may have been born in the early 330s or perhaps the late 340s.[2] Jerome's family encouraged him to pursue a classical Latin education, and he studied in Rome under the famous rhetorician Aelius Donatus in about 360. Once trained in rhetoric, Jerome began a career in civil service, but after undergoing religious conversion and a monastic calling around 370 he went to Aquileia in northern Italy and then to the Syrian desert near Antioch. Here he began his study of the Hebrew language under the tutelage of a Jewish convert to Christianity. After several years of increasing conflict with his fellow monks, he settled in Antioch, where he received ordination as a priest in 377. Moving on to Constantinople, he studied under Gregory of Nazianzus and later relocated to Rome in 382. Due to his increasing reputation as a biblical scholar proficient in Greek, Latin, and Hebrew, Jerome

---

1. *Ep.* 129.5 (CSEL 56:172), English translation kindly provided by Dr. Bernard Prusak, Villanova University, 2009. Other English translations of Jerome's letters are from *St. Jerome: Letters and Select Works*; others are from *The Letters of St. Jerome*, and others are my own.

2. See the critical biographies of Cavallera, *Saint Jérôme*; Kelly, *Jerome*; and Rebenich, *Jerome*.

served as secretary and scholar in residence to Pope Damasus. However, within three years he was forced to leave Rome under suspicion of inappropriate motives with several women who had become his patrons.[3] Jerome ventured to Palestine and settled in the city of Bethlehem in 386, where he and his patron Paula established two respective monasteries and lived out the rest of their lives. Jerome continued his massive literary productions of commentaries, translations, and correspondence until his death in 419. Woven deeply into Jerome's massive literary works is the thread of Christian replacement of and supremacy over those who had earlier been the people of God. This theology of displacement, known as Christian supersessionism, was for Jerome a standard narrative of the Christian church. As we shall see, he gave that inherited narrative new layers and twists, igniting controversy and creating points of contact between himself and Jews.

DEFINING CHRISTIAN SUPERSESSIONISM

Christian supersessionism is the belief that the Jewish people and religion have been entirely replaced by the Christian people and religion, and that divine favor rests only with those (both Jew and Gentile) who follow Jesus as God's messiah. Jews therefore can find religious legitimacy only as members of the Christian church.

R. Kendall Soulen has described three types of supersessionism found in Christian history.[4] First, "economic supersessionism" teaches that the Jewish people prepared the way for the Christian church in the economy of redemption through their Old Testament religion, consisting of shadows and types in preparation for fulfillment in Jesus Christ. This version looks at the Old Testament cultus as foundational and temporary, divinely intended for replacement by the New Testament message. Consequently there is no validity to any current practice of Jewish laws and piety since the presence of Jesus has rendered all such rituals obsolete. This position does not attribute inherent sinfulness to the Jews and their religion; it simply renders post-Christian Judaism as an obsolete phase in the ongoing work of God—its time has expired.

Second, "punitive supersessionism" logically proceeds from economic supersessionism by declaring God's judgment on the Jewish people because

---

3. "He was convicted in an Episcopal court of clerical misconduct stemming from allegations of opportunism and sexual impropriety" (Cain, "Jerome's *Epitaphium Paulae*," 108).

4. Soulen, *God of Israel*, 29–33.

of their rejection of Jesus as messiah. The Christian church displaces the Jews due to the largely Gentile acceptance of the Jewish messiah and thereby enjoys God's favor, while the Jews in their rejection fall under God's wrath. This formulation places God in the role of the Jew hater. Faithful Christians therefore must imitate the divine attitude of retribution against the Christ-killing Jews. Christian proclamation of punitive supersessionism claims divine authority for its stance since to do otherwise would be to also risk divine disfavor. Reflecting this notion of punitive supersessionism is the *Adversus Judaeos* tradition, a body of literature written by generations of Christians who opposed the continuance of the Jewish race and religion.[5] These diatribes began in the second century and continued uninterrupted into the period of Late Ancient Christianity and beyond.

Soulen labels a third category as "structural supersessionism," in which the standard canonical narrative of the Christian church omits any reference to the God of Israel and the people of Israel. He asserts that the accepted story of the Bible rests on four main points in the plot line: creation, fall into sin, redemption in Jesus through the church, and the consummation of all things in eternity. Consequently, the narrative of Genesis 4 through Malachi is entirely absent. This version of the Bible's storyline becomes universalistic in scope and has no need for the unique people of Israel. In fact, the Jews are rendered utterly irrelevant. It is this Jewish-free account that is embedded in the historic Christian creeds, which omit the role and significance of the people of Israel in the canonical and ecclesiastical story. A positive word about Israel's past, present, or future is rare if present at all. When this non-Israel narrative is repeated by the Christian church, the embedded theology of replacement is reinforced. It is not surprising that Christian supersessionism and its attendant anti-Judaism have traveled together to the present day. Although the most obvious and egregious examples of supersessionism are found as expressions of the punitive type, economic and structural supersessionism serve as quiet supporters.

In the fourth century, Christian writers had little conception of theological self-definition apart from the supersessionist paradigm. While some authors might be cited for their virulent rhetoric of displacement in line

---

5. Listings of these works from the earliest texts to the Middle Ages are found in Williams, *Adversus Judaeos*, and Schreckenberg, *Die christlichen Adversus-Judaeos-Texte*. Some early authors include Barnabas, Justin Martyr, Tertullian, Hippolytus, Cyprian, Origen, Aphrahat, Pseudo-Ephraim, and Chrysostom, along with dialogues of Christians against Jews.

with punitive supersessionism, such as Ambrose[6] or John Chrysostom,[7] such extreme sentiments reveal the widespread influence and magnitude of a theology of contempt within the established church: "The *adversos Judaeos* tradition represents the overall method of Christian exegesis of the Old Testament. Any sermons, commentaries, or teachings based on scriptural exegesis of the Old Testament . . . will reflect this tradition of anti-Judaic midrash."[8] In this milieu Jerome was trained and prepared to replicate the Christian message couched in the all-too-familiar vocabulary of replacement and denigration.

JEROME AS INNOVATIVE SUPERSESSIONIST

Jerome expresses Christian supersessionism in complex ways. Like other Christian supersessionists, he refers to the Jews in both threatening and triumphalistic tones, typical of economic and punitive supersessionism. However, he cannot wear the label of structural supersessionist since he simultaneously and paradoxically rejects the legitimacy of the Jewish religion and holds a strong appreciation for Jewish connections to the Scriptures. Jerome rhetorically distances himself from Jews yet, at the same time, stays in close proximity to them: "If it is expedient to hate any men and to loathe any race, I have a strange dislike to those of the circumcision. For up to the present day they persecute our Lord Jesus Christ in the synagogues of Satan. Yet can anyone find fault with me for having had a Jew as a teacher?"[9] He denigrates the Jews for their rejection of the Christ, yet he honors their guardianship of what he calls the "Hebrew truth" (*Hebraica veritas*) and elevates them as teachers of Christians. Jerome embodies a fascinating contradiction that lead to three questions: How can he maintain Christian superiority and yet depend upon the Jews for their Hebrew Scriptures? Why would he argue vehemently for christological fulfillment of Old Testament passages and simultaneously defend certain contemporary Jewish interpretations of the same Old Testament books? What would motivate Jerome to pursue a life of monastic study in the ancient homeland of the Jews, and

---

6. He encouraged the burning of a synagogue in Callinicum (Parkes, *Conflict of the Church*, 166–68).

7. See Wilken, *John Chrysostom and the Jews*, 95–127.

8. Ruether, *Faith and Fratricide*, 121. For a brief survey of fourth-century writers, see Flannery, *Anguish of the Jews*, 47–65.

9. *Ep.* 84.3 (CSEL 55:123).

even hire them to teach him the Hebrew language, grammar, geography, and hermeneutical insights? I propose to answer these questions by examining the ambivalent expression of Jerome's attachment to and antipathy of the Jews and by offering proposals to explain his position.

First, I will examine his choice of texts for the Christian Old Testament. Jerome performs an unusual feat in his single-handed argument against the divine inspiration of the Septuagint and the elevation of the Hebrew text as the basis for his new Latin translation of the Old Testament. Following in the steps of Origen's third-century text-critical scholarship, Jerome furthers the task of purifying the sacred texts. Such a project brings him into tension with some church leaders, who castigate Jerome as an innovator of dangerous doctrines. Not only does he consult the Hebrew text of the Christian Old Testament (as Origen and others had done), but he claims its superiority over the supposedly inspired Greek text of the Septuagint. Jerome's position evolves over a number of years from a preference for the Septuagint to a settled conviction that the Hebrew Old Testament is the most accurate source for his new Latin translation. While there is some disagreement about Jerome's actual knowledge of the Hebrew language, most agree that he knew Hebrew well enough to legitimize his scholarly works. Various motivations may be behind Jerome's motivation for reverting to the Hebrew. It may be that he desired the stability of the Hebrew text in contrast to the multiple editions of the Septuagint, or perhaps he wanted to produce a truly Christian translation, unlike the Jewish, pre-Christian Septuagint. By rejecting the supremacy of the Septuagint, and with it the authority of the apocryphal books, Jerome stirs up fierce debate within the Christian church for years to come. An old friend, Rufinus, becomes an enemy over this issue, and the two exchange heated letters in which Rufinus castigates Jerome for hiring Jews as tutors who allegedly trick Jerome into introducing Jewish influences into Christianity. Jerome faces similar opposition from Augustine, who considered the Septuagint authoritative and sufficient. He urges Jerome to cease his Hebrew translation and maintain the Septuagint as the source in order to maintain a church unity centered on the supremacy of the Septuagint and established tradition.

His path to the Hebrew text was not a straight line, however. The ambivalence of Jerome's textual supersessionism surfaces when the entire range of his statements about the Greek and Hebrew texts are considered. Namely, he makes contradictory statements about the Septuagint—sometimes commending it, but usually condemning it. He consistently chooses the Hebrew text when the Septuagint differs, and as an answer to his critics he composes *Hebrew Questions on Genesis* to defend his textual selection and to illustrate the rich resources found only in the Hebrew. Only rarely have Christians cared to consult the Jewish text, and now a Christian monk argues in favor of it. With such actions Jerome blurs the traditional boundaries between Jews and Christians. At the same time, he inscribes the differences between Christianity and Judaism by arguing that the Hebrew text provides stronger support for christological interpretations of the Old Testament, in that the apostles quoted from the Hebrew rather than the Septuagint in certain significant passages.

The second expression of Jerome's ambivalent stance that I will examine is his hermeneutic of recovering ancient Jewish interpretations for Christian consumption. Jerome reflects his Christian predecessors and contemporaries by utilizing a hermeneutic of displacement in order to legitimize the Christian religion. In typical supersessionist fashion, he positions the fulfillment of promises to Israel as exclusively, and allegorically, for the Christian church. In contrast, he simultaneously employs historical exegesis of the dire predictions of judgment on Israel and directs fulfillment squarely on the guilty Jews, those of the past as well as those of his own time. Jerome's settled presupposition is that the spiritual church replaces carnal Israel, and such reasoning legitimizes his rereading of the Jewish promises as destined for the church and his rereading of the Jewish curses as for the Jews alone. In many of Jerome's writings he reviles the view, held by both Jewish Christians and some Gentile Christians (whom he names "Judaizers"), of a Jewish restoration to the land of Israel as a carnal reading and elevates a spiritual interpretation that sees the Christian church as the true referent. Such spiritualized readings are the common heritage of early Christian interpreters who embrace a supersessionistic hermeneutic and develop the rhetoric of contempt, of which Jerome is heir and to which his writings add in great measure.

Like most Christian supersessionists, Jerome lays claim to the heritage of Israel, selectively appropriating Jewish covenants while leaving only a denigrated "carnal" remainder behind for those from whom he borrows. He erects and reinforces the borders between Jews and Christians by selectively applying the blessings to the Christian church and assigning the curses to the Jews. Jerome is set apart from his contemporaries by his agility to travel back and forth across the border between Christians and Jews to retrieve valuable information for his own use. Acting as both judge and jury, Jerome selects texts and interpretations by navigating between Jewish historical and Christian allegorical readings. His method of selecting which meanings are for the Jews and which apply to Christians is inconsistent and unpredictable. He condemns the Jewish religion, castigates Christian Jews as imposters, and seems to prohibit others from enjoying the type of relationship he establishes for himself with the Jews and their traditions. Such bold moves were novel yet unsettling to the Christian community of the fourth century. They also reflect the depth and color of Jerome's complex supersessionism. In this stance of innovation and ambivalence, Jerome places himself as the supreme mediator of sacred texts and the master architect of the boundary between Christians and Jews.

The third expression of Jerome's pioneering supersessionism I will explore is his attempt to inscribe Christian identity onto the Jewish homeland. When Constantine's mother, Queen Helena, selected sacred places in Palestine for Christian churches, the sacred land of Israel officially became the Christian holy land. Christianized Palestine enriched the lives of believers who made pilgrimage to three sacred places: Jerusalem's Church of the Resurrection (later known as the Holy Sepulcher), the Church of Eleona on the Mount of Olives (associated with the ascension), and the Church of the Nativity in Bethlehem, Jesus' birthplace. After years of residing in several cities throughout the Roman Empire, Jerome is mystically drawn to the ancient homeland of the Hebrew people. His pilgrimage becomes permanent when he establishes a monastery in Bethlehem and lives out his remaining years. Jerome believes that he and other like-minded Christians who settle in Palestine as pilgrims are the rightful heirs of the Jewish homeland. His supersessionist mindset not only embraces the hermeneutical notion of being a part of the new Israel, but he expands the notion to include the sacred space of Bethlehem in his image of a properly constructed Christian identity. Like the biblical heroes in Joshua's time, he and other Christians displace the disobedient people of the land and take up their residence as God's new people. He further Christianizes the map of Palestine by denigrating Jewish cities in their ruined condition and substituting the idealized towns sanctified by Jesus' presence as recorded in the gospel accounts. These places become the Christians' promised land, suitable as pilgrimage sites for believers throughout the Roman Empire and made more accessible by Jerome's new translation of Eusebius' travel atlas. His letters invite fellow Christians to join him in walking through the holy land as if he were Moses or Joshua leading his followers into the promised land. Jerome continues to perplex his readers when at times he considers the true holy land to be the spiritual Jerusalem in heaven. In another layer of complexity, Jerome situates Bethlehem over against Jerusalem as the most sacred space in the holy land. As in other expressions of his supersessionism, Jerome again reveals his seemingly contradictory disposition in the concept of the sacred space.

The conjunction of text, exegesis, and land form a fascinating web of complexity in Jerome's formation of Christian supersessionism. In spite of Jerome defining the boundaries that separate Jews and Christians in traditional terms, he continually crosses them at will to form relationships for his personal benefit and his readers' instruction. In the land of the Jews he hires Jewish rabbis to teach him more of the Hebrew language as well as the meaning of geographical names known only in the Hebrew tongue. Jerome uses rabbis as living encyclopedias of Judaica to mine their prized resources of inaccessible knowledge. His presence in the land naturally feeds his hunger for Judaic background, rabbinic interpretations, and firsthand knowledge that provides source material for his commentaries. To his readers, Jerome lives on both sides of the fence—simultaneously appreciating the Jews for what he can gain from them and deprecating them for what they have done to his Christ. In order to obtain the resources he desires, he creates a personal gateway in the fence to which he alone possesses the key.

In summation, Jerome is set apart from other contemporary Christian writers in the particular depth and complexity of his sustained ambivalence toward the Jews. His position is inherently unstable, and such instability reveals itself in intriguing ways. While maintaining his basic stance of sole Christian legitimacy, he regards the Hebrew language as a divinely chosen means of communication, the Jews as privileged preservers of sacred truth, and their holy land as radiating the sacred impress of divine history and the supernatural power of sacramental presence. He builds relationships with Jewish people in his attempt to profit from their trusted linguistic, theological, and geographical insights. Conversely, Jerome speaks against the Jewish other with vicious language, assigning them and their religion to damnation. The very existence of Jewish Christianity is to him an oxymoron, since he allows no middle ground between the two religions except his own. Jerome is an enigma—he both blurs the line between Christians and Jews yet inscribes it more deeply. The language of supersessionism allows him to sustain these contradictions, and yet his rhetoric of Jewish necessity has within it a constructive path ahead.

Chapter 1

A Survey of Recent Scholarship

As a fourth-century Christian writer, Jerome's attitude of hostility to the Jews comes as no surprise. Christian theology had bred a sense of superiority for several centuries before him, and Christian culture had begun to legislate its dominance since the time of Constantine. However, before a study can be made of Jerome's statements about the Hebrew text, Jewish exegesis, and the ancient Hebrew homeland, the larger backdrop of the Christian culture of supersessionism must be considered as it has been studied in recent times. The context of Jerome's Christianity and its interface with the Jewish people and their religion has been the subject of several centuries of scholarly thought. In order to understand Jerome's statements about Jews, and to provide the proper context for appreciating his selective appropriation of their resources coupled with his active relation with living Jews, I will summarize the history of Christian and Jewish relations in the early centuries of the church.[1]

REVIEW OF THE SCHOLARSHIP OF CHRISTIAN SUPERSESSIONISM

This review will examine four historical phases of scholarship and include the important literature in each period as well as an appraisal of the presuppositions behind each position. Without an awareness of the flow of thought by historians and theologians, one cannot appreciate the difference between late ancient Christians' conception of themselves in relation to the Jews and those who afterward read the literature with attentiveness to subsequent history and theological strategies. With an appreciation of the

---

1. My survey is partially based on that of Jacobs, "Lion and the Lamb," 97–105.

progress of scholarship and its theological implications, there is a growing hope for meaningful conversation and understanding in the contemporary discussions between Christians and Jews.

The First Phase: Christian Supersessionism of Judaism

The critical study of early Christianity began in the nineteenth century with Adolf von Harnack, whose work set the stage for much of the scholarship of the twentieth century.[2] His 1902 publication of *Die Mission und Ausbreitung des Christentums in den Ersten Drei Jahrhunderten* pioneered the way for much of the subsequent scholarship of ancient Christianity. His "uncritical reading of Judaism through the filter of Christian polemic" resulted in his own emulation of the supersessionism found in the early texts.[3] Scholars now realize that his Christian supersessionism inspired him to draw conclusions about Judaism of the early centuries without any historical evidence. As an example of his prejudicial stance against Jews, Harnack writes:

> As Christianity is the only true religion . . . it follows that it can have nothing in common with the Jewish nation and its contemporary cultus. The Jewish nation in which Jesus Christ appeared, has, for the time at least, no special relation to the God whom Jesus revealed. Whether it had such a relation at an earlier period is doubtful . . . but certain it is that God has now cast it off, and that all revelations of God, so far as they took place at all before Christ . . . must have aimed solely at the call of the 'new people', and in some way prepared for the revelation of God through his Son.[4]

Further, Harnack asserts several positions that successive scholarship accepted at face value, one of which is that the synagogue's expansion throughout the Roman Empire prepared the way for Christianity's arrival and acceptance, and in this way the Jews served to prepare the fertile ground in which Christianity grew. He also states that the synagogue had transformed itself from a temple-based cultus into a universal moral influence and laid the groundwork for the acceptance of the universal Christian message, thus demonstrating that in many ways the servant Israel worked for the good of

---

2. Harnack's educational background and his importance as a foundation for recent patristic study is developed by Chestnut, "Century of Patristic Studies," 36–45.

3. White, "Adolph Harnack and the 'Expansion,'" 108.

4. Harnack, *History of Dogma*, 148.

the exalted Christian church. Harnack argues that Judaism sought converts with missionary zeal from the Gentile areas into which it penetrated. Finally, reflecting his position of Christian superiority and Jewish weakness, Harnack views ancient Christian polemics against Jews as purely fictitious rather than real since he reasons that the Jews would not have been able to mount such attacks in their deteriorating condition. Shaye Cohen reveals that the weak ground of Harnack's argument was the underlying Christian supersessionism that dominated nineteenth-century Protestantism in Germany: Harnack's "theological history was (at least here) more theology than history, and a theologian does not need footnotes."[5]

The following narrative, reflective of Harnack's influence, summarizes the dominant conversation in the nineteenth and early twentieth centuries about early Christian history and the church's relation to the Jews.[6] Christianity arose within Judaism of the first century. Christians, both Jewish and Gentile, had ongoing contact with Jews in society and in the synagogue until a crucial turning point in history—the destruction of the Jewish temple in 70 C.E. This social disruption forced Christian Jews to separate from their fellow Jews, who were under Roman persecution, and to flee from such persecution in Jerusalem for safety in the Transjordian city of Pella. Their exit effectively negated Jewish influence in the new Christian church, signaled their demise, and elevated Gentiles to leadership in the emerging Christian church. The final Jewish Revolt in 135 C.E. served to cement the split between Jews and Christians, institutionalizing differences between rabbinic Judaism and proto-orthodox Christianity. The growing Gentile influence in the church established itself in the major cities west of the land of Palestine and included cultural and philosophical adaptations from the Greco-Roman world, whereas the Jews remained defeated and lived throughout Diaspora cities in their self-imposed isolation. From this point in history, Christian contact with Jews surfaced only in debate or to enhance Gentile understanding of the Old Testament. Additionally, this model portrays rabbinic Judaism as a parallel movement to orthodox Christianity, which had quickly institutionalized itself in resistance to mainstream Christianity in the first century. The Council of Jamnia (Yavneh) brought unanimity to the diverse Judaisms that existed prior to the destruction of the temple by affirming the dominant position of rabbinic Judaism. The "curse on the Minim [Christians]" finalized the split

---

5. Cohen, "Adolph Harnack's 'The Mission and Expansion of Judaism,'" 168.
6. This is based on Reed and Becker, "Introduction," 4–5.

from the Jewish side by excluding Jewish and Gentile Christians from the synagogue. Jewish contact with Christians was rare as evidenced by vague references in the Talmud, and Christian contact with Jews was just as rare. Such supposed relations were merely rhetorical devices to serve Christian interests but had little historical verity.

It was with this narrative in mind that scholarship in the nineteenth and early twentieth centuries read the early Christian texts. Such a reading simply reflects the tenor of the primary sources, as these scholars consider their writings to be essentially historical and theologically correct. Further, they encourage the rhetoric of triumphalism by naming the Jewish religion in the first century "Late Judaism," revealing an assumption that first-century Judaism was near its demise. This account of Late Judaism begins its description of "Early Judaism" with the era of divine revelation and covenant kingship (1200–539 B.C.E.). However, Israel forfeited divine blessing after its exile (539 B.C.E.–70 C.E.) and thus began the slow dying process that resulted from its own disobedience.[7] The creation of the term "Late Judaism" as an infirm and dying organism prepared the way for its replacement by the young and energetic "Early Christianity." Thus, these scholars repeat the arguments of early Christian writers that history validated God's selection of the Christians as worthy replacements after the destruction of the Jewish temple in 70 C.E. and the final defeat by Rome in 135 C.E.

In summary, the supersessionist presuppositions of these historians led to the definition and codification of historical nomenclature and historiographic categories. Only later will other scholars point out evidence of Judaism's continued growth and conclude that those who neglected such data were shaped by their own paradigm of theological supersessionism, as Cohen pointedly observes: "The fact that Judaism continued to flourish and develop for millennia after the period of 'late Judaism' did not affect the currency of the term, because the term derived not from historical analysis but from theological belief."[8] Since supersessionism had been embedded in the theological world of such scholars, it is not surprising to find their historical evaluations permeated with such an outlook. Harnack and

---

7. Jaffee, *Early Judaism*, 16. See the timeline chart of the various names used by scholarship (17). Jaffee surmises that the term was first used by Wilhelm Bousset in 1903 (22–23 n. 7). Gabriele Boccaccini writes, "The continued vitality of Judaic worlds for centuries after the emergence of Christianity as its own family of religious worlds reminds us that what is late Judaism for Christian theology is just the beginning for the history of Judaism" (*Middle Judaism*, 16).

8. Cohen, *From the Maccabees to the Mishnah*, 7.

many European Christians not only exude Christian supersessionism but also exaggerate it by effectively silencing the reality of the Jewish voices. They strip the Jews of their historical reality and perform the ultimate act of supersession—rendering the Jews essentially non-existent. This form of hyper-supersessionist triumphalism was soon to find itself in a struggle for its own survival.

The Second Phase: Christian and Jewish Separation with Continuity

The early twentieth century saw several writers engage early Christian and Jewish relations with a far different tone than Harnack's. The most notable author was James Parkes, whose writings dramatically reversed the course of scholarship established by Harnack. Parkes pioneered the exploration of the Christian roots of anti-Semitism in *The Conflict of the Church and the Synagogue: A Study in the Origins of Antisemitism*, published in 1934, after many of the Russian pogroms in Eastern Europe but prior to Nazi Germany's rise. His work not only challenged the prevailing supersessionist tone of Christian scholars, but it identified supersessionism with anti-Semitism, tracing the roots of anti-Semitism from the New Testament until the time of Visigoth Spain. In an even more devastating blow, Parkes laid the blame for anti-Semitism directly on the New Testament documents. His radically revised view challenged traditional supersessionistic readings. While his book was prophetically insightful, it was politically ineffective in the face of the coming world war. Its real strength was that it prepared the groundwork for the postwar period's fresh perspective, namely, that two religions emerged at the end of the first century, each a viable religion in its own right. Notably, his third chapter is titled "The Parting of the Ways," pointing to the concept that other scholars would later develop.[9]

A French Jewish scholar set another new and surprising course while personally in flight from Nazi persecution. Jules Isaac lost his wife and daughter during the war, which prompted his desire to examine the Christian roots of the anti-Semitism that he personally faced in Christian Europe. His book, published in 1943 before the end of the war, places the blame for anti-Semitism on Christians, who he suggests have misread their own New Testament. His original preface says: "The reader may wonder to what religion the author belongs. This is easy for him to answer: none. But

---

9. Reed and Becker, "Introduction," 10 n. 31.

his whole book witnesses to the fervor that inspires and guides him, fervor for Israel, fervor for Jesus, son of Israel."[10] His concluding proposition states:

> Whatever the sins of the people of Israel may be, they are innocent, totally innocent of the crimes of which Christian tradition accuses them: they did not reject Jesus, they did not crucify him. And Jesus did not reject Israel, did not curse it: just as 'the gifts . . . of God are irrevocable' (Rom. 11:29), the evangelical law of love allows no exception. May Christians come to realize this at last.[11]

This bold approach is quite astonishing—a Jewish scholar actually defends the Christian New Testament as philo-Semitic. Unlike Parkes, who pronounced the New Testament texts guilty, Issac attempted to rescue the Christian texts by sanitizing them. However, only after the brutal effects of the Holocaust became known would a chorus of voices emerge to forge a new path. It was that historic tragedy that cut short this period of scholarly research and began a radical rereading of the underlying supersessionist attitudes in both primary texts and scholarly minds.

The Third Phase: Christian and Jewish Separation with Equal Legitimacy

The Jewish Holocaust changed the direction of Late Ancient Christian scholarship. Since that time, many historians and theologians (both Christian and Jewish) have placed blame for the Holocaust on an overt anti-Judaism and an incipient anti-Semitism found in New Testament texts and early Christian writings. Their proposed trajectory begins in the first century and leads to Nazi Germany. Postwar scholars began the discussion to consider "whether Christianity itself was, in its essence and from its beginning, the primary source of anti-Semitism in Western culture."[12] The nearly unanimous answer was yes. Christian texts and Christian religion were forced to take some or all of the blame. Answers range from anti-Judaism in the New Testament documents to the later developments by a Gentile-dominated church that institutionalized an anti-Semitic supersessionism in church and state laws. A broad range of proposals surveyed below reveals the ongoing evaluative discourse in both Jewish and Christian traditions.

---

10. Isaac, *Jesus and Israel*, xxiv.
11. Ibid., 385.
12. Gager, *Origins of Anti-Semitism*, 13.

A Survey of Recent Scholarship

Building on the seminal work of Parkes, who initiated the idea of two separate religions, scholars began to develop the notion of a living and vigorous Jewish voice behind the well-known Christian rhetoric. Jewish French scholar Marcel Simon proposed such a view of Jews in actual conflict with Christians in his book, published in 1948 soon after World War II, in direct response to the anti-Semitism revealed in the Holocaust. In contrast to those Christian supersessionistic historians who had painted Judaism as a dying religion, Simon regards the Jewish religion as filled with immense vitality. He stridently challenges Harnack's characterization of imaginary Jewish foes and argues for an actual and energetic Judaism that debated with and even proselytized Christians. Simon contends that vigorous attempts to curtail contact between Jews and Christians in the early centuries, as well as the establishment of imperial laws against Jewish missionary endeavors, are an obvious sign that such activities actually existed. He also notes the important difference between anti-Jewish polemic (where Christians argue about their theological differences with Jews) and anti-Semitism (where Christians express hostility toward Jews in light of their theological and racial differences). His emphasis on the attractiveness and vitality of Judaism spoke in direct opposition to the consensus of scholars who had already pronounced its weakness and irrelevance. Simon's contribution develops Parkes's pioneering concept of "the parting of the ways." Thus began a new approach to Jewish and Christian relations, marked by the separation and independence of Jews and Christians during their mutual religious development—a development that saw marginal polemical contact. A noted historian observes Simon's impact: "Having set out to change the consensus reigning at the time he first wrote, Simon achieved that goal to such an extent that his reconstruction become the dominant view."[13] Scholars thereafter began to follow Simon's lead and use words like "single," "early," and "decisive" to describe the separation between Christians and Jews. It is important to note that Simon did nuance the discussion of Jewish and Christian separation with words like "progressive" and "gradual" to describe the emergence of Talmudic Judaism and the split with Christians.[14] His contribution to twentieth-century scholarship lies in redirecting the discussion away from the consensus of a supersessionist model of victory and defeat to a view of separate religions with equal vitality. This "parting" paradigm came to dominate the field by the late twentieth century, as

---

13. Baumgarten, "Marcel Simon's *Verus Israel*," 473.
14. Simon, *Verus Israel*, xi–xii.

Judith Lieu observed in 1994: "By now the model appears to have become a truism which needs no justification."[15] Scholars tended to begin with this notion as a presupposition that influenced their conclusions, as will be seen in the following survey of leading authors and their unique contributions to this new model.

Alan Segal's *Rebecca's Children* explains the "two ways" using a family metaphor found in both Jewish Midrash and in the Christian New Testament:

> It is a startling truth that the religions we know today as Judaism and Christianity were born at the same time and nurtured in the same environment. Like Jacob and Esau, the twin sons of Isaac and Rebecca, the two religions fought in the womb. Throughout their youth they followed very different paths, quarreling frequently about their father's blessing.[16]

Segal places their parting after the final Jewish revolt, with both siblings constructing firm boundaries to protect themselves from mutual contamination, and sees a parting that was neat and clean with each side insulated from the other.[17] His work is an attempt to construct a model of initial contact and early separation. Since Segal chooses to emphasize the difference between the two religions, his conclusion of an early and clean separation is buttressed by selective evidence of partings rather than a comprehensive treatment of ongoing evidence of contact.

In 1989, James Dunn chaired the Second Durham-Tubingen Research Symposium on Earliest Christianity and Judaism. His concluding summary of those presentations noticeably moves the discussion away from the simple and clean break as presented by earlier historians:

> "The parting of the ways" properly speaking, was very "bitty", long drawn out and influenced by a range of social, geographical, and political as well as theological factors. On the one hand, we must beware of thinking of a clear or single "trajectory" for either Christianity or Judaism; and we should also avoid using imagery that necessarily implies an ever-widening gap between Christianity and Judaism. On the other hand, "Christianity" *did* emerge from a Jewish matrix, and "Christianity" and "Judaism" *did* become

---

15. Lieu, "Parting of the Ways," 102.
16. Segal, *Rebecca's Children*.
17. Ibid., 173.

separate and distinct, so that the basic image, "the parting of the ways", is appropriate.[18]

Dunn's earlier work on the subject, entitled with the plural *Partings*, provides more specifics about those partings.[19] He proposes three movements that eventually yielded an irreversible separation. The first two are described in the book of Acts, occurring when followers of Jesus broke away from temple worship beginning with the death of Stephen and when Paul took the message of Jesus to Gentiles. The third parting resulted when Christians affirmed the divinity of Jesus. Dunn notes that contact did take place between Jews and Christians as recorded by Ignatius, Barnabas, and Justin and as mentioned in the Talmud, placing such interaction between the Jewish revolts (70–132 C.E.) and noting that "whatever interaction there continued to be [was] at the margins."[20] In summary, Dunn argues for a decisive parting, as the traditional model suggests, but he relegates Jewish and Christian dialogue to the fringes. He seems to concentrate on the notion of discontinuities, thereby paying little attention to the contact between Jews and Christians, naming the contact as "marginal" and therefore inconsequential to meaningful discussion.[21] Once again, the presupposition of a definitive parting creates the framework for the discussion of the evidence.

Several other scholars represent similar perspectives. Porter and Pearson present a case for understanding the ancient split between Christians and Jews as based mainly on ethnic differences, arguing that the church progressively became more Gentile and left its Jewish past behind. Their proposal is for an extremely early theological split during the time of Jesus, for which they find confirmation by later official Roman witnesses.[22] Reflecting a similar model, Stephen Wilson sees a Jewish-Christian dialogue in the early years (70–170 C.E.) but considers such relationships to have greatly diminished in the following centuries. He reads the early evidence as demonstrating a "degree of variety and complexity in Jewish-Christian interaction that was to become increasingly rare."[23] As in the case of Dunn, Wilson's vision may be clouded by an already determined parting model

18. Dunn, *Jews and Christians*, 367–68.
19. Dunn, *Partings of the Ways*.
20. Ibid., 238.
21. Dunn corrects himself in the second edition of this book.
22. Porter and Pearson, "Why the Split?"
23. Wilson, *Related Strangers*, xiv. He criticizes Ruether's single christological cause, citing a variety of reasons for the parting that form the basis of his book (xv, 301).

that predisposes him to explain contacts between Jews and Christians as "rare" and therefore inconsequential. In a desire to further nuance the partings, Wolfram Kinzig discusses four levels of separation between Jews and Christians: doctrinal (i.e., distinctive christological creeds) and theological (shared beliefs) separation in the area of theoretical reflection, and institutional and popular piety levels of separation in the domain of religious practice. He argues that some separations occurred early (doctrinal, institutional) and were brought about by the leaders, while other divisions occurred later (practical piety) due to popular practice, which lagged behind the official stance of separation.[24]

In reaction to this consensus, Miriam Taylor argues that the supposed discussions between Christians and Jews are rhetorical devices without historical foundation.[25] Taylor sees Simon's "conflict model" as too stereotypical to be real since it uses images of Jews and Judaism. Her stated desire becomes her interpretative presupposition—to remove any reason that Christian anti-Semitism may have to justify itself. She therefore refuses to see any historicity in the accusations made by Christians and states that Christians invented their anti-Jewish attacks without any Jewish provocation. Taylor suggests that if the texts are read as reflecting reality, then Christians would be justified in their caustic responses because the Jewish threat would be real. With such a provocation from the Jews, guilt for Christian anti-Semitism would be removed. However, she argues that if the texts are read as merely rhetoric, then Christians alone are to blame. Her account has met with several critiques of her thesis, including that of Wolfram Kinzig, who points out numerous omissions of scholarly literature, factual errors in the primary sources, and faulty assumptions.[26] Taking the same stance as Taylor, David Rokeah denies the reality of polemical texts between Jews and Christians after 135 C.E., stating that "no Jewish work has been preserved which might have caused their composition or which reacted to them."[27] Such arguments on the negative side of the "rhetoric versus reality" debate have reminded scholars to be cautious in assuming that there must be historical veracity behind every anti-Jewish polemic.

Other scholars discuss the subject of the Christian and Jewish division with a more nuanced approach. William Horbury, a leading proponent of

---

24. Kinzig, "'Non-Separation,'" 27–29.
25. Taylor, *Anti-Judaism and Early Christian Identity*.
26. Kinzig, review of *Anti-Judaism*. See also the reviews by Paget and Kaminsky.
27. Rokeah, *Jews, Pagans, and Christians in Conflict*, 211.

the parting model, argues for a mediating position, choosing to see "an interplay between stereotypic views and more genuine perception."[28] Stephen Spence presents a work on first-century Rome that elevates the social dimension of the relationship between synagogue and church into the discussion. He argues that it is wrong to appraise the parting on ideological grounds alone, since life is not lived in that abstract arena. Instead, a combination of concrete, local, and social realities must be evaluated to provide a glimpse of life on the ground.[29]

While some scholars were defining and defending the parting model, others were searching out its cause, in particular the roots of theological anti-Semitism. Like Parkes before her, Rosemary Ruether pointedly lays the blame for Christian anti-Semitism on the New Testament documents. Rather than cleansing the texts of anti-Semitism as Isaac and others attempted, Ruether endeavors to expose their true interpretation as embraced by the early anti-Judaic Christian leaders. She rejects the separation of theological anti-Judaism and sociological anti-Semitism which had been proposed by Simon: "For Christianity, anti-Judaism was not merely a defense against attack, but an intrinsic need of Christian self-affirmation. Anti-Judaism is a part of Christian exegesis."[30] Her work created an important shift in the view of the role of the New Testament in shaping anti-Semitism through discussion of the gospels' blame of Jewish leaders for Jesus' death and Paul's rejection of the Mosaic law.[31] Gregory Baum, himself a Christian convert from Judaism, initially wrote to defend the sanctity of the New Testament's attitude toward Jews.[32] However, Ruether challenged his thinking, and nine years later he admitted that her influence and that of others finally caused him to change his mind.[33] This recasting of the Christian message has found

---

28. Horbury, *Jews and Christians in Contact and Controversy*, 24.

29. Spence, *Parting of the Ways*. His use of the rational choice theory, as developed by Rodney Stark, attempts to inject new insights into a purely textual discussion (2–11).

30. Ruether, *Faith and Fratricide*, 181.

31. For other examples, see her chapter "The Growing Estrangement" (64–116).

32. Baum, *Is the New Testament Anti-Semitic?* He reveals his debt to Jules Isaac's work and spirit by carrying it forward: "Many passages from the New Testament read out of context do seem to express resentment against the Jews. We must study these texts to come to the true meaning of the sacred authors. We must also examine the positive evaluations of the Jewish people in the writings of the New Testament" (8).

33. Baum, preface in Ruether, *Faith and Fratricide*, 3. On pages 4–6 he recants his earlier work, *Is the New Testament Anti-Semitic?*

some acceptance in Jewish and Christian theological scholarship.[34] Ruether revived Parke's innovations and established the evaluative stance present within Christian circles.

In summary, post-Holocaust scholars have attempted the difficult task of reframing the relation of Jews and Christians in the early centuries. In their effort to preserve the legitimacy of both groups, they have employed a host of metaphors to describe the separation while maintaining a stance of equality. Such images include the following: two circles that initially overlap and then move apart forming two separate circles; a textile whose strands have separated; a broad river with two currents that carve out two smaller streams; familial metaphors of mother-daughter or arguing siblings; and a main highway with arterial roads.[35] The parting model has dominated scholarly discussion since the Holocaust. However, as scholars continue to consider the primary texts in light of the parting concept, they are beginning to doubt its adequacy. Their questions about serious problems in the parting model are beginning to unseat established thought. A new direction is emerging in a yet undetermined path.

The Fourth Phase: Christian and Jewish Continuity and Interchange

The latest trend in early Christian and Jewish scholarship attempts to chart a new course away from the dominant parting model. As recent scholars step back to examine the evidence of Christian and Jewish interaction in light of a supposed parting, they express skepticism of the dominant paradigm and offer constructive alternatives toward an understanding that better explains all of the data. For example, John Gager characterizes the parting model's long tradition as "bad history" and "distorted."[36] Judith Lieu, at the forefront of much of the recent discussion, is dissatisfied with the parting notion because of its universalizing tendency to draw conclusions about Judaism and Christianity instead of focusing on the variety of experiences lived out in the specific and local situations. Using several case studies, she effectively dismantles the neat categories of the theologically oriented parting model and introduces her own paradigm: "In trying to make sense

---

34. For an attempt to reinterpret the New Testament texts and later Christian misunderstanding of them, see Bibliowicz, *Jews and Gentiles in the Early Jesus Movement*.

35. For charts that map nine models, see Goodman, "Modeling the 'Parting of the Ways,'" 119–29.

36. Gager, "Parting of the Ways," 64.

of the uncertainties of the early history of Christianity it may prove to be theologically less satisfying but sociologically more persuasive to picture a criss-crossing of muddy tracks which only the expert tracker, or poacher, can decipher."[37] Her metaphor is less linear than the parting scheme and sees continual interaction between both groups, with boundaries being difficult to set in universal terms. It is noteworthy that her work persuaded James Dunn to change his mind about his previous stance. In the second edition of his work on the partings of the ways, he reverses his earlier position of a 135 C.E. split, admitting, "In the fifteen years since I wrote *Partings*, however, I have come to recognize that the process was still more complex than I first envisaged."[38] The significance of Dunn's admission must be given serious consideration. His reconsideration of the evidence led him to propose a much longer process of separation and to position the decisive break between Christians and Jews in the post-Constantinian era. Dunn's admission reveals the current climate of reevaluating categories and repositioning conclusions about early Christian and Jewish relations.

Representing Jewish studies, Martha Himmelfarb takes up a similar sentiment by citing evidence, both archaeologically and textually, of continued Jewish and Christian interaction in the fourth century that belies the official line propagated by both rabbis and church fathers. She criticizes Jewish scholarly tradition: "Historians have perhaps not been suspicious enough of the story rabbinic Judaism tells about its own emergence as the dominant form of Judaism in the Roman world."[39] These recent movements toward reevaluation of the scholarly tradition attempt to freshly examine all the evidence of interplay between Christians and Jews that earlier scholars either ignored or marginalized.

In summary, the last seventy years have seen the discussion progress from a paradigm of parting (advancing from a "single" and "early" to "multiple" and "late") to a fresh look at all the evidence, especially the points of contact between Christians and Jews. No one has personified

---

37. Lieu, "'Parting of the Ways,'" 119. She explores this in more detail in *Image and Reality*.

38. Dunn, *Partings of the Ways*, xii. "I accept Judith Lieu's critique that the imagery of 'ways' parting is too simple.... What I began to see more clearly, however, is that if the beginning of the process of the partings of the ways was much less clear-cut, then the outcome of the process was even less clear-cut and the final parting a lot longer delayed than I had allowed" (xii, xix). He describes first-century evidence of Jewish and Christian disagreement in "From the Crucifixion to the End of the First Century."

39. Himmelfarb, "Parting of the Ways Reconsidered," 56.

this reevaluation of the evidence more than Daniel Boyarin. He offers the metaphor of a wave theory "of shared and crisscrossing lines of history and religious development.... In this model, convergence is as possible as divergence."[40] Boyarin does not ignore the obvious differences between Jews and Christians (both Jewish and Gentile), but he is quick to point out the intertwined relationships between them that are revealed only in a subtle reading between the lines of Jewish and Christian texts. In a more recent work, Boyarin describes the borders between Judaism and Christianity as "contact zones" with hybridity that were erected by heresiologists, both Jewish and Christian. These writers are seen to have carved out their own domains in reaction to the other, especially by attacking as heretics those who straddled the fence between both groups (with Jewish Christians labeled "Judaizers" by Christians and Christian-like Jews named "Minim" by Jews).[41] He argues against some sort of natural "parting of the ways" and for "an imposed *partitioning* of what was once a territory without border lines."[42] Inherent in Boyarin's reconstruction is interaction and interpenetration between Jews and Christians as well as the creation of parallel boundaries. He sees the dialogue continuing well past traditional parting dates, suggesting that "Judaism and Christianity were not separate entities until very late in Late Antiquity."[43]

The radical revision of established tenets begun by the scholars mentioned above received further impetus in a colloquium at Princeton University in 2002 entitled "The Ways that Never Parted," and the subsequent book containing many papers from the conference, edited by Adam H. Becker and Annette Yoshiko Reed.[44] The dominant theme of this scholarly trend is to examine the ongoing dialogue and development of each religion, rather than concentrating on differences between Jews and Christians and their consequent acts of separation. They believe that too often the notion of parted ways has been assumed and reread back into the texts. In addition, they highlight evidence from the third and fourth centuries of close interaction between Jews and Christians that earlier scholars had either ignored or dismissed as irrelevant. This new direction commences

40. Boyarin, *Dying for God*, 8, 9.
41. Boyarin, *Border Lines*, 17–22. See also his "Semantic Differences." His earlier article "Justin Martyr Invents Judaism" illustrates his thesis.
42. Boyarin, *Border Lines*, 1.
43. Boyarin, "Semantic Differences," 78.
44. Reed and Becker, *Ways that Never Parted*.

by deconstructing the parting model's rigid definitions and by reevaluating the primary textual and archaeological evidence in order to read new social constructions of identities.[45] For example, some of their specific problems with the parting model include the historicity of the Council of Yavneh (Jamnia), the nature of the Birkat Ha Minim (the Curse on the Heretics), and the historicity of the Jerusalem church's flight to Pella during the First Jewish Revolt. Many of these scholars dehistoricize supposed events and consider them to have been constructed by the ancient authors, both Christian and Jewish, for propagandist purposes. Most significantly, this new wave of scholars rejects a major presupposition of many earlier writers of "the equation of rabbinic Judaism and proto-orthodox Christianity with 'Judaism' and 'Christianity' in a global sense."[46]

Such scholars wish to equalize the discussion by elevating the silenced voices of shared experiences. While they acknowledge that most writers who defend the parting model do admit qualifications for that construction, they consider that such qualifications "serve, in the end, to dilute the explanatory power of the model as a whole—and, as a result, to raise questions concerning its heurism for historical research and its undue influence on the contemporary practice of scholarship."[47] In addition, they offer a proposal for a decisive separation between Christians and Jews in the fourth rather than the second century, while suggesting that the division was never as complete as the earlier model suggests. These authors see convergences and further partings with further convergences that continue down through later centuries. Reed and Becker hesitate to label this new trajectory as an established model, since they claim that the critique of the old one is ongoing.[48]

For example, Paula Fredriksen addresses the issue directly by resisting the entire concept of two ways, since the category originated with

---

45. Reed and Becker rehearse Parkes's admitted qualifications of his own parting model, from which their critique of it begins, and point out that subsequent scholars failed to consider Parkes' warning in establishing a rigid parting scheme (*Ways that Never Parted*, 17).

46. Ibid., 19; see also 5–6.

47. Ibid., 18.

48. Ibid., 23. "The contributions in this volume demonstrate the inadequacy of any monolithic model that seeks to theorize the relationships between 'Judaism' and 'Christianity' without considering the socio-cultural and discursive specificities that shaped interactions between Jews and Christians in different cultural contexts, geographical locales, and social strata" (x).

the "winners" who dictated terms to all those who came after. Her move is to think outside the winners' box and suggest that "to get some critical purchase on the ancient literature . . . we need to re-incarnate the charged rhetoric of the *contra Iudaeos* tradition within the lived human context of ancient civic life."[49] This contextual analysis attempts to compare the rhetoric of the texts with the social reality of the day. She concludes that the parting model misinterprets the situation between Jews and Christians and most of the Mediterranean culture as well through the seventh century. On a familiar note often sung by those who deconstruct the parting model, Fredriksen says: "The constant reiteration of civil and ecclesiastical legislation suggests the opposite [of a parting]: legal prescription cannot yield social description."[50] She concludes that a parting between Jews and Christians did not exist until the invasion of Islam.

In light of the foregoing discussion, I have described this fourth phase in scholarship as a move to emphasize the "continuity and interchange" between Christians and Jews. While I admit that such a label may tend to simplify a complex discussion, I believe that it correctly identifies the contemporary direction in early Christian and Jewish studies. It is obvious that the scholars mentioned above resist a simple description of the relationship between Jews and Christians and point out the tangled details that challenge the dominant model. Most writers expend effort to dismantle the parting model but are hesitant to construct a new one.[51] James J. D. Dunn suggests that "the simplest imagery to use is the process in which the parts of a garment pull over time, the threads that begin to break under the stresses of 'wear and tear,' or the popping of rivets as heavy seas put unbearable strain on the metal plates of a ship, and so on."[52] Adele Reinhartz attempts to illustrate this complexity by expanding on the parting of the ways metaphor:

> What we have is a fast-moving, multi-lane highway. Cars and their passengers move in and out of these lanes as speed, destination, weather, and roadwork require; they travel in the same direction at various points as they merge and diverge, exit and double back.

49. Fredriksen, "What 'Parting of the Ways'?," 36–37. See also Fredriksen and Lieu, "Christian Theology and Judaism," where she further advances the argument by showing the dependence of Christians on Jews as the other in the construction of self-definition.

50. Ibid., 62.

51. Reed and Becker said that it was "neither the right time nor the right place to propose a new model" in their book first published in 2003.

52. Dunn, "From the Crucifixion to the End of the First Century," 29.

Yet the lanes themselves are marked off from each other, and the exit signs are clearly labeled. If the highway does not finally split in two until the beginning of the fourth century, neither does it move along without its share of exits and parallel routes.[53]

This contemporary stage brings scholars into a new conversation of complexity and creativity as they "part ways" with former modes of analysis and look for fresh ways to plot the past and instill direction for the future.

ASSESSMENT OF THE PROGRESS OF SCHOLARSHIP

The discussion of early Christian and Jewish relations has progressed from the echoing and amplifying of ancient supersessionist views by nineteenth-century European scholars to a dawning of non-supersessionist historiographical viewpoints encompassing equality and shared legitimacy. The challenge for scholars within the fourth phase is to construct a new model that would achieve some sort of consensus, one that embraces the diversity of interplay between Christians and Jews while at the same time refuses to discount the lines of separation and distinction inscribed by the Christian authors of ancient texts. Judith Lieu attributes the frustration of achieving this goal to a failure in identifying the parting of "ideas, or people, or systems" and to the difficulty of understanding the evidence presented in the texts, specifically, who is doing the labeling and who is being labeled. She also questions the frequency of Jewish and Christian interaction, and this uncertainty leads her to express skepticism regarding the conclusion: "That the ways parted at different places, at different times, and in different ways is now obvious, but equally unproductive of greater understanding. The dividing of paths does not determine who will choose to walk along them, nor who will journey without regard to their different destinations."[54] Rejecting the entire category of parting, Adiel Schremer explains: "When discussing the subject of Jewish relations with nascent Christianity from the point of view of early rabbinic sources, the concept of the 'parting of the ways' is misguided and inapplicable: it presupposes two *equal* parties, and this is a deeply Christianizing notion. Contrary to this implied view . . . the discourse that emerges from the early rabbinic material is that of

---

53. This summary is explained in detail by Reinhartz, "Fork in the Road?," 292–93.
54. Lieu, *Christian Identity in the Jewish and Graeco-Roman World*, 306.

exclusion."⁵⁵ I suggest that the difficulty in formulating a coherent model of Christian and Jewish relationship reveals the depth of complexity and unpredictability in the accounts of personal interaction that are recorded in the early Christian writings, especially those of Jerome.

It is within this tangled milieu that I see Jerome's relations to the Jewish text, exegesis, and land. Listening to his varied rhetoric and observing his personal contact with Jews resists easy formulation and confirms that a rigid explanation of Jerome's relation to Jews, either by classic supersessionism or a parting of the ways, is an utter impossibility. I interpret Jerome's texts with an eye to both his rejection of the Jewish religion in light of his Christian supersessionism and his agreeable dependence upon his Jewish teachers as sources of truth for the Christian church.

Scholarship has made significant progress in the last two hundred years—from the first attempt that inherited and reflected the early Christian texts' attitudes of replacement and lack of mutual contact, to the later refinement of two separate but equal religions rivaling for adherents, to the present rereading of the texts without a predetermined separation. The reimagining of Christian and Jewish relations continues to envision a future that nuances Christian supersessionism and builds bridges of understanding and appreciation for both.

RECENT SCHOLARSHIP ON JEROME

Since the early 1990s, scholars have explored new horizons in studies about Jerome. A brief critical biography has been written by Stefan Rebenich that includes fresh translations of Jerome's varied literary works. Rebenich's aim "is to reflect upon and revise some elements of the traditional portrait of Jerome that even today determine his representation across various denominational and ideological borderlines."⁵⁶ In the field of textual studies, Adam Kamesar focuses his research on Jerome's *Hebrew Questions on Genesis* to determine Jerome's motivations behind this work as well as his broader translations of the Old Testament from the Hebrew texts.⁵⁷ Kamesar also surveys the earlier work of Origen and finds a Septuagint based approach dominating Origen's writings, in spite of the inclusion of Hebrew in his *Hexapla*. Kamesar then offers his argument that Jerome's conversion to the

---

55. Schremer, *Brothers Estranged*, 98.
56. Rebenich, *Jerome*, ix.
57. Kamesar, *Jerome, Greek Scholarship, and the Hebrew Bible*.

superiority of the Hebrew came much earlier than scholars had previously supposed. Further, he argues that Jerome included rabbinic views as an essential part of Christian biblical interpretation only after "critically sifting" the material for his readers.[58] This work intricately explores Jerome's sophisticated approach toward presenting the Hebrew text alongside the Septuagint and his eventual elevation of the Hebrew text above the Greek. Kamesar raises the level of awareness regarding Jerome's linguistic and textual inclinations and aptitudes. Along a similar line is the work of C. T. R. Hayward, whose translation of Jerome's *Hebrew Questions on Genesis* includes an illuminating introduction and commentary.[59] While less of an analysis of Jerome's motivations and abilities, this work illustrates the breadth of learning that Jerome acquired from his Jewish teachers and his justification for passing this knowledge onto his Christian readers. Hayward argues that Jerome wrote to deflect his critics' suspicion concerning his Jewish sympathies and "to show his detractors that Jewish understanding of the Scriptures is often correct."[60] This valuable work affords ample resources to illustrate Jerome's attraction to rabbinic traditions and textual readings.

Others scholars have written about Jerome's construction of his literary persona. In particular, Mark Vessey explores the strategies that Jerome employs in his self-description as a fourth-century author. Vessey finds in Jerome's writings that Jerome "is most clearly seen putting on his public faces, the masks in which he will appear—and through which he will speak—to his various audiences."[61] The most popular mask of Jerome is that of a Christian writer, in particular, a writer cast in the mold of Origen for the Latin church. Vessey's most recent work is a reception study of Jerome, where he locates the end of *jeromanesque* with Erasmus, who began to dismantle a millennium of "myth, legend, and pious invention" and replace it with the beginning of "the Jerome of philology, history, and biography."[62] Another recent study of Jerome by Megan Hale Williams looks at his life and work "as a cultural program."[63] She addresses the challenge of understanding Jerome as scholar and monk, two seemingly opposite identities fused into one by Jerome.

---

58. Ibid., 179.
59. Hayward, *Saint Jerome's Hebrew Questions on Genesis*.
60. Ibid., 14.
61. Vessey, "Jerome's Origen," 137. See also his article "From *Cursus* to *Ductus*."
62. Vessey, "Jerome and the *Jeromanesque*," 229.
63. Williams, *Monk and the Book*, 261.

Juxtaposing Jerome's elevation of scholarship regarding the Hebrew text as a Christian duty alongside his emphasis on ascetic constraints necessary to obtain Hebrew knowledge, Williams presents Jerome's "carefully fashioned construct" of himself as "an implicit but unchallengeable authority as arbiter of biblical truth."[64] Her valuable work illumines Jerome's association with Jewish teachers and continues the work begun by Kamesar in drawing out the implications of such interreligious associations. However, her intent is to examine this relationship in light of Jerome's role as scholar and monk. She thus concludes that Jerome's closeness to Jews was deliberately cast by him as "monastic self-mortification" to balance the impression made by his scholarly efforts.[65] Several recent works on Jerome have been by Andrew Cain, who edited a volume based on the conference "Jerome of Stridon: Religion, Culture, Society and Literature in Late Antiquity," at Cardiff University in 2006.[66] This volume includes discussions of Jerome as a hagiographer, writer of letters, and theologian, as well as Jerome's biblical scholarship with papers on philology, exegesis, and translation. It concludes with topics relating to the fifth through the sixteenth centuries. The editors note that "scholarship on Jerome is thriving like never before," with an "unprecedented flurry of research activity, especially in the past two decades."[67] Of the eighteen articles, two deal specifically with issues related to Jerome and the Jews.[68] This work represents the breadth of scholarship and international interest currently active in studies about Jerome. Andrew Cain also published his own work specifically on Jerome's letters, arguing that they reflect propaganda designed to elevate Jerome's status among his readers. Cain's book examines Jerome's "sophisticated use of literary artistry to construct spiritual and intellectual authority for himself through an idealized epistolary self-presentation."[69] While limited to Jerome's letters, this work positions Jerome's self-promotion as largely defensive, responding to the critics who disliked his extreme ascetic notions or his Hebrew based exegesis.

Centering on the issue of Jerome and the Jews, several recent works merit attention. Hillel Newman has produced a detailed work that remains

64. Ibid., 123.
65. Ibid., 231.
66. Cain and Lossl, *Jerome of Stridon*.
67. Ibid., 1.
68. Cameron, "Rabbinic Vulgate?"; and Newman, "How Should We Measure Jerome's Hebrew Competence?"
69. Cain, *Letters of Jerome*, 6.

untranslated from Hebrew,[70] but he has subsequently written several articles that investigate Jerome's knowledge of the Hebrew language and his relationship to Jews and their homeland. Newman's linguistic skill in Hebrew and Latin lend weight to his arguments in favor of Jerome's knowledge of Hebrew, and Newman's critical readings of earlier scholarship coupled with creative readings of Jerome's texts provide fresh proposals. In particular, Newman argues persuasively that Jerome attacks Christian millenarians in order to deflect charges brought against himself for his close relationship to Jews.[71] In a similar vein, Michael Graves has advanced the knowledge of Jerome's use of Hebrew[72] and has contributed to the discussion of Jerome's attacks on Christian Judaizers who adopted Jewish interpretations of Old Testament prophecies.[73] Finally, Andrew Jacobs looks at late antiquity through the lens of postcolonial criticism, proposing that Jerome (among others) exhibited his power over the Jews by his knowledge of them, which simultaneously produced an attraction to them. Jacobs highlights Jerome's discourse about his Jewish teachers as it constructs his Christian identity, one that produced a complex mix of contradictory sentiments composed of "desire and need for the Jewish other that authenticated Christian power and its fear and anxiety generated by Jewish otherness."[74] It is this "double vision" of "mistrust and appropriation" that Jacobs articulates in Jerome's utilization of Jewish knowledge for Christians.[75]

With this review of the scholarship of supersessionism and Jerome, we are better prepared to analyze Jerome's traditional anti-Jewish stances and rhetoric accompanied by his unconventional acts of appropriation. Both of these paradoxically prepare the way for the creation of alternative supersessionist structures. In particular, his continual need for Jewish resources forces him to maintain personal relationships with living Jews. While Jerome writes as if he is delegitimizing the Jews, he acts as one justifying their existence. These unintended juxtapositions serve to illustrate the fragility of Christian supersessionism and pave the way for contemporary opportunities for Christian and Jewish interaction.

---

70. Newman, "Jerome and the Jews."
71. Newman, "Jerome's Judaizers."
72. Graves, *Jerome's Hebrew Philology.*
73. Graves, "'Judaizing' Christian Interpretations."
74. Jacobs, *Remains of the Jews,* 14.
75. Ibid., 60.

Chapter 2

"Return to the Source"
Jerome's Ambivalent Pursuit of Jewish Scripture

IN A LETTER TO Marcella, a widowed patron in Rome, Jerome responds to her questions about one of the psalms by rejecting the Septuagint's readings and preferring another basis of the original text: "Therefore, it remains for us to return to the source, the Hebrew words, and see how they are written."[1] Such words likely sounded radical for Latin-speaking Christians in the fourth century, who were using sacred texts of the Old Testament written in Latin that had been translated two hundred and fifty years earlier from the Greek language. Jerome equipped himself for a lifelong battle against the ingrained Christian tradition. He learned the Hebrew language, secured ancient Hebrew scrolls, hired Jewish teachers, visited the forbidden territory of synagogues, settled in the ancient Israelite homeland, and obtained financial support for his literary endeavors. As a result of these iconoclastic actions, Jerome revised the narrative of Christian supersessionism by redirecting the source of the Christian Old Testament to the Hebrew texts.

Jerome's life reads in one particular way like no other Christian writer in the first thousand years of the Christian church—he elevates the authority of the Hebrew Old Testament and its contemporary Jewish exegetical interpretations, providing a place for the excluded Jews among the voices of Christian interpretive tradition. This fact about Jerome was understood in his own time. A younger contemporary, Augustine, acknowledges Jerome's Hebrew erudition twice in his *On Christian Doctrine*, calling him "the learned Jerome" and "an expert in both languages [Hebrew and Latin]."[2]

---

1. *Ep.* 34.4 (CSEL 56:249).
2. Augustine, *On Christian Doctrine*, 111 (4.7.15), 129 (4.20.41).

In a later work Augustine recognizes the uniqueness of Jerome's translation skills: "In our time has come the Presbyter Jerome, a most learned man and a scholar of all three languages; and he has translated these same Scriptures into Latin, not from the Greek but from the Hebrew."[3] No other contemporary Christian, including Augustine, attempted to bridge the gap that separated the Greek- and Latin-speaking Christians from the Jews who spoke Hebrew. Jerome penetrated the region that had been off limits for centuries. Fourth-century Christian culture breathed an increasingly anti-Jewish sentiment, as reflected in the *Adversus Judaeos* tradition since the beginning of the church. From the second century the Gentile Christian church defined itself as the true Israel; that is, the Gentile church inherits the role and destiny of God's ancient people and with it the Jewish Scriptures.[4] What began as a position of replacement later led to a theology of contempt. As the Roman Empire became more influenced by Christianity, its laws took on a similar anti-Jewish stance.[5] For example, Constantine outlawed proselytizing by Jews in 315, and soon after Emperor Constantius forbade marriages of Jews and Christians. In 388 Emperor Theodosius reversed his decision that would have forced Christians to pay for the damage they caused to a Jewish synagogue. Thus, the Jewish people and their religion fell under assault from the state as well as the church. No one embodies this anti-Jewish spirit of Christian supersessionism more than Jerome's contemporary in Constantinople, John Chrysostom. His sermons against the Jews reflect the dominant views of the post-Constantinian Christian church: the Jews are cursed as Christ-killers; avoid them at all costs![6]

Yet, tucked away in a monastery in Palestine, a monk steeped in Jewish insights authored translations and commentaries on the Old Testament Scriptures grounded in the Jewish traditions. Jerome stands firmly in his commitment to Christian superiority over Judaism and staunchly defends the church's creedal authority. His steadfast Christian orthodoxy was recognized when, almost a thousand years later, he was made one of

---

3. Augustine, *City of God*, 884 (18.43).

4. The concept of the Gentile church as the "true Israel" is first found in Justin in his *Dialogue with Trypho*: "For we are the true spiritual Israel and descendants of Judah, Jacob, Isaac, and Abraham" (11.5). See Richardson, *Israel in the Apostolic Church*, 9–14.

5. For a general description of fourth-century Christians who set the tone of Jerome's world (Eusebius, Hilary, Chrysostom, Ambrose, Epiphanius) and the church councils and civil laws that culminated in the Theodosian Code of the fifth century, see the seminal work of Parkes, *Conflict of the Church and the Synagogue*, 151–95.

6. Wilken, *John Chrysostom and the Jews*.

the four doctors of the Western church.[7] However, Jerome's supersessionism was of a different sort than his contemporaries. With his mission to "return to the source," Jerome set himself against the prevailing tradition. The Christian church in the West had been reading Latin translations since the second century. There may have been a single Latin translation of the Bible that was copied repeatedly, resulting in corrupted copies, or perhaps there existed multiple translations of biblical books. One thing was clear: confusion among the copies brought confusion among Christians.[8] This state of affairs caused Pope Damasus to charge Jerome with revising the Old Latin translation. He began his series of fresh translations in 384 with the gospels, followed by the Psalter and several other books of the Old Testament, and he used the Greek Septuagint, which was considered the authoritative source for the Christian church. Some six years later, around the year 390, he reversed this practice and began to use the Hebrew text as his exclusive source.[9] Over the next fifteen years Jerome produced translations of each of the Old Testament books. Such a replacement of the traditional Christian Greek Old Testament with a Hebrew one put him in dialogue with his Jewish contemporaries and at odds with his Christian friends. This daring move by Jerome eventually convinced the later Christian church to "return to the source," but the process was fettered by misunderstanding, hatred, personal insults, and ecclesiastical disunity. In this chapter I will consider Jerome's displacement of the traditional Christian Old Testament and appropriation of the traditional Hebrew text as expressed in his commentaries, his prologues to his translations, and his correspondence. These writings reveal Jerome's strategies, apologies, and controversies with his critics as well as his ambivalent approach to textual displacement. It is of major significance that one individual should attempt to reorient the foundation of textual authority from an enshrined Greek model to a largely unknown and at times despised Jewish one, and that on his own authority.

---

7. Ambrose, Augustine, Jerome, and Gregory I were so named in 1298.

8. The "Old Latin" (*Vetus Latina*) refers to all of the translations and citations of the earliest form of the biblical Latin texts. Scholars are divided over the question of an early, single Latin version with multiple recensions or multiple translations with multiple recensions (Kedar, "Latin Translations," 300–301; Schulz-Flugel, "Latin Old Testament Tradition"; Burton, *Old Latin Gospels*. For more information, see http://www.vetus-latina.de/en/index.html).

9. Chronology is based on the work of Williams, *Monk and the Book*, 267–301.

"Return to the Source"

JEROME'S PREFERENCE FOR THE HEBREW TEXT

Jerome, settling in Bethlehem in 386, continued his earlier translation project of the Old Testament from the Greek Septuagint, using Origen's *Hexapla* located nearby in the coastal city of Caesarea. His choice of the source text was dictated by the prevailing view of the Christian church, whose traditions reinforced the dogma that God had inspired the Septuagint before the coming of Christ for later use by Gentile Christians. While Jerome claims to have translated all of the Old Testament books from the Septuagint,[10] extant evidence exists for only the Psalter, Job, and the prologues to the Song of Songs, Proverbs, Ecclesiastes, and Chronicles.[11] The years surrounding 386–390 are significant, for these mark a change in Jerome's source text from the Greek to the Hebrew.

Progressive Awakening

Scholars are divided on the timing and motivation behind Jerome's alteration of foundational texts.[12] Some argue that the year 390 represents a personal rejection of the Septuagint, renouncing his earlier commitment to the inspiration of the Septuagint and beginning his translation from what he now considers the Hebrew truth (*Hebraica veritas*). For example: "It is a fascinating study to observe how every one of his points is slowly clarified and how the value of the Septuagint is more and more reduced until, at the end, he pronounced judgment against the Septuagint and against the theory of inspiration."[13] Others see a much earlier date for Jerome's conversion to Hebrew and place it during the time he spent in Rome, c. 382–85.

---

10. For example, *Ep.* 71.5 (CSEL 55:6): "Doubtless you already possess the version from the Septuagint which many years ago I diligently revised for the use of students" and *Ep.* 134.2 (CSEL 56:263): "We are experiencing a great shortage of Latin speaking scribes in this province and that is why I am unable to obey your orders, especially regarding the edition of the Septuagint which has been marked with asterisks and obelisks; also, I have lost a large part of my earlier work because of someone's dishonesty" (White, *Correspondence between Jerome and Augustine*, 228).

11. Rebenich, *Jerome*, 53–54. Rebenich assumes that Jerome translated only those books rather than the entire Old Testament.

12. Summarized by Kamesar, *Jerome, Greek Scholarship, and the Hebrew Bible*, 41–50.

13. Schwarz, *Principles and Problems of Biblical Translation*, 28.

Primary evidence for this view is found in the letters written during this period, wherein he exhibits a clear preference for the Hebrew.[14]

The crux of the argument centers on how to interpret Jerome's positive statements about the Septuagint during the years before his apparent conversion to a more Hebraic approach about the year 390. The following passages demonstrate his affection for the Septuagint. Living in Rome in 384, he writes: "I am not discussing the Old Testament, which came from the Seventy Elders in the Greek language.... This may be the true translation which the Apostles have approved."[15] In a prologue to his translation of Chronicles from the Greek, written in 389, he says: "The seventy translators, who were filled with the Holy Spirit, translated the true text," and they changed the Hebrew text "on the authority of the Holy Spirit."[16] A change in Jerome's tone can be detected in his commentary on Ecclesiastes written in 389. Here the Hebrew is in play alongside the Greek. In the preface he explains:

> Translating from the Hebrew, I have adapted my words as much as possible to the form of the Seventy, but only in those places in which they did not diverge far from the Hebrew. I have sometimes referred also to Aquila, Symmachus, and Theodotion, so as not to deter the reader's interest by too much novelty, nor, on the other hand, to follow the rivulets of opinions, omitting, against my conscience, the source of truth.[17]

His conscience whispers to him that the source of truth is the Hebrew text. It is this new consciousness that will soon direct all of Jerome's future literary endeavors.

At the same time he was translating from the Greek, he was writing letters with answers based on the Hebrew by providing exegetical solutions to questions from Pope Damasus and several others.[18] This evidence contradicts the view that his initial conversion to Hebrew did not occur until c.

---

14. Graves, *Jerome's Hebrew Philology*, 87 n. 43.

15. *Preface to the Four Gospels* 16–20; *Biblia Sacra* 1515. English translations of the prologues are by Kevin P. Edgecomb (http://www.bombaxo.com/prologues.html).

16. *Prologue to Paralipomenon from LXX* (PL 29:402).

17. *Commentary on Ecclesiastes*, preface (CCSL 72:249).

18. Letters 18A, 20, 25, 26, 28, 29, 30, 32, 34, 36, 37. The concept of Hebrew truth first appears in a letter written in 383: "It is from the Hebrew codices that the truth must be extracted" (*ex Hebraeis codicibus veritas*) (*Ep*. 20.2 [CSEL 54:105]). According to Markschies ("Hieronymus und die *Hebraica Veritas*," 147–48), the exact phrase *Hebraica veritas* first appears in 393 (*Ep*. 49.19 [CSEL 54:383]). The concept appears to be present before the technical term is used.

390, when he began his Old Testament translations from Hebrew. A better explanation for the apparent contradiction between Jerome's adherence to the Septuagint and his devotion to the Hebrew is that this awareness came to him gradually, beginning with a nascent phase and growing stronger over time. In the years before 390, his preference for the Hebrew text motivated him to favor Origen's hexaplaric recension rather than the others, especially that of Lucian. His simultaneous attachment to both languages is reflected in his writings, and attempting to resolve the ambivalence is difficult.[19] It would seem that expediency, coupled with a text-critical preference for Origen's hexaplaric revision (as opposed to the other recensions), was Jerome's rhetorical approach during these years. Kamesar summarizes: "Since all theological and exegetical discussion took place on the basis of that translation [the Septuagint], he was not about to burn his LXX and cut himself off from the rest of the Christian world."[20] This approach did not last for long.

In the year 392 Jerome began translating the Old Testament using the Hebrew text as his source.[21] Writing to a friend a year later about his recent translation of the prophets, he puts in no uncertain terms which source text bears the truth: "If you read the books of the sixteen prophets which I have rendered into Latin from the Hebrew . . . and compare the old version with my rendering, you will then clearly see that the difference between them is that between truth and falsehood."[22] It is important to remember that Jerome had no conception of what scholars now take for granted, namely, that the Septuagint reflects a different Hebrew text type from the Hebrew text Jerome read. This other source text underlying the Septuagint agrees at times with Hebrew manuscripts that were discovered in the twentieth century near the Dead Sea. Jerome presupposed that there was only one Hebrew source and that it was fixed, in contrast to the state of the Septuagint. His quest for that original text is the presupposition behind his passion for the *Hebraica veritas*.[23]

---

19. Kamesar proposes that Jerome had a dual allegiance to the two texts and argues against a supposed conversion in 390 (*Jerome, Greek Scholarship, and the Hebrew Bible*, 49–58).

20. Ibid., 55.

21. Eventually his entire translation of the Old and New Testaments would be called the Latin Vulgate. In his own writings, he uses the term "Vulgate" to refer to the common Latin translation used in his day. See Tkacz, "*Labor Tam Utilis*."

22. *Ep.* 49.4 (CSEL 54:349).

23. Muller, *First Bible of the Church*, 25–45. See also Williams, *The Monk and the*

Unashamed Reversal

The Christian world of the late fourth century contentedly presupposed that the Greek Septuagint was inspired by God for use by the Gentile Christian church, in spite of contrary claims found in the *Letter of Aristeas* and Philo. Early Christian writers asserted this, and later writers embellished it. Jerome confronted it and demolished it. "The most serious charge Jerome had to face while translating the Old Testament according to the Hebrew text consisted in the argument that he was rejecting the divinely inspired version of the Septuagint and *eo ipso* [by that itself] Judaized the Old Testament."[24] One aristocratic Roman Christian accused him of sacrilege, not for any doctrinal error against the Christian creeds, but for Jerome's translation of a word in the prophets.[25] Most of the prologues to his translations contain justifications for resorting to the Hebrew, and a few of his letters are apologetic in his own defense.[26] For example, responding in about 405 to the questions from a Gothic pastor about many of Jerome's translations, he replies: "I am criticized, as you say, for having avoided this rendering in my Latin translation."[27] As this letter reveals, Jerome's translation had not only reached into the heart of the Roman Empire, but his work had created enough discussion and agitation to prompt such a lengthy letter full of exegetical questions to the translator in faraway Bethlehem. Jerome's reply to one who was upset over his view of the Hebrew superiority was was to deny the Septuagint's inspiration and to strongly defend the Hebrew text's supremacy.

The reason for such conflict stems from the entrenched view of the Septuagint's superiority at that time. The standard narrative concerning the Septuagint originates from the *Letter of Aristeas*, dated c. 170 B.C.E.[28]

Book, 67–73 and Jellicoe, *The Septuagint and Modern Study*, 29–58. Jellicoe's book builds on the classic study by Swete, *An Introduction to the Old Testament in Greek*. The most recent comprehensive work is by Marcos, *The Septuagint in Context*.

24. Rebenich, "Jerome: The 'Vir Trilinguis' and the 'Hebraica Veritas,'" 63.

25. Jerome translated Jonah 4:6 using the word "ivy" for the Hebrew word *qiqeion* instead of the Old Latin's "gourd." See his explanation in his *Commentary on Jonah* 4:6 (CCSL 76:414–16).

26. Under the classification of "apologetic," Cain lists three of Jerome's letters (57, 106, 112) that specifically deal with exegetical and translational subjects (Cain, *Letters of Jerome*, 209–10). Many others contain references to the Hebrew text.

27. Ep. 106.54 (CSEL 55:275).

28. *Letter of Aristeas*, 7–34. Critical approaches invalidate the historicity of the letter, for example, Wasserstein and Wasserstein, *Legend of the Septuagint*, 25–26.

King Ptolemy II Philadelphus (285–246 B.C.E.) of Egypt sponsored the translation to add the Jewish texts to his vast library in Alexandria, and he commanded that the Jewish high priest in Jerusalem send seventy-two translators to render the Hebrew Torah into Greek. The *Letter* describes their scholarly work and the collation of their manuscripts into a finished text.[29] Later writers, both Jewish and Christian, mention this narrative and add their own embellishments.[30] Philo of Alexandria (c. 15 B.C.E.–50 C.E.) describes the story from the *Letter* and injects the idea of the translators' divine inspiration, considering the translators to be prophets.[31] However, Josephus (37–100 C.E.) omits any mention of its inspiration in his description of the Septuagint's conception.[32] Rabbinic texts contribute further to the legend by describing how the translators met in isolated cells and, adding another miracle, how they produced a unanimous translation in every single detail.[33]

Early Christian writers found the Septuagint ideally suited for use by Gentiles. They reasoned that it was commissioned by a Gentile king, sanctified by apostolic use in the New Testament, and rejected by the Jews of the early Christian era. It is not surprising that Gentile Christians, emboldened by the prevailing supersessionism, appropriated the sacred text of the Jews used in the Diaspora. Those who defended, perpetuated, and embellished the legend include Justin Martyr (100–165) who innovates that, in addition to the Pentateuch, the prophetic books were also translated and included in the Septuagint.[34] The concept of its divine inspiration and inherent

---

29. The story of the Septuagint consists of a frame around another story, constituting only one sixth of the letter. Gruen proposes that it was written to celebrate the strength of the Jewish community in Alexandria even to the extent of subtly mocking the Ptolemaic king ("Letter of Aristeas and the Cultural Context of the Septuagint").

30. The following chronological survey of authors is found in Muller, *First Bible of the Church*, 46–83.

31. *De Vita Mosis* 2:26–44.

32. *Antiquities of the Jews* 12.11–118.

33. Baraitha in Megilla 9a–b; also Mekhilta on Exodus 12:40; Massekhet Sepher Torah 1:8–9; Massekhet Sopherim 1:7–8; Midrash Tanhuma Exodus 19 (cited in Wasserstein, *Legend of the Septuagint*, 55–75). Segal argues that the Talmudic mention of altered translations (or mistranslations) has no historical basis; rather it betrays the theological agenda of the rabbinic sages: "The assumption that second- or third-century Palestinian rabbis would have preserved authentic memories of the original text of the Alexandrian Torah is contradicted by the literary and archaeological evidence" ("*Aristeas* or Haggadah," 172).

34. *First Apology* 31.2–5; *Dialogue with Trypho* 68.7–8, 71.1–2.

perfection, probably borrowed from Philo,[35] is first seen in the writings of Irenaeus (120–203): "For all of them read out the common translation [which they had prepared] in the very same words and the very same names, from beginning to end, so that even the Gentiles present perceived that the Scriptures had been interpreted by the inspiration of God."[36] Clement of Alexandria (150–215) mentions its divine origin: "It was not alien to the inspiration of God, who gave the prophecy, also to produce the translation, and make it as it were Greek prophecy."[37] Tertullian (155–220) is silent about the miracle but is the first Christian writer to refer to Aristeas,[38] and Pseudo-Justin (c. 260–300) is the first Christian to mention the isolated cells along with the miracle.[39] Origen (185–254) is silent about its inspiration and similarly Eusebius (260–340) writes about God's providence in the translation but not the miracle.[40] Cyril of Jerusalem (315–386) is the first Christian to include all twenty-two Old Testament books in the miraculous translation.[41] Finally, Jerome's contemporary Epiphanius (315–403) provides the longest description of the legend and innovates by situating the translators as working in pairs in the miraculous story.[42]

Jerome began to dismantle the entrenched Christian attachment to the Septuagint using the following strategy. First, he denied the myth of divine origin by delegitimizing its veracity:

> I do not know who was the first author whose lie constructed seventy cells in Alexandria in which they were divided and yet all wrote identical words, since Aristeas ... and long after Josephus, have reported no such thing, but write that they were assembled in a single hall and conferred together, not that they prophesied. For it is one thing to be a prophet and another to be an interpreter; in one case the Spirit predicts future events, in the other

---

35. Seidman, *Faithful Renderings*, 53. "The account of the composition of the Septuagint undergoes both a political and a semiotic shift ... for the Fathers, the Septuagint is a perfect document *despite* its having been composed by Jews" (54).

36. *Against Heresies* 3, 21, 2.

37. *Stromata* 1.22.

38. *Apology* 18.5–9.

39. *Cohortatio ad Graecos* 13.

40. *Praeparatio Evangelica* 8.1–9.

41. *Catecheses* 4, 33–35.

42. *De Mensuris et Ponderibus* 3.2–17.

erudition and command of language translate those things which he understands.[43]

Jerome makes a careful distinction between being a translator and a prophet, since the gift of prophecy necessarily entails the presence of the Spirit, who guarantees divine authority. Jerome works backwards to diffuse that authority by denying the translators' gift of prophecy. Although Jerome never divulges the source of his doubts about the Septuagint myth, I am inclined to agree with Naomi Seidman's suggestion that Jerome, knowledgeable of contemporary rabbinic opinion, agreed with their assessment of the Septuagint's inaccuracy. Her reading of the Talmud sees the rabbis teaching that the Septuagint contained intentional mistranslations provided by divine inspiration that were intended to deceive Christians: "The Talmud present[s] the composition of the Septuagint as an elaborate Jewish trick."[44] Jerome admits his awareness of fourth-century rabbinic opinion about the *Letter*: "The Jews say it was done wisely in deliberation so Ptolemy, the worshipper of one god, might not yet discover a double divinity with the Hebrews . . ."[45] It is not unreasonable to assume that he borrowed their view and adapted it to his Christian purpose. Thus armed with insight garnered from his trusted Hebrew teachers, Jerome launched an attack from within the Christian church on the received Christian text of the Old Testament. "Remarkably enough, Jerome knows—indeed he seems to be the *only* Father who knows—the (apparently still oral!) rabbinic LXX tradition."[46] The motivation for his Christian call to "return to the source" of the Septuagint's origins might very well have originated, or at least been stimulated, through his contacts with contemporary Jewish informants.

Second, he stressed that the original text of the Septuagint had been hopelessly corrupted by later recensions. In a prologue to the second translation of Chronicles from the Hebrew in 396, Jerome says the Septuagint is "corrupted and violated."[47] He then describes exactly how the original Septuagint text is corrupt in its three recensions used by Christians throughout the Roman Empire. Those in Egypt used the recension of Hesychius, those in Constantinople and Antioch used that of Lucian, and those in the area of

---

43. *Prologue to Pentateuch* 26–30; *Biblia Sacra* 3–4; see also *Prologue to Paralipomenon* 17–20; *Biblia Sacra* 546–47.

44. Seidman, *Faithful Renderings*, 64; see also 12.

45. *Prologue to Pentateuch* 21–25; *Biblia Sacra* 3.

46. Seidman, *Faithful Renderings*, 71.

47. *Prologue to Paralipomenon* 6; *Biblia Sacra* 546.

Palestine used Origin's *Hexapla*. There are also differences, due to copying errors, within the three recensions.[48] The book of Daniel provides for him a prime example of such confusion:

> The churches of the Lord and Savior do not read the prophet Daniel according to the Seventy translators, but they use instead the edition of Theodotion, but I do not know why this happened.... This one thing can I affirm, that it is considerably out of harmony with the true text, and it is repudiated by correct judgment.[49]

By using this edition of Daniel, Jerome alleges that Christians are unwittingly trusting in the work of a Jew, since Theodotion "was an unbeliever, after the coming of Christ."[50] He further explains the multiple recensions and the mother of all the editions:

> There is one edition which Origen and Eusebius of Caesarea and all Greek writers call the *koine*, that is, the common or vulgar text, and which now goes mostly by the name Lucian; the other is the Septuagint, which is also to be found in the Hexapla ... [which] is the pure and unadulterated version of the Septuagint.[51]

Jerome's intends his new translation to correct this confusion of multiple recensions and the shameful inconsistency of the Christian church in accepting and using them. The other texts led to embarrassment among Christians when they argued with Jews—the playing field was rendered uneven. If Christians would debate from the same sacred text, presumably Christians would not lose, or at least, might not be embarrassed, when the Septuagint differed with the Hebrew scrolls: "The Jews generally laugh when they hear our version of this passage of Isaiah.... But how shall we deal with the Hebrew originals in which these passages and others like them are omitted, passages so numerous that to reproduce them all would require books without number?"[52] Jerome thus marshals an apologetic reason for

---

48. *Prologue to Paralipomenon* 6–16; *Biblia Sacra* 546.

49. *Prologue to Daniel* 1–8; *Biblia Sacra* 1341.

50. *Prologue to Commentary on Daniel* (CCSL 75A:774). Scholars have recently overturned the view that regarded the three recensions as reactions against the Christian use of the Septuagint. They now argue for recensions based on a growing favor toward the Masoretic text type and different translation methods (Kreuzer, "From 'Old Greek' to the Recensions").

51. *Ep.* 106.2 (CSEL 55:248–49). Some spelling modified from Melten, "Letter of St. Jerome to the Gothic Clergymen," 516.

52. *Ep.* 57.11 (CSEL 54:522–23).

his new translation among Christians, since he himself knows firsthand the strength of debating from the same texts. He also demonstrates his Christian authority over the Jews—what Andrew Jacobs refers to as "academic imperialism" over the Jews and their text.[53] It seems paradoxical for Jerome to argue against Christians for a standard Hebrew text and at the same time to argue with Jews about the meaning of that standard text. Swirling about Jerome are contradictory currents of trust and distrust. He vehemently rejects the Christian tradition of the Septuagint's divine authorization, yet he passionately embraces the textual tradition of a people whose hermeneutics he distrusts. His discordant emotions isolated him from both Christian and Jewish associates and probably alienated him from the very ones he sought to engage.

Third, in an amazing turn from his rejection of the inspiration of the seventy translators, Jerome reasons that they purposefully hid christological prophecies from the pagan king:

> The Jews say it was done wisely in deliberation, so Ptolemy, the worshipper of one god, might not yet discover a double divinity with the Hebrews; he made them do so chiefly for this reason, because he was seen to fall into the dogma of Plato. Accordingly, wherever anything sacred in Scripture is witnessed of the Father and Son and Holy Spirit, they are either translated otherwise, or they have passed over all in silence, so they might both satisfy the king, and might not divulge the secret of the faith.[54]

He writes similarly elsewhere that the translators were unwilling to reveal "those things which promised the coming of Christ, lest the Jews might appear to worship a second God also,"[55] and again, the seventy "hid these [mysteries of their faith]."[56] From Jerome's perspective it seems that the Jewish translators were secret believers in Christ before his coming and that they deliberately omitted cardinal truths of the Christian faith. While this may not be an instance of the inspiration of the texts in Jerome's mind, it certainly sounds like some sort of pre-Christian illumination of the official Jewish translators from Palestine. So instead of looking at the seventy as merely scholarly translators, Jerome heightens their "spirituality" by speculating that they are Jewish Trinitarians. This type of ambivalence is typical

---

53. Jacobs, *Remains of the Jews*, 83.
54. *Prologue to Pentateuch* 21–25; *Biblia Sacra* 3.
55. *Hebrew Questions on Genesis*, preface (CCSL 72:2).
56. *Commentary on Isaiah*, preface (CCSL 73:1).

of Jerome's writing and reveals an essential element of his person that will be discussed later.

While Jerome systematically attempted to dispel Latin-speaking Christians' attraction to the Septuagint, he also argued in favor of the Hebrew text's superiority.[57] As Michael Grave states, "Jerome was the only figure in the early church who regarded the original text of the Old Testament as authoritative over against the Septuagint."[58] Jerome's point is simple and direct—the New Testament authors quoted from the Old Testament at least five times with no corresponding passage in the Septuagint, only in the Hebrew. His list includes Matthew 2:15 ("Out of Egypt have I called my son") with Hosea 11:1; Matthew 2:23 ("He shall be called a Nazarene") with Isaiah 11:1; John 19:37 ("They will look on him whom they have pierced") with Zechariah 12:10; John 7:38 ("Rivers of living water shall flow from within") with Proverbs 18:4; 1 Corinthians 2:9 ("Things which no eye has seen, nor ear heard, nor has arisen in the heart of man, which God has prepared for those who love him") with Isaiah 64:4. His argument seems flawless: "Therefore let us ask them where these are written, and when they are unable to say, we will produce them from the Hebrew texts."[59] Without saying it, the weight of his argument stands on apostolic authority. The apostles quoted something not in the Septuagint, rendering the Septuagint either deficient or flawed; therefore the text from which they do quote, the Hebrew, must have ultimate authority, in fact, divine authority. That is why in Jerome's mind this act of concealment is close to blasphemy: "How can the Septuagint leave out the word 'Nazarene,' if it is unlawful to substitute one word for another? It is sacrilege either to conceal or to set at naught a mystery."[60]

In addition, these passages from Jerome's letters make it abundantly clear that divine truth is to be found only in the Hebrew sources: "For as the true text of the Old Testament can only be tested by a reference to

---

57. For a detailed examination of Jerome's use of Old Testament quotations, see Kato, "Jerome's Understanding of Old Testament Quotations in the New Testament."

58. Graves, *Inspiration and Interpretation of Scripture*, 104.

59. *Prologue to Pentateuch* 16–17; *Biblia Sacra* 3. Muller oddly supposes that Jerome would retranslate Greek into Hebrew: "Due to the impossibility of finding the quotation in Jn 7.38 either in the Septuagint or in the Hebrew Bible, Jerome demands that the passage should be translated back to the Hebrew" (*First Bible of the Church*, 85). He bases this on his translation of Jerome's Latin as "thus is the turning back to the Hebrew books" (*Prologue to Paralipomenon* 30–31; *Biblia Sacra* 547).

60. *Ep.* 57.7 (CSEL 54:515–16).

the Hebrew, so the true text of the New requires for its decision an appeal to the Greek"[61]; "Thus you, too, should adhere to the true version lest, while adopting a spurious reading, you lose sight of what the prophet has written."[62] That "true version" is stated in the next section of the same letter: "Since we are investigating the truth, we simply must adhere to what we find in the Hebrew,"[63] Jerome is now signaling that the fight for texts is underway. No longer will he keep it to himself and his ascetic community in Bethlehem. His publications announce his agenda and urge others to follow him as those who "return to the source" with him. Jerome places the Jewish sacred text in Hebrew above the Christian sacred text in Greek. In a chronological reordering he displaces a Christian tradition with a Jewish one, and in doing so endows the Hebrew text with Christian authority.

A final example reveals Jerome's attempt to persuade others of his position of Hebrew textual superiority, he makes a subtle yet blatant attempt of actually receiving divine approval. In his work that honored his patron Paula after her death, Jerome places words in her mouth that confess it was God who taught her about the Hebrew word and its truth rather than Septuagint's wording from Psalm 132:6: "The Hebrew word 'zoth,' as I have learned from your instruction . . . " Andrew Cain explains that

> what is interesting about this passage, apart from the fact that Paula speaks authoritatively as a textual critic of the Bible, is that she ascribes this philological insight to God himself ("te docente"), whom she is now addressing, and not to any human agent, namely Jerome, and thus this is a clever little piece of apology for Jerome's methodology of Hebrew verity.[64]

JEROME'S PREFERENCE FOR THE HEBREW CANON

While the actual term "canon" may only be traced back to Athanasius (295–373), the concept of a body of sacred books finds precedent both in the Jewish and Christian collections of sacred Scriptures. By the time of Jerome in the fourth century, the Christian canon of the Old Testament was

---

61. *Ep.* 71.5 (CSEL 55:6).
62. *Ep.* 106.41 (CSEL 55:267).
63. *Ep.* 106.78 (CSEL 55:287).
64. Cain, *Jerome's Epitaph on Paula*, 22. Cain explains that Jerome actually mistranslates the Hebrew in this verse (254–56).

unstable and varied based on geographical location. "No two Septuagint codices contain the same apocrypha, and no uniform Septuagint 'Bible' was ever the subject of discussion in the patristic church."[65]

Athanasius established a three-tiered approach to sacred texts inherited from the Jews.[66] The first level contained those jointly regarded as sacred Scripture by Jews and Christians. Although the number of these texts varied depending on a combination of two-part texts into one, the documents remained fixed (with the exception of Esther in the earliest centuries) and were considered the Christian Old Testament canon. The second group of texts consisted of those approved for reading in the churches and therefore labeled ecclesiastical (deuterocanonical). The third collection, called apocrypha (meaning "hidden" from church use), was considered heretical and banned from the churches and the attention of Christians. Adding to the confusion of scholars, some ancient writers label the second tier as apocryphal, while others, Jerome among them, combine both the second and third as apocryphal. Jerome was the first Christian writer that we know of to also label the second group as apocryphal.[67]

The division of texts into three tiers of descending value was not consistently reflected among the Christian churches. Eastern writers maintained a loose division between the categories, while western church leaders in Jerome's time were erasing the distinction between canonical and the ecclesiastical. The western church revered the Old Latin and the Septuagint, both of which contained apocryphal texts, and this fact explains why certain regions of the church adopted a larger canon than others: the canons of the western councils of Rome (382), Hippo (393) and Carthage (397 and 419) included several apocryphal books. "Churches in north Africa, which from the beginning of the third century exercised an increasingly important role in Western Christianity, had apparently reached a settled acceptance of apocryphal writings and received them at full parity with the other Scriptures."[68] In contrast, the Eastern council of Laodecia (364) maintained the Jewish canon. Jerome's call for a Western canon that emulated the Jewish canon was met with resistance.

Jerome's views on the Old Testament canon parallel his views on the Old Testament text. While I believe that both concepts are inextricably

---

65. Ellis, "Old Testament Canon in the Early Church," 678.
66. *Easter Letter 39*.
67. Hengel, *Septuagint as Christian Scripture*, 50 n. 80.
68. Ellis, 673.

"Return to the Source"

linked to the *Hebraica veritas*, I suspect that the former is a result of the latter—the conviction about the Hebrew canon naturally flows from the preference for the superiority of the Hebrew text. In his prologue to one of the earlier translations from the Hebrew in 392, Jerome clearly enumerates his preferred canon of the Old Testament. His strategy is not to simply list the names of the books, but to lay the groundwork to justify his list. Thus he begins by explaining the significance of the number of the letters in the Hebrew alphabet (twenty-two) as the mystical number of the Levites (Num 3:39) and as the basis for the acrostic poems (in Psalms, Proverbs, and Lamentations). He even sees meaning in the number of the five doubled Hebrew letters (final letters) and the number of the five doubled Hebrew books (1–2 Samuel, 1–2 Kings, 1–2 Chronicles, Ezra-Nehemiah, Jeremiah-Lamentations): "Therefore, just as there are twenty-two elements, by which we write in Hebrew all that we say ... thus twenty-two scrolls are counted, by which a just man is instructed in the doctrine of God."[69] He then lists the scrolls in three sections: five in the Law, eight in the Prophets, and nine in the Holy Writings. He mentions that some argue for a twenty-four-book canon by dividing two books. Rather than criticize that calculation, Jerome defends it on the basis of the twenty-four elders in Revelation 4:4. Such reasoning from the New Testament may seem unusual in light of his Jewish-centered precedent seen earlier, but this move is natural for one steeped in Christian supersessionism. He can move back and forth within two canons since the church has inherited Israel's canon. In this subtle justification for an alternate number, Jerome demonstrates his assimilating practice of fourth-century supersessionism.

Aware that some Christians very probably would react with skepticism and even quarrel with his canonical proposal, Jerome explicates further his Jewish-centered approach to both text and canon: "This prologue to the Scriptures may serve as a helmeted introduction to all the books which we have turned from Hebrew into Latin, so that we may be able to know that whatever is outside of these must be set apart among the apocrypha."[70] Jerome describes this particular prologue with a word for defensive warfare, "helmeted," no doubt ready for the onslaught of attacks on his textual and canonical views. He already faces "the barking dogs which rage against me with rabid mouth."[71] With those enemies in mind, he constructs his defense

---

69. *Prologue to Kings* 19–22; *Biblia Sacra* 364.
70. Ibid., 52–54; *Biblia Sacra* 365.
71. Ibid., 78; *Biblia Sacra* 366.

of the Jewish canon. After listing what is included in his canon, Jerome completes his argument by listing what is outside his canon. He calls such texts "the apocrypha" and includes the books of the Wisdom of Solomon, the book of Jesus son of Sirach (Ecclesiasticus), Judith, Tobit, the Shepherd of Hermas, and the first and second book of the Maccabees—these are "not in the canon."[72] Whose canon omits these, the Jewish canon or Jerome's? Jerome constructs this prologue to blend his own views so closely to the Jews that the two are the same. In another prologue he defends his combining the books of Ezra and Nehemiah into one by appealing to the Jewish canon:

> It should not disturb anyone that the book published by us is a single work, nor should they be delighted by the dreams of the third and fourth books of the apocrypha [1–2 Esdras], for also in the Hebrew copies the words of Ezra and Nehemiah are confined to one scroll; and what is not contained in the Hebrew, or numbered among the twenty-four elders, is to be rejected.[73]

Once again Jerome heads in the direction of the authority of the Jews, borrows it, possesses it, and then transforms it into a new canonical authority for the Latin-speaking Christian church.

Although Jerome's affection for the Hebrew text undoubtedly began while he lived in Rome (382–85), he continued to translate from the Septuagint while he gradually moved to a firmer stand for an exclusively Hebrew source text. In a similar fashion, the texts written before he began his translations of the Hebrew Scriptures reveal a more tolerant attitude toward the apocryphal books. His appreciation of these works is evident by his repeated quotations of the books of Susanna, the Hymn of the Three Hebrew Children, Tobit, Ecclesiasticus, the Wisdom of Solomon, Bel and the Dragon, and 2 Maccabees.[74] Such approbation is also found in his early New Testament commentaries. For example, in commentary composed in 387, Jerome mentions Matthias, a name occurring only in 1 Maccabees 2:26–27. His stated source for this name is "the treasury trove of Scripture."[75]

---

72. Ibid., 54–56, *Biblia Sacra* 365.

73. *Prologue to Ezra* 18–21; *Biblia Sacra* 638.

74. Jerome's earlier correspondence provides an example of one of his favorite sources, the Wisdom of Solomon: *Ep.* 14.6 quotes Wis 1:11; *Ep.* 14.9 quotes Wis 6:6; *Ep.* 39.3 quotes Wis 4:8–14; *Ep.* 54 quotes Wis 4:13; *Ep.* 58 quotes Wis 4:8; *Ep.* 60.10 quotes Wis 4:9; *Ep.* 75.2 quotes Wis 4:11–14; *Ep.* 78.25 quotes Wis 6:6; *Ep.* 79.6 quotes Wis 4:9, 13 (Skehan, "St. Jerome and the Canon of the Holy Scriptures," 261–62).

75. *St. Jerome's Commentaries on Galatians, Titus, and Philemon*, 178.

Other commentaries on New Testament books dating to 387 (Galatians, Ephesians, Titus, and Philemon) reveal similar quotations of apocryphal writings. However, after the early 390s the situation changes. His Old Testament commentaries dated from 390 to 392 (Micah, Nahum, Habakkuk, Zephaniah, and Haggai) contain references to the apocryphal works, but his citations do not reflect the assumption that the books have canonical status. In a prologue to his Latin translation of Solomon's writings, Jerome elucidates his notion about the canon: "Just as the church reads Judith, Tobit, and the books of Maccabees, but does not receive them among the canonical Scriptures, so also one may read these two scrolls for the edification of the people, but not for confirming the authority of church doctrines."[76] Here is a significant distinction—texts have two purposes: to prove church teaching and to edify church constituents. Jerome's primary concern is to establish the Christian church's dogma on the foundation of the Jewish Scriptures. His secondary concern is to help Christians grow in their faith. Such priorities mirror Jerome's own pursuits. He is a monk and a scholar first; pastoral work is a lower priority left mainly to others.

However, Jerome does give counsel to one Laeta, daughter-in-law of his patron Paula, that reveals the danger of the apocryphal texts:

> Let her avoid all the apocryphal writings, and if she is led to read such not by the truth of the doctrines which they contain but out of respect for the miracles contained in them, let her understand that they are not really written by those to whom they are ascribed, that there are many faulty elements in them, and that it requires great skill to look for gold in mud.[77]

In contrast, he gives unquestioning sanction to the writings of Cyprian, Athanasius, and Hillary: "... let her peruse [these writings] without fear of stumbling"[78] Jerome places the writings of other Christians above the apocryphal texts. It seems that their authority has lessened and Jerome has dragged them into the "mud." One scholar parochially laments that Jerome has dragged the Christian church itself into the proverbial mud:

> Jerome changed his views on the subject of the Canon during his long and tempestuous career ... in addition to the mischief he did by his ungoverned rhetoric in his quarrels with other theologians, he did a much greater mischief by giving the sanction of his great

---

76. *Prologue to the Books of Solomon 19–21; Biblia Sacra 957.*
77. *Ep. 107.12 (CSEL 55:303).*
78. *Ibid.*

fame as a scholar to a theory of the Canon which, whatever its merits, was not that of the primitive Church.[79]

In his allegiance to the Jewish canon, Jerome did indeed redirect the tradition of the early church. Sullied with the charge of Judaizing, Jerome relentlessly "returned to the source" of the Hebrew text that he had embraced, namely, the community of fourth century Jews who preserved the tradition Jerome considered to be hallowed. There he also learned that the texts were embedded in a canon. Inextricably bound to each other, text and canon emerged as Jerome's twins in his effort to restore Hebrew truth to the Christian church.

JEROME'S ARGUMENTS OVER TEXT AND CANON

These radical positions on text and canon produced a wave of personal attacks upon Jerome. Much of his writing, especially the prologues to his translations of the Old Testament, contains self-justification directed at his opposition. For example: "I respond only to my detractors, who bite me with dog's teeth, slandering me in public, speaking at corners, the same being both accusers and defenders, when approving for others what they reprove me for."[80] In a similar tone: "I am forced, through each of the books of holy Scripture, to respond to the slander of adversaries who accuse my translation of being a censure of the Septuagint."[81] In a letter he complains: "Why do my enemies tear me to pieces, and the gross swine, silent though I am, grunt against me?"[82] These opponents remain nameless, except for two. They were fellow Christians, one a younger priest with sincere questions who discovered that he was dealing with a short-tempered monk, the other a beloved friend turned enemy.

Conflict with Augustine

As a young priest and later bishop in North Africa, Augustine (354–430) corresponded with Jerome over a period of about twenty-five years (394–419). Their letters reveal the intricacies of their personalities and a relationship that is "from the psychological, intellectual, and religious points of

---

79. Howorth, "Influence of St. Jerome on the Canon," 321.
80. *Prologue to Paralipomenon* 32–35; *Biblia Sacra* 547.
81. *Prologue to Job* 1–2; *Biblia Sacra* 731.
82. *Ep.* 119.11 (CSEL 55:468).

view, one of the most fascinating in antiquity."[83] Among the several topics discussed in their seventeen extant letters is a heated discussion concerning Jerome's translation of the Old Testament. The first letter is from Augustine, who expresses gratitude for Jerome's helpful translations of important texts as well as a candid request that Jerome revert to the Septuagint as his source for Old Testament translation rather than the Hebrew. Failing to get a response to his questions, Augustine sent another letter four years later expressing similar sentiments. The first letter never arrived in Bethlehem, and the contents of the second were divulged in Rome by a misdirected courier. A copy of that letter was eventually delivered by a friend of Jerome's who discovered such on an island in the Adriatic. This sort of confusion, whether from unintentional mishaps of delivery, loss, or crossing of letters, compounded the tension expressed in these letters, ranging from interpretational differences to personal insults.[84]

In his first letter Augustine requests:

> When it comes to translating the sacred canonical writings into Latin, I would like you simply to do what you did when you translated the book of Job, in other words to add signs indicating the points where your translation differs from that of the Septuagint, which has such great authority. I would be very surprised if anything could still be found in the Hebrew texts which had escaped the notice of all those translators who were such experts in that language.... I do think that their work should without doubt be accorded preeminent authority in this field.[85]

Thus the battle for authority spread to North Africa, a conflict that Jerome had already commenced in Palestine by proclaiming the *Hebraica veritas* superior to the Septuagint. In another letter Augustine explains his concern if Jerome's translation is adopted. It is not a matter of the truth of the Scriptural text, but rather the unity of the church:

> I feel that many problems would arise if your translation began to be read regularly in many churches, because the Latin churches would be out of step with the Greek ones.... If, however, someone

---

83. Kelly, *Jerome*, 217.

84. For a survey of each letter and the difficulties of chronology, see White, *Correspondence between Jerome and Augustine*, 19-34; also Furst, *Augustins Briefwechsel mit Hieronymus*, 139-45, 223-24.

85. Augustine's *Ep.* 28.2 (CSEL 34:105-7); White, *Correspondence*, 66. English translations are from White.

> were to object to some unusual expression in the version translated from the Hebrew and were to allege that it is wrong, it would be almost impossible to get hold of the Hebrew texts to use in defense of the point to which he objected.... In addition, if Hebrew scholars were consulted, they might give a different answer and so you might appear indispensable as the only one who could prove them wrong—but I would be amazed if you could find anyone to arbitrate between you.[86]

To Augustine, the challenge presented by Jerome's new text is not to be met by obtaining the Hebrew texts and learning the Hebrew language in order to secure its meaning. For him the concern centers primarily on church authority and only secondarily on textual authority. He could not think of a worse position to be in—the debate might be reduced to Hebrew scholars, over whom Augustine had little authority, versus Jerome, who was in faraway Bethlehem, and even then was a fallible authority. It was far safer for Augustine to keep the status quo: a standard text and a unified church.

Such a scenario did in fact take place in North Africa. Augustine relates an incident that caused a major disturbance at the church of Oea (modern Tripoli). The bishop had publically read the prophet Jonah from Jerome's new Latin translation in which a word sounded unfamiliar to the congregation.[87] Local Jewish rabbis were subsequently consulted who actually favored the Old Latin's translation: "The man was forced to correct the passage in your version as if it were inaccurate since he did not want this crisis to leave him without a congregation. This makes even us suspect that you, too, can be mistaken occasionally."[88] This anecdote reveals the power of a Hebrew word in light of the stability of Christian tradition. Unity in the church was valued over accuracy of the text, especially when such accuracy was questioned by a Christian enamored by a Hebrew word regarded inaccurate by Jews. Augustine paints solitary Jerome into a corner and positions his own rabbinic colleagues as Jerome's enemies.

Jerome's responses are pointed and biting. First, he points out Augustine's blatant inconsistency in using a Greek text with insertions made by a blaspheming Jew (Theodotion):

---

86. Augustine's *Ep.* 71.3 (CSEL 34:253); White, *Correspondence*, 92.
87. The old word "having been read by so many generations, was ingrained in their memories" (Augustine's *Ep.* 71.4 [CSEL 34:252]; White, *Correspondence*, 92).
88. Ibid.; White, *Correspondence*, 93.

"Return to the Source"

> I am surprised that you are not reading the Septuagint in the original form as it was produced by the Seventy, but in an edition corrected, or corrupted, by Origen using daggers and asterisks and that you are not following the translation, undistinguished though it may be, of a Christian, especially when he has removed those additions which came from the edition of a Jew and blasphemer after Christ's passion.[89]

Jerome pits himself, a Christian, against the Jewish translator in an easy two-way contest—Augustine would be a fool not to choose Jerome.[90] Jerome centers the argument on authority: either his and the Hebrew text, or the recension and the Jew. Next, he answers Augustine's criticism of his attempt to improve on the ancient Septuagint by reversing Augustine's logic. Why would Augustine himself write comments on the Psalms if many others had done so already?

> If the Psalms are unintelligible you must admit that it is possible for you, too, to be mistaken about them, but if their meaning is clear, it is hardly likely that those commentators should have got them wrong. And so, either way your interpretation will be redundant. On this principle no one will dare to express their view once their predecessors have spoken.[91]

Lastly, Jerome focuses his attention on the translation difference that raised an uproar in Oea. He justifies his rendering, even casting aspersion on the Jews who sided against Jerome: "If your Jews, as you claim, whether out of spite or ignorance, said that the Hebrew edition contained the same as the Greek and Latin editions, it is clear that they are either ignorant of Hebrew literature or that they deliberately lied so as to make fun of the gourd planters."[92] Once again, Jerome elevates his own authority above the Jews and above Augustine (referred to as "your Jews"). Both parties are pitted against Jerome, who "it is clear" is correct. Jerome acts as judge and jury with the only possible outcome being his victory.

In Augustine's final letter about such matters, he takes on a more subdued tone:

---

89. *Ep.* 112.19 (CSEL 55:389); White, *Correspondence*, 133.

90. Fredriksen observes how Jerome uses his *adversus Judaeos* rhetoric to rebut Augustine (on this and other issues) in *Augustine and the Jews*, 290–302. It is ironic, yet typical, that Jerome would accuse him of something that he is accused of by Augustine.

91. *Ep.* 112.20 (CSEL 55:390); White, *Correspondence*, 135.

92. *Ep.* 112.22 (CSEL 55:393); White, *Correspondence*, 137.

> On the question of our translation, you have now persuaded me of your positive reasons for translating the Scriptures from the Hebrew; you wanted to make known to the public what had been left out or corrupted by the Jews. But I ask you, please, to inform me which Jews did this–whether it was those who translated before the coming of the Lord and if so, which ones, or which one, or whether it was those later translators who might be thought to have removed some things from the Greek texts or to have corrupted them.[93]

Augustine's probing question might be read as if he is prepared to abandon the Septuagint altogether. I suspect that he knows that the answer to his question is that the later Jews are the corrupters, because he continues to believe that the original Septuagint should be the basis of Jerome's translation. Thus he continues later in this letter: "I am very keen to see your translation of the Septuagint as it will enable us to get away, as far as possible, from the terrible defects of the Latin translators who attempted this work whether qualified to do so or not."[94] Augustine still reverts back to the inspired Septuagint: "The reason I was unwilling for your translation from the Hebrew Bible to be read in the churches was that I wanted to avoid introducing it as something new and as a rival to the authority of the Septuagint."[95] The argument is essentially one of authority: the church's authority expressed by possession of the text of the Septuagint, or Jerome's authority symbolized by and centered in the Jewish text. Augustine sides with the church. In the last mention of textual matters, Jerome adds a postscript to a letter to explain why he has not sent Augustine a copy of his Latin translation from the Septuagint ten years after Augustine asked for it:

> We are experiencing a great shortage of Latin speaking scribes in this province and that is why I am unable to obey your orders, especially regarding the edition of the Septuagint which has been marked with asterisks and obelisks; also, I have lost a large part of my earlier work because of someone's dishonesty.[96]

Why would Jerome have procrastinated for ten years in even answering Augustine's request?[97] Perhaps Jerome actually did not have such a copy, as

93. Augustine's *Ep.* 82.34 (CSEL 34:385); White, *Correspondence*, 173.
94. Augustine's *Ep.* 82.35 (CSEL 34:386); White, *Correspondence*, 174.
95. Ibid.
96. *Ep.* 134.2 (CSEL 56:263); White, *Correspondence*, 228.
97. Augustine's request was in 405 (his *Ep.* 82); Jerome responded in 416.

he says, or perhaps he feared that Augustine might use such a translation for the purpose of criticizing Jerome, since Augustine continued to be convinced of the Septuagint's inspiration and superiority to the Hebrew text.[98]

Schulz-Flugel offers an interesting insight into the reasons behind these personal differences. She suggests that Augustine's basic objection stemmed from his theory of language, which was rooted in the Stoic teaching of *res et signa* (reality and signs). Since language is merely a sign, not the real thing, Jerome's term *Hebraica veritas* equates the truth of Scripture with the Hebrew language—an utter impossibility for Augustine: "Within this context a recourse *ad fontes* becomes irrelevant: a Latin version—on the condition that errors and mistakes are eliminated—is as more or less a suitable instrument for understanding as the Hebrew, which is a human text as well, corrupted by human sin."[99] She describes Jerome's theory of language as based on the pre-Aristotelian idea of the power entrenched in the spoken and written word resting in the link between "being" and "name." For example, Jerome finds mystical truth embedded in Hebrew words, revealed in the order of the Hebrew words and even disguised in the shape of Hebrew letters. With such intransigent philosophical differences, reconciliation was impossible. In the end, both men maintained their stance with slight compromise: Augustine accepted Jerome's new Latin translation as another expression of the inspired voice of God, and Jerome continued to refer to the Septuagint.

Jerome's urging may have caused Augustine to supplement his translations, but it never changed Augustine's view of Septuagintal priority. One of Augustine's later books, written in 419 and entitled *Questions on the Heptateuch*, reveals that at times he preferred the reading of the Hebrew text in a particular verse. However, when faced with the opportunity to elevate it above the Septuagint, as Jerome did, he never does: "The Greek text is always consulted even if, as Augustine clearly admits, the Hebrew text on many occasions is as authoritative or clearer."[100] Augustine, an apparent friend of Jerome,[101] was never convinced of Jerome's argument for the supremacy of the Hebrew text.[102] For Augustine, on the issue of authority, the church won.

98. Lossl considers Jerome's answer "a feeble excuse" ("Shift in Patristic Exegesis," 159).
99. Schulz-Flugel, "Latin Old Testament Tradition," 660.
100. La Bonnardiere, "Did Augustine Use Jerome's Vulgate?," 44.
101. For an investigation of their friendship, see Burrus, "'In the Theater of This Life.'"
102. For Augustine's later view on the Septuagint, see his *On Christian Doctrine*,

Conflict with Rufinus

Rufinus of Aquileia (345–410) and Jerome first met as young men studying together in Rome. Rufinus later studied in Egypt under a disciple of Origen, Didymus the Blind. From there he moved to Jerusalem and established a monastery on the Mount of Olives in 381 and later moved to Italy, where he began translating Christian texts, including the works of Origen, into Latin. His old friend Jerome became part of a movement to ostracize the followers of Origen due to his supposed heterodoxy.[103] Their friendship ruptured when Jerome bitterly castigated Rufinus as a heretic. Both men gathered forces against each other and issued written defenses of their respective positions.[104] In 401, Rufinus wrote a highly polemical two-volume treatise to defend his orthodoxy in which he assails Jerome for a similar unorthodox practice—translating a new Latin version of the Scriptures from the Hebrew rather than from Greek: "Perhaps it was a greater piece of audacity to alter the books of the divine Scriptures which had been delivered to the Churches of Christ by the Apostles to be a complete record of their faith by making a new translation under the influence of the Jews."[105] Rufinus maligns Jerome for disregarding the traditional Old Testament Septuagint as well as for befriending Jews. It seems to Rufinus that Jerome is reversing the direction of Christian supersessionism by reverting back to Jewish texts:

> There has been from the first in the churches of God, and especially in that of Jerusalem, a plentiful supply of men who being born Jews have become Christians; and their perfect acquaintance with both languages and their sufficient knowledge of the law is shown by their administration of the pontifical office. In all this abundance of learned men, has there been one who has dared to make havoc of the divine record handed down to the Churches by the Apostles and the deposit of the Holy Spirit?[106]

Rufinus wonders why no converted Jew has done what Jerome has dared to do. Jerome seems to be reversing the direction a convert should travel of leaving Judaism behind in all its forms and joining with the new Israel.

42–43 (2.15.53–56); and *City of God* 15.14.2; 18.34; CCL 48, 587, 45–464; 639, 31–32.

103. See Clark, *Originest Controversy*.

104. Rebenich, *Jerome*, 41–51. For an analysis of Jerome's writings, see Lardet, *L'Apologie De Jerome Contre Rufin*.

105. *Apology Against Jerome* 2.32 (PL 21:387).

106. Ibid., 2:33 (PL 21:388).

"Return to the Source"

The Jewish converts that Rufinus knows act like true Christians, submitting entirely to the Christian church's tradition without bringing the "havoc" of Jewish influence, as Jerome has done in his reverting to the Hebrew text and canon. Namely, Jerome has removed the apocryphal books from the Christian canon:

> For instance, the whole of the history of Susanna, which gave a lesson of chastity to the churches of God, has by him been cut out, thrown aside and dismissed. The Hymn of the Three Children, which is regularly sung on festivals in the church of God, he has wholly erased from the place where it stood. But why should I enumerate these cases one by one, when their number cannot be estimated?[107]

For Rufinus it is not only Jerome's dangerous views on the canon that are alarming; it is Jerome's unorthodox position on the Septuagint that lies at the heart of his errors. Reflecting the dominant Christian tradition,[108] Rufinus continues:

> The Seventy translators, each in their separate cells, produced a single, consistent version, under the inspiration, as we cannot doubt, of the Holy Spirit; and this version must certainly be of more authority with us than a translation made by a single man under the inspiration of Barabbas.[109]

Rufinus chooses damning rhetoric to castigate Jerome, who, instead of submitting to the tradition of Spirit-inspired Septuagint translators, has supplanted the role of translator and received his inspiration from the spirit of one opposed to Christ!

Earlier in this book Rufinus berates Jerome for hiring a Jew whom Jerome had named Baranina:[110] "From that other friend of yours, Barabbas, whom you chose out of the synagogue rather than Christ...."[111] In biting paronomasia, Rufinus turns Jerome's Jewish teacher into the rebel who was released in place of Jesus, and Jerome is painted as one of the traitorous Jews who said, "Give us Barabbas." Rufinus thus labels Jerome a Jewish traitor.

---

107. Ibid.
108. Rufinus names Ambrose, Hilary, Lactantius, and Didymus as fellow supporters of this Christian tradition (ibid., 2:35 [PL 21:390]).
109. Ibid.
110. Previously named by Jerome in his *Ep.* 84.3 (CSEL 55:123).
111. *Apology Against Jerome* 2.12 (PL 21:367).

The anti-Jewish attacks continue with subtle allusion to the story of Jesus' betrayal for thirty pieces of silver: "Now therefore after four hundred years the truth of the law comes forth for us, it has been bought with money from the Synagogue."[112] Rufinus moves from accusation to sarcasm regarding the translation of Jonah 4:6: "Let us change the inscriptions upon the tombs of the ancients, so that it may be known by those who had read the story otherwise, that it was not a gourd but an ivy plant under whose shade Jonah rested."[113] Jerome's perverse translation disturbs, from Rufinus' perspective, even the dead in their finely decorated sarcophagi, which are now in need of renovation due to Jerome's single word.[114]

In Rufinus' final attack he fashions Jerome as a victim of Jewish influence. Four times he blames the Jews by saying:

> This action is yours, my brother, yours alone. It is clear that no one in the church has been your companion or confederate in it, but only that Barabbas whom you mention so frequently. What other spirit than that of the Jews would dare to tamper with the records of the church which have been handed down from the Apostles? It is they, my brother, you who were most dear to me before you were taken captive by the Jews, it is they who are hurrying you into this abyss of evil. It is their doing that those books of yours are put forth in which you brand your Christian brethren, not sparing even the martyrs, and heap up accusations speakable and unspeakable against Christians of every degree, and mar our peace, and cause a scandal to the church. It is they who cause you to pass sentence upon yourself and your own writings as upon words which you once spoke as a Christian. We all of us have become worthless in your eyes, while they and their evil acts are all your delight.[115]

Rufinus considers Jewish influence to be so enticingly irresistible that Jerome has succumbed to its devilish powers. Blame for Jerome's apostasy is here transferred to the Jews, the source of "evil." In typical supersessionistic fashion, Rufinus embodies the Christian position on the text of the Old Testament and its entire displacement by the Christianized Septuagint.

---

112. Ibid., 2:35 (PL 21:39).

113. Ibid.

114. "For nearly two hundred years Christians in the west had seen a certain picture on graves, sarcophagi, church walls, and innumerable other places" (van der Meer, quoted in Fredriksen, *Augustine and the Jews*, 419 n. 1).

115. *Apology Against Jerome*, 2:37 (PL 21:393–94).

Jerome responds to this attack by acknowledging that he had hired a Jewish teacher named Baranina, not Barrabas. He goes on to reverse Rufinus' serious charge of submission to Jews by clarifying his relationship and compares it to his critical reading of Origen: "I did not say that he was my master; but I wanted to verify my study of sacred Scripture to prove that I had read Origen just as I had heard it also from the Jew."[116] Jerome insists that one reason he translated from the Hebrew was to engage the Jews in debate and "for the refutation of the Jews, even those very copies which they themselves admit are very faithful, so that, if they are ever in an argument with Christians, they may not have an avenue of escape, but may be struck down in the main with their own weapon."[117]

Jerome goes on to express consternation to Rufinus over a letter, falsely attributed to him, revealing his remorse in translating the Old Testament from Hebrew into Latin and his belittling of the Septuagint. Jerome sarcastically responds: "I wonder why he did not say in the same letter that I was a homicide, an adulterer, sacrilegious, and a parricide, and any foul name that the mind can think of in its silent meditation."[118] Evidently the reputation of Jerome had spread to faraway North Africa, where Eusebius of Cremona reports that bishops had gathered to discuss this alleged letter. That such a letter would be composed about the subject, and that African clergy would be greatly upset is a remarkable indication of both Jerome's influence and his fierce opposition. He replies with a surprisingly mild rejoinder: "Did I say anything against the Septuagint translators, whose work I revised very carefully many years ago . . . whose Psalms I constantly sing and meditate upon?"[119]

Jerome then expands his defense by quoting from nine prologues that he had previously written to his Old Testament translations. His main argument is mentioned in the prologue to Kings: "I beg you not to consider my work as a condemnation of the ancients. In the tabernacle of God, each and every man offers what he can. Some offer gold, and silver, and precious stones; others offer cotton stuff, purple garment, scarlet cloth, and hyacinth. We do well if we offer skins and goats' hairs."[120] Jerome then interprets his

---

116. *Apology Against Rufinus* 1.13 (CCSL 79:12). English translations are from Jerome, *Dogmatic and Polemical Works*.
117. Ibid., 3.25 (CCSL 79:97).
118. Ibid., 2.24 (CCSL 79:60).
119. Ibid.
120. Ibid., 2:26 (CCSL 79:64).

own parable and sarcastically admonishes Rufinus: "Notice how puffed up I am with pride against the Septuagint translators that I admit that they offered gold, and precious stones, and the purple robe in the tabernacle of God, and I goat's skins and hairs?"[121] Jerome claims the high ground by denying the allegations of outright rejection of the Septuagint, yet he never yields ground on his primary allegiance to the Hebrew text. After quoting from his Daniel prologue, in which he explains how Christians use Theodotion's Greek translation instead of the Septuagint, he is puzzled over the inconsistency: "Yet I wonder why he reads Theodotion, the heretic and Judaizer, and despises the translation of any Christian sinner without distinction."[122] In typical fashion, Jerome belittles himself as a sinner yet Christian to exaggerate the difference from Theodotion, the heretical Jew. As he did with Augustine, Jerome offers up a choice between two authorities, and the deck is always stacked in his favor.

In conclusion, Jerome freely offers his own translation to Rufinus with the notice that it comes with a high price tag:

> From all of this, it is clear that the edition of the Septuagint translators, which has been established by the antiquity of its readers, is useful to the churches, since the Gentiles heard of the coming of Christ before he came; and that the other translators are not to be reproved because they translated not their own, but sacred volumes; and that my good friend should accept from a friend and a Christian an edition that he has sought to transcribe from the Hebrew at great cost to himself.[123]

Subtly, Jerome seems to imply that if the Septuagint is "useful to the churches," then his own translation will be even more useful.

JEROME'S INCONSISTENCY REGARDING TEXT AND CANON

The discussion thus far might make it appear as though Jerome progressed in his textual and canonic beliefs with an eventual repudiation of the Septuagint and everything related to it. However, the actual situation is more complex and potentially more confusing. Jerome is never one to be neatly categorized. He writes in favor of the Septuagint text and canon at the same

---

121. Ibid.
122. Ibid., 2:33 (CCSL 79:70).
123. Ibid., 2:35 (CCSL 79:72).

time that he is elevating the Hebrew truth to supremacy. As scholars of Jerome have noticed, his "comprehensive statements regarding the canon ... are not ... entirely consistent."[124]

Defending the Septuagint

The following statements from Jerome's letters, prologues, and apology expose his other side. He defends, recommends, and sees God's hand in the very work that he criticizes. From his correspondence in 393 he lists his Old Testament canon.[125] While it does omit the apocryphal texts, he places Ruth after Judges rather than with the Megilloth of the Hebrew list, and he puts Daniel with the prophets in contrast to placement by the Hebrew canon.[126] Both of these arrangements show a parallel to the Septuagint's order. In a letter from 396 he honors the Greek version but continues to keep it subservient to the Hebrew: "The Septuagint has rightly kept its place in the churches, either because it is the first of all the versions in time, made before the coming of Christ, or else because it has been used by the apostles (only however in places where it does not disagree with the Hebrew)."[127] Again, he answers a Gothic clergyman who asks him about the name of God, which is used twice in his particular copy of Psalm 71. Throughout the lengthy letter Jerome consistently argues for the Hebrew text yet goes on to say that the Septuagint reading, which agrees with the Hebrew, also uses the name of God three times, since "the threefold occurrence in the Septuagint of the name of our Lord and God very clearly indicates the mystery of the Holy Trinity."[128] It would seem that he goes out of his way to approve of the Septuagint when it affirms Christian teaching, even as he does when he suggests that the seventy translators hid their Trinitarian doctrine from the pagan king. A final example, addressed to Augustine, attempts to alleviate Jerome's harsh stance against the Septuagint: "If someone does not wish to read my version, he will not be forced to do so against his will. Let

---

124. Skehan, "St. Jerome and the Canon of the Holy Scriptures," 263.

125. *Ep.* 53.8 (CSEL 54:454–62).

126. See Table 1 at the end of this chapter. Note that Job is placed after Deuteronomy, possibly due to the Jewish tradition of Mosaic authorship (*Baba Bathra* 14b).

127. *Ep.* 57.11 (CSEL 54:523–26). This is not accurate, since the New Testament quotes from the Septuagint when it differs from the Hebrew of the MT.

128. *Ep.* 106.44 (CSEL 55:268).

him drink the old wine with enjoyment and reject my unfermented wine."[129] One wonders how a Christian would be "forced" to read Jerome's version, but perhaps this reveals more about Jerome's unspoken desire. In 396 he claims to be using an edition of the Septuagint "corrected from the Greek" for public ministry in his monastery: "I always explain these things in the gatherings of the brothers."[130] Here, Jerome the churchman and traditional Christian continues to respect the wishes of his fellow monks who likely have not been persuaded of his Hebrew truth. As he had written, he is not one to "force" the version on those who would not appreciate it.

Jerome consistently alleges that he never desires that people ignore or disregard the Septuagint, but rather he offers his new translations as a supplement to it: "Do we condemn the old texts? By no means; but we work in the Lord's house as best we can after the endeavors of our predecessors."[131] He frames his words so as not to offend the traditional sensibilities of Christians:

> If anyone is truly more pleased by the edition of the Seventy interpreters, he already has it corrected by us [Jerome's earlier translations based on the Septuagint]. For it is not as though we build the new so that we destroy the old. And yet, when one will have read most carefully, he will know our things to be better understood, which have not soured by having been poured into a third vessel, but have rather reserved their flavor by having been entrusted to a new container immediately from the press.[132]

He uses a compelling image to convey that the flavor of the original is present but diluted in the Septuagint. He cannot help but inject that discerning pallets might prefer something stronger. In a final example of Jerome's hesitating ambivalence, he responds to Rufinus' argument that he has completely rejected the Septuagint:

> Did I say anything against the Septuagint translators, whose work I revised very carefully many years ago, and gave to the students of my own language, and expound daily in the convent of my brethren; whose Psalms I constantly sing and meditate upon? Was I so foolish as to wish to forget in my old age what I learned in my youth? All of my treatises are interwoven with their testimonies.

---

129. *Ep.* 112.19 (CSEL 55:389).
130. *Prologue to Paralipomenon* 35–37; *Biblia Sacra* 547.
131. *Prologue to Pentateuch* 35; *Biblia Sacra* 4.
132. *Prologue to the Books of Solomon* 22–24; *Biblia Sacra* 957.

> My commentaries on the twelve prophets are an explanation of both my version and that of the Septuagint.[133]

To summarize: "Jerome continued to cite the LXX version both as a basis for oral instruction as well as in his scholarly works even until the end of his career.... Often the LXX is the basis of his spiritual application of the text."[134] However, Jerome never allows it to rise above the Hebrew text.

Defending the Christian Apocrypha

Jerome confuses his readers by making pronouncements about the apocryphal books that seem to contradict his contemporaneous statements about their rejection. This leads one scholar to conclude: "We do not see any real change in Jerome's attitude to the canon.... Jerome makes apparently contradictory statements about the O.T. canon at different times in his life."[135] It is noteworthy, but not contradictory to his sentiments, that Jerome includes many quotations and allusions to the apocryphal texts during his years in Bethlehem, when his devotion to the Hebrew truth escalates.[136] However, it is one thing to quote an apocryphal text, but it is another thing to consider it as canonical Scripture.

To demonstrate this inconsistency, consider several of his letters. In 394 Jerome delicately includes a reference to Judith: "In the book of Judith—if anyone is of opinion that it should be received as canonical—we read...."[137] In 397 Jerome refers to Judith as comprising a "sacred volume,"[138] and in 400 he places Baruch in the same category as the prophets: "I would cite the words of the psalmist ... and those of Ezekiel ... and those of Baruch [5:5], 'Arise, arise, O Jerusalem,' and many other proclamations made by the trumpets of the prophets."[139] Jerome occasionally prefaces his quotation of apocryphal books with phrases that would seem to indicate a

---

133. *Apology Against Rufinus* 2:24 (CCSL 79:61).

134. Braverman, *Jerome's Commentary on Daniel*, 33, 34.

135. Brown, *Vir Trilinguis*, 67. Gallagher concurs: "All of our evidence indicates that he always considered them outside the canon" and that Jerome used the negative term *apocrypha* "to emphasize all the more forcefully the normative status of the Hebrew canon" ("Old Testament 'Apocrypha' in Jerome's Canonical Theory," 233).

136. See Skehan, "St. Jerome and the Canon of the Holy Scriptures," 278–85.

137. *Ep.* 54.16 (CSEL 54:483).

138. *Ep.* 65.1 (CSEL 54:617).

139. *Ep.* 77.4 (CSEL 55:42).

canonical status. Writing in 404, Jerome quotes from Ecclesiasticus 13:2, which is preceded with the words "for does not the Scripture say,"[140] and in 407 he includes a quotation from Ecclesiasticus 22:6 introduced by "holy Scripture says."[141] Similarly, Jerome's commentary on Isaiah, written in the year 410, names Ecclesiasticus as "holy Scripture"[142] and Wisdom of Solomon 1:4 is likewise called "Scripture" in his final work in 415 on Jeremiah.[143]

How can this evidence be reconciled with the following notion, which seems to exonerate Jerome of these contradictions?

> No one year represents a radical change for Jerome. His metamorphosis is gradual. Moreover, considering his entire life's work, his practice with regard to the canon is similar to his practice regarding the text: throughout his life he continues to cite passages from books which he considers non-canonical. However, he certainly cites them comparatively less after 390, and often with critical reservations.[144]

The evidence presented above contradicts this scholar's conclusion.

Furthermore, in about 405 Jerome produced Latin translations of Tobit and Judith at the request of some friends. Why would he make such works available if he devalues their importance and actually advises against their reading? He defends this project with a curious combination of anti-Jewish sentiment and pro-Christian traditionalism: "For the studies of the Hebrews rebuke us and find fault with us, to translate this for the ears of Latins contrary to their canon. But it is better to displease the judgment of Pharisees and obey the commands of bishops."[145] Did Jerome placate his church associates in order to alleviate some pressure building against his Hebrew canon? Regarding the book of Judith, he seems to justify himself with recourse to Christian tradition (unknown beside this reference): "Because the Nicene Council is considered to have counted this book among the number of sacred Scriptures, I have acquiesced to your request."[146] Here

---

140. *Ep.* 108.21 (CSEL 55:422).
141. *Ep.* 118.1 (CSEL 55:435).
142. *Commentary on Isaiah* 3:12b (PL 24:67A).
143. *Commentary on Jeremiah* 18:18 (PL 24:798D).
144. Braverman, *Jerome's Commentary on Daniel*, 44.
145. *Prologue to Tobit* 6–7; *Biblia Sacra* 676,
146. *Prologue to Judith* 4–5; *Biblia Sacra* 691. The following book contains many such references to Jerome's apocryphal citations: Penna, *San Gerolamo*, 387–89.

the authority of the church reigns supreme over his own instincts and convictions.

RESOLUTION OF JEROME'S APPROACH TO TEXTUAL SUPERSESSIONISM

Scholars have long recognized Jerome's inconsistent positions on the Old Testament text and canon. Some confusion can be dispelled by distinguishing earlier quotations from later, with the obvious explanation that Jerome must have undergone a metamorphosis of sorts regarding Hebrew sources. What continues to elude a satisfying explanation is those statements made in the latter part of his life that seem to betray his mature notions that elevated Hebrew truth. One scholar observes this antinomy: "This ambivalent attitude [about the LXX] is never really resolved in Jerome's mind."[147] The same scholar ventures an answer as to why Jerome cites apocryphal texts as "Scripture" while he is actually devoted to the more restrictive Hebrew canon: "A simple solution is plausible: Jerome ... was very probably quoting from memory and did not take the time to check them in a manuscript copy, especially as, with all his quotations from the apocryphal books, he was merely using them to illustrate a minor point in his overall argument."[148] Are we to suppose that the scholarly Jerome was forgetful, not instinctively knowing whether something was found in canonical or apocryphal texts, or did not take the time to look it up? I do not find this solution plausible.

Rather than simply observing Jerome's ambivalent statements or leaving the contradictions stand as they are, I find it more satisfying to view Jerome's words as revealing the inherent contradictions necessitated by supersessionism. Jerome's ambivalence is not a puzzle to be solved but a reflection of his agenda. He positions himself in the unstable space between traditional Christians devoted to their Septuagint and traditional Jews devoted to their Hebrew text. This placement forces Jerome to produce statements that betray his dependence on Jews and Christians and to publish attacks on Jews and Christians so as to isolate himself from both. Compromising statements result from Jerome's dramatic stance against his own tradition, which forces him to negotiate a safe space through inconsistent attitudes to his own tradition. Contradictory statements about Jews result from his unique form of supersessionism, which intensifies both the

147. Brown, *Vir Trilinguis*, 60.
148. Ibid., 66–67.

Christian dependence on the Jews and the Christian appropriation of the Hebrew text. Jerome's situation finds him largely isolated from his own tradition on an island of literary seclusion. It is in the position of a solitary supersessionist that I situate Jerome—solitary by his own making.

It is illuminating that Jerome presents himself as the lone Christian capable of traversing the gulf between Christians and Jews. One looks in vain for evidence of his call for others to create social contacts with contemporary Jews or for younger monks in his monastery to further his research into Jewish sources. Instead, Jerome's path to the next generation is a dead end, or rather a living end; he himself is the focal point of the process as well as the goal. His body of writings stand as his self-proclaimed tribute. In his book *On Illustrious Men*, a work describing the achievements of 135 famous individuals beginning with Simon Peter, Jerome lists himself last. It is of no surprise that, as far as we know, no one dared to assume his mantle. Jerome's intentions are not to create disciples; he rather positions himself in the role of a prophet. He considers himself to be a new kind of translator, one who sees and understands better than the seventy: "We write after His passion and resurrection, not so much prophecy as history. For in the one are told what things were heard, in the other what were seen. What we understand better, we also translate better."[149] Consider Jerome's role in contrast to the Septuagint translators: he is a post-crucifixion Christian who is enlightened by the Spirit, skillful in Hebrew, Greek, and Latin, with courage to shatter entrenched traditions and to enlighten the church to truth concealed in the Hebrew text. What character is Jerome portraying in this portrait? I suggest that Jerome replaces the Septuagint myth with one of his own making, and this one postures himself in the role of the translating prophet. Even though he denies the gift of prophecy ("We write ... not so much prophecy"), he admits to the role of a surrogate for the original authors of the Hebrew text. For at the end of the same prologue, he desires to be inspired by the Spirit in order to translate effectively: "Now I entreat you that ... you might help in your prayers, how I might, by the same Spirit by whom the books were written, be able to translate them into the Latin language."[150] He embodies the legend he demythologized, impersonating those traditionally Spirit-inspired translators. He wishes to become a Spirit-guided translator, compared not to the seventy but to the original prophets who prophesied by the Spirit. Jerome claims the pres-

---

149. *Prologue to Pentateuch* 38–39; *Biblia Sacra* 4.
150. *Prologue to Pentateuch* 47; *Biblia Sacra* 4.

"Return to the Source"

ence of the Spirit in his writing of commentaries, since choosing between alternate meanings in the Septuagint and Hebrew cannot be done without divine enablement: "For always in expounding holy Scripture we require the coming of that one [i.e. the Holy Spirit]."[151] To summarize, Jerome carefully constructs himself like an Old Testament prophet but calls himself an enlightened translator who is inspired by the Spirit.[152]

Jerome's self-portrait as a prophet, guided by God and answerable only to God, lends further support to his contradictory language. The intensity of his supersessionism finds justification in his perceived calling by God. The following examples demonstrate his self-acclaimed prophetic authority, which allows him to speak unpredictably and dogmatically, exclusively knowing how to speak to each side of the issue. First, while living in Rome (382–85), Jerome composes letters in response to questions by Pope Damasus regarding exegetical difficulties, in which he always references the Hebrew text as the source of truth. Possibly Jerome purposefully published the letters later, after his translation from the Hebrew had begun, in order to prove "not only that his exegetical expertise was in great demand in high places within the church, but also that his controversial Hebrew scholarship came with a papal seal of approval."[153] What more could a prophet need than the voice from Rome saying, "With you I am well pleased"? Second, in a commentary written in 389, Jerome explains his approach as midway between outright abandonment of the Septuagint tradition and a wholehearted embrace of the Hebrew truth:

> I note, briefly, that I have followed no one's authority, but in translating from the Hebrew I have adapted myself to a great extent to the usage of the Seventy translators, but only in those places in which they did not diverge far from the Hebrew. Occasionally also I have made reference to Aquila, Symmachus and Theodotion, so as neither to discourage the reader's interest by excessive novelty, nor on the other hand to forsake the source of truth against my own conscience and follow the streamlets of opinion.[154]

With this prophet-like tone, Jerome constructs his position not only between the extremes of either Greek or Hebrew versions, but also as a

---

151. *Commentary on Micah* 1:10 (PL 25:1218).

152. For similar instances of Jerome claiming to be inspired by the Spirit, see his prefaces to the commentaries of Jonah and Hosea (Williams, *Monk and the Book*, 129 n. 76).

153. Cain, *Letters of Jerome*, 64.

154. *Commentary on Ecclesiastes*, preface (CCSL 72:249).

supremely discerning translator who alone understands the proper renderings. He alone is able to navigate that middle space between the two texts. Jerome writes "prophetically," leading the Christian church out of its comfortable space of a Septuagintalized text and into the new world of a Hebraized and now Christianized text.

A third example of Jerome's authoritarian spirit is found in the way he pontificates on the right Scripture for the right audience: "For the reading of the Septuagint should be used in the churches, because of its antiquity, whereas the scholars should, for the sake of the accuracy of the Scriptures, not forget the true version."[155] Here the authority of antiquity (tradition) is pitted against that of scholarship (truthfulness). Both domains, the church and the monastic community, have influence. Jerome positions himself as the key who is able to unlock the proper text for saint and scholar. The implication is that they are not be able to make that decision for themselves, or that if they do confusion will result, since congregants do not care about scholarship and scholars do not care about tradition. Jerome, as an innovative supersessionist, unlike others who live only in one realm, considers himself well suited to traverse both domains. A fourth example pits Jerome against the gospel writer Matthew, whom Jerome thinks has misapplied the words of the prophet Zechariah to God as the speaker instead of the prophet: "In this instance according to my judgment—and I have some careful critics with me—the evangelist is guilty of a fault in presuming to ascribe to God what are the words of the prophet."[156] In a surprising move, Jerome situates his own authority above that of the New Testament author. For one who regularly defended the Scriptures against the charge of error, this statement is quite revealing. The spirit of the prophet Matthew has become subject to the prophet Jerome.

In conclusion, I have argued that Jerome's construction of Christian supersessionism is both novel and traditional and that his new approach to Hebraize the Christian Old Testament brings with it unintended violations of supersessionism's underlying presuppositions. By simultaneously embracing the superiority of the Christian church and the necessity of interaction with Jews, Jerome created a new approach to an old tradition. He reinforced Christian supremacy in language designed to repress Jewish legitimacy. However, his depiction of the Jews as preservers of the sacred text and guardians of the divine truths within that text subtly empowers

155. *Ep.* 106.46 (CSEL 55:269).
156. *Ep.* 57.7 (CSEL 54:512).

the very people he delegitimizes. Christianity's stereotyped Jew, blind and misguided as well as pernicious and dangerous, must give way to Jerome's additional depiction of the Jew as preserver and transmitter of the sacred text. In spite of Jerome's hostility to the Jews because of their rejection of Christ, he still injects a humanizing value of religious worth alongside his rejection of Jewish theology.

Jerome's readers are therefore faced with a choice: accept the tradition of Septuagintal superiority and its implicit rejection of Jewish legitimacy, thereby rejecting Jerome's approach as misguided at best or deviously subversive at worst, or reject the prevailing Christian tradition and begin the novel and dangerous journey toward acceptance about the Hebrew language, text, and canon. Such a path might take the reader on a personal awakening to Jewish people, Jewish religion, and Jewish culture through the unspoken approval of a Christian writer's example. Jerome's praxis betrays his indebtedness to the Jews in spite of his rhetorical rejection of their religious status.

The historical consequences of Jerome's influence are sparse but distinct. As far as is known, the only contemporary writer who adopted Jerome's new translation was Julian of Aeclanum (c. 380–455), whose exegetical commentaries also used the Hebrew text as his authority instead of the Septuagint.[157] Andrew Cain notes the irony: "Jerome's Vulgate translation of the Bible, in many respects his greatest scholarly achievement, was a colossal failure in its own time."[158] Jerome's Latin translation did not find general acceptance until the ninth century, and yet "up to the thirteenth century monks and priests were still copying and reading Old Latin versions of the Scriptures."[159] Ecclesiastical resistance to Jerome's translation was finally reversed by the Council of Trent in 1546, when the Western church endorsed it as the authoritative Bible for the Roman Catholic Church.[160] The Hebrew-based text for which Jerome had argued so vehemently continues to undergird the translations and exegetical endeavors of the Western church's scholars and churches. Jerome's attempt to revise the Western church's canon into a Hebraic form found limited success. With

---

157. Lossl, "Shift in Patristic Exegesis," 166–70.

158. *Commentary on Galatians*, 15.

159. Rebenich, "Jerome: The 'Vir Trilinguis' and the 'Hebraica Veritas,'" 50.

160. "It is the irony of history that Jerome's translation into Latin, later called the Vulgate, was endowed with the same authoritative significance that the Church had for centuries attempted to bestow on the Septuagint by means of the legend of its creation" (Muller, *First Bible of the Church*, 88 n. 43).

Augustine's influence, the Western church's three councils in 393, 397, and 419 approved the Septuagint canon as did Pope Innocent I in 405.[161] The same church body that later adopted Jerome's translation failed to adopt his canon: "The irony [that Jerome's translation was endowed with authority] is augmented by the fact that in the meantime the Apocrypha had become incorporated into the Latin canon."[162] It was not until the time of the Reformation that the canon question was reconsidered and adopted in Jerome's direction by the Protestant churches. These dual moves toward Jerome's translation and canon are slight but definite projections toward a Jewish orientation. Only in the centuries following the Reformation would the Christian church begin to affirm its debt to the Jewish people.

161. Sparks, "Jerome as Biblical Scholar," 534.
162. Muller, *First Bible of the Church*, 88 n. 43.

Table 1: Canonical Lists of Old Testament Books

Hebrew (Talmud)	Prologue to Kings (392)	Jerome's Letter 53 (393)	Council of Rome (382)	LXX (Codex Vaticanus)
Genesis–Deuteronomy	Genesis–Deuteronomy	Genesis–Deuteronomy	Genesis–Deuteronomy	Genesis–Deuteronomy
Joshua	Joshua	Job	Joshua	Joshua
Judges	Judges	Joshua	Judges	Judges
Samuel (1–2)	Ruth	Judges	Ruth	Ruth
Kings (1–2)	Samuel (1–2)	Ruth	Kings (1–4)	Samuel (1–2)
Jeremiah	Kings (1–2)	Samuel (1–2)	Chronicles (1–2)	Kings (1–2)
Ezekiel	Isaiah	Kings (1–2)	Psalms	Chronicles (1–2)
Isaiah	Jeremiah	Twelve	Proverbs	1 Esdras
Twelve	Ezekiel	Isaiah	Ecclesiastes	Ezra–Nehemiah
Ruth	Twelve	Jeremiah	Song	Psalms
Psalms	Job	Ezekiel	Wisdom of Solomon	Proverbs
Job	Psalms	Daniel	Sirach (Ecclesiasticus)	Ecclesiastes
Proverbs	Proverbs	Psalms	Isaiah	Song
Ecclesiastes	Ecclesiastes	Proverbs	Jeremiah–Lamentations	Job
Song	Song	Ecclesiastes	Ezekiel	Wisdom of Solomon
Lamentations	Daniel	Song	Daniel	Sirach (Ecclesiasticus)
Daniel	Chronicles (1–2)	Esther	Twelve (Hosea–Malachi)	Esther
Esther	Ezra (1–2)	Chronicles (1–2)	Job	Judith
Ezra–Nehemiah	Esther	Ezra–Nehemiah	Tobit	Tobit
Chronicles (1–2)			Esdras (1–2)	Twelve
			Esther	Isaiah
			Judith	Jeremiah
			Maccabees (1–2)	Baruch
				Lamentations
				Epistle of Jeremiah
				Ezekiel
				Susana
				Daniel
				Bel & Dragon

Chapter 3

"Back to the Hebrew Truth"
Jerome's Ambivalent Quest for Jewish Truth

FEW AUTHORS IN THE early centuries of the Christian church break with the prevailing disdain that Christian supersessionism heaped upon the Jews. One of them is Jerome. In answer to a letter from two Christians from Goth who presented numerous questions to Jerome about the differences between their Septuagint-based Psalter and Jerome's Gallican Psalter, he responds: "Therefore in the Old Testament, if there is a difference between the Greek and Latin, we flee back to the Hebrew truth, so that whatever flows from that spring, this we seek in the stream."[1] In a striking feat of iconoclasm, Jerome shatters the image of the rejected Jewish people and their ancient languages, texts, and traditions, and turns the Christian church "back to the Hebrew truth" in order to stabilize the Christians' heritage as rooted in the Old Testament. Few others navigate the boundary separating the Jews and the Christians as surprisingly and skillfully as does this late ancient Christian ascetic.

Some Christians considered Jerome suspect because of his unusual affection for the truth of the Jewish Scriptures mediated by contemporary Jews, what he calls the "Hebrew truth" (*Hebrica veritas*). His method for obtaining this truth was to gather relevant information, not only from written works of Jewish tradition or other Christian works, but from Jewish teachers whom he hired for that purpose.[2] The breadth of material that he included from his Jewish sources is remarkable and is scattered throughout his letters, his commentaries, and his translation of the Old Testament. Jerome's association with Jewish teachers finds few parallels in Christian

---

1. *Ep.* 106.2 (CSEL 56:249).
2. Newman, "Jerome and the Jews," 5.

history up to his time and for a thousand years thereafter. The only other Christian writer before Jerome who had fairly similar Jewish associations was Origen.[3] Although he did include the Hebrew text in the *Hexapla*, Origen never considered the Hebrew text as authoritative for Christian doctrine.[4] It has been conjectured that one of Jerome's contemporaries in the East, Eusebius of Emesa, might have pushed Jerome to elevate the Hebrew Test. In Eusebius's commentaries, he consulted the Hebrew text through Jews without knowing the language himself but he never considered the Hebrew the authoritative.[5] These two Christian exegetes no doubt influenced the trajectory of Jerome, who eventually violated traditional Christian boundaries in his quest for the Hebrew truth.

I believe that Jerome constructs late-fourth-century Christian identity by reshaping Christian supersessionism into a more relational model of appropriation and appreciation, leading to ambiguity and contradiction. Jerome rejects the exclusively spiritual Christian interpretation of the Old Testament. Much like those in the "Antiochene" tradition of literal exegesis, he insists on the historical or literal exposition of the Old Testament in order to provide a legitimate basis for the spiritual interpretation. I will survey his writings to demonstrate such an emphasis on reclaiming Jewish exegesis, with its emphasis on historical exposition, as a necessary and integral part of Christian doctrine, and I will then draw conclusions of his views about Jews and Judaism and how they define Jerome and his place in the history of Christian supersessionism.

JEROME'S LAUDATORY DISCOURSE ABOUT HEBREW TRUTH

Jerome figures prominently as one of the few Christian writers in ancient Christianity who turned to the Jews for their understanding of the Old Testament as the foundation for a genuinely Christian understanding. He frequently validates his own research by appealing to the "Hebrew truth." As Megan Williams notes, this phrase represents more than simply the

---

3. Origen was the first Christian scholar to use the Hebrew text consistently in the *Hexapla* to correct the Septuagint. His actual knowledge of the Hebrew language is uncertain. See McKane, *Selected Christian Hebraists*, 22–31.

4. Salvesen, "Convergence of the Ways?," 241. For more information about Origen's contacts with Jewish rabbis see De Lange, *Origen and the Jews*.

5. Kamesar, *Jerome, Greek Scholarship*, 43 n. 11; Law, *When God Spoke Greek*, 152–54.

Hebrew text of the Old Testament.⁶ It includes written Jewish materials that aided his interpretation of the Scriptures, Jewish teachers whom he employed as tutors, and any references to Jewish sources consulted by earlier Christian writers (such as Origen and Eusebius of Caesarea). While scholars have debated Jerome's proficiency in the Hebrew language and the veracity of his Jewish contacts, the consensus is that "there seems to be little real doubt that Jerome had some contact with the Jews of his day, and most scholars are willing to accept that Jerome could at least read Hebrew."⁷ The following is a survey of Jerome's favorable opinions toward Hebrew sources of truth from his correspondence, the prologues to his translation of the Old Testament, his commentaries, and several of his other works.

Jerome's Letters

Jerome's voluminous correspondence provides a personal look at a monk who communicated regularly with his patrons, friends, and associates. This review of his letters is presented in chronological order, examining letters written from about 380 to 412.⁸ His correspondence reveals no progression to philo-Semitism, but rather a thirty-year pattern of appreciation for the language and text of the Hebrew Old Testament and interaction with the people who transmitted their language and traditions to him. In the first example, Jerome bestows highest honor on the original language of the Old Testament since "universal tradition" teaches that the Hebrew language is the original tongue before the confusion of languages at Babel spread a variety among the nations.⁹ In the same letter he points to the source of his unique knowledge as found in a Jewish teacher: ". . . a man from whom I rejoice to have learned a great deal." Jerome presents to this letter's recipient, Pope Damasus, the Jewish teacher's interpretation of an Old Testament passage with the urging "that you may perceive this man's

---

6. Williams, *Monk and the Book*, 89. She notes that the phrase occurs over one hundred times, mainly in Jerome's exegetical books (90).

7. Graves, *Jerome's Hebrew Philology*, 7; see also Williams, *Monk and the Book*, 226–30; Rebenich, "Jerome: The 'Vir Trilinguis' and the 'Hebraica Veritas,'" 58–65; and Hasselhoff, "Revising the Vulgate," 209–21.

8. A complete list of Jerome's letters on this subject is in Hosmer, "Epistles of St. Jerome."

9. *Ep.* 18A.6.7 (CSEL 54:82).

interpretation."[10] In another letter to the pope, Jerome places Jewish interpretation alongside Christian interpretations for the meaning of the word *hosanna*. He then surveys several Christian interpretations and implores Pope Damasus to "forsake the rivulets of opinion [of Christians] and hasten back to the source [Hebrew] whence it was taken by the Evangelists . . . it is from the Hebrew codices that the truth must be extracted."[11] This is the first statement of Jerome's evident preference for what he later calls the "Hebrew truth." In another letter Jerome uses a culinary image to compare the Hebrew language to coarse food in contrast to the Latin literary tradition of savory delicacies. Using Hebrew as an edible food comes as a surprise, since Jerome's asceticism prides itself on relinquishing such luxuries in favor of the monastic ideal.[12] Another letter reveals Jerome's desire to obtain certain books from the synagogue in Rome from a Jewish friend.[13] These texts cannot have been copies of the Hebrew Old Testament (which he already possessed), but must have been Jewish works of biblical interpretation or midrash.[14]

In a letter to his first patron, Marcella, a wealthy Roman widow, Jerome defines the role of the true exegete as one who understands the sense of the original author, necessitating a knowledge of the original language.[15] In a lengthy letter to a former Roman senator turned monk, Jerome argues repeatedly that the Hebrew, not the Greek Septuagint, contains the words that are quoted in several New Testament texts.[16] He elsewhere uses a simple analogy to illustrate his impulse to return to the original languages of each testament: "For as the true text of the Old Testament can only be tested by a reference to the Hebrew, so the true text of the New requires for its

---

10. *Ep.* 18A.10–15 (CSEL 54:86–96).

11. *Ep.* 20.1-2 (CSEL 54:104–5).

12. *Ep.* 29.1 (CSEL 54:232–33). Megan Williams enlarges upon this theme in *The Monk and the Book*, arguing that Jerome presents himself in a contradictory way, claiming the monastic values of asceticism yet acting like a Roman scholar and rhetorician.

13. *Ep.* 36.1 (CSEL 54:268).

14. Braverman suggests that they were works of Jewish midrash (*Jerome's Commentary on Daniel*, 8); Graves follows Vaccari's suggestion that they were a "non-biblical aggadic text" (*Jerome's Hebrew Philology*, 92 n. 62). A term that Jerome uses for his Jewish teachers is the Greek word *deuterotes*, which he says is a translation of the Hebrew word *esna* and is linguistically related to the terms Mishna and Tanna (Williams, *Monk and the Book*, 224).

15. *Ep.* 37 (CSEL 54:286–89).

16. *Ep.* 57 (CSEL 54:503–26).

decision an appeal to the Greek."[17] Jerome writes a letter defending his use of Origen, Apollinaris, and Didymus along with his justification for hiring a Jewish teacher: "What trouble and expense it cost me to get Baranina to teach me under cover of night. For by his fear of the Jews he presented to me in his own person a second edition of Nicodemus. ... Yet can anyone find fault with me for having had a Jew as a teacher?"[18] Here Jerome casts the Jew in the role of an inquirer as well as a teacher. Jerome becomes Jesus, representing the truth that the Jew seeks under cover of darkness regardless of his fear of fellow Jews. This teacher is not a Jewish missionary spreading indoctrination to Jerome, as some detractors such as Rufinus might wish to perceive him; rather he is a potential convert sharing his Hebrew knowledge with Jerome, who stands in the position of stability. Jerome's knowledge of the Hebrew language and Jewish worship methods became a tool to impart to others, including his patron Paula, who "succeeded so well that she could chant the psalms in Hebrew and could speak the language without a trace of the pronunciation peculiar to Latin."[19] It might be asked where Jerome learned to chant the Psalms. A possible answer is that Jerome attended synagogue services, since chanting was a liturgical practice involving musical tones that he would have heard repeatedly and learned during his attendance.[20]

Jerome's later years reveal the same constancy of dependence and appreciation of Jewish tutors. As we have seen, he defends himself to Augustine concerning his translation from Hebrew by asking Augustine to consult the Jews in order to check the accuracy of his translation: "My work on the Old Testament is ... authentic, for in it I did not include my own ideas but only translated the divine texts as I found them in the Hebrew. If you do not believe me, ask the Hebrew scholars."[21] In a clear statement of his dependence and submission to Jews, Jerome positions himself under the authority of those who speak the language of the sacred text. His positioning implicitly infuses the relationship as one of legitimacy and indebtedness. It is not surprising then that Jerome commends the giving of alms

---

17. *Ep.* 71.5 (CSEL 55:6).
18. *Ep.* 84.3 (CSEL 55:123).
19. *Ep.* 108.27 (CSEL 55:345).
20. Graves, *Jerome's Hebrew Philology*, 91.
21. *Ep.* 112.20 (CSEL 55:391); White, *Correspondence between Jerome and Augustine*, 136. English translations are from White.

to poor Jews and Samaritans.²² In a letter written in 412, seven years before his death in 419, he recalls his first attempt to learn the Hebrew language:

> In my youth when the desert walled me in with its solitude I was still unable to endure the promptings of sin and the natural heat of my blood; and, although I tried by frequent fasts to break the force of both, my mind still surged with [evil] thoughts. To subdue its turbulence I betook myself to a brother who before his conversion had been a Jew and asked him to teach me Hebrew.²³

Jerome links the study of Hebrew with control over his inner struggles, thereby elevating it as a spiritual discipline. I find it curious that he learns Hebrew not from a Jew but from a Jewish Christian, whom he does not describe negatively here, whereas elsewhere he castigates such people as mingling Jewish practices with Christian worship. He is a fellow Christian monk who is presented as the bridge leading Jerome into the as-yet-un-explored world of Hebrew truth. Rather than seeking out a Jew to begin his quest, Jerome finds his connection to the hidden truth through one in between. This same section of his letter includes a retrospective comment about his attempt to learn Hebrew: "I thank the Lord that from this bitter seed of learning I now pick sweet fruits." The value of mining Hebrew truth far exceeds his exertion in the process. This final comment, highlighting the sweetness, fittingly summarizes the tone of his correspondence.

Jerome's Translation Prologues

The prologues to Jerome's translations of many Old Testament books offer another glimpse of his positive views of Hebrew truth. He composed each of these to introduce his particular translation and justify its need. He then sent the prologue along with the translation to those who had requested it. In these enlightening texts, Jerome justifies his translation from what he considers to be the Hebrew originals. For example, he defends his radical departure from the tradition of basing translation on the Greek Septuagint by appealing to the New Testament authors' similar practice of quoting from the Hebrew Old Testament: "Therefore let us ask them [defenders of the Septuagint] where these are written, and when they are unable to

---

22. *Ep.* 120 (CSEL 55:472–515).
23. *Ep.* 125.12 (CSEL 56:131).

say, we may produce them from the Hebrew books."[24] Such an appeal is made repeatedly to his critics, asking them to check the accuracy of his translation by asking contemporary Jews, whom Jerome considers worthy linguistic judges of their own language and of Latin: "They may ask the Hebrews and their authors, whether they accept or reject the faithfulness of my translation."[25] As we have seen, he rejected the books of the Apocrypha on the basis that they "are not in the canon"[26]—that is, the Jewish canon. This stance positions Jerome against the accepted Christian canon as found in the Septuagint. Jerome encourages his critics to inquire of Jews living at that time rather than to consult the Hebrew text (which they were probably not even able to translate). Thus Jerome invests a certain degree of trust in those Jews who had been rejected by Christian theology. His prologues continue to invite fellow Christians to engage Jewish leaders: "Consult the teachers of the many different cities."[27] Jerome empowers the Jews with authority in these matters as can be seen in his use of the present tense, i.e., "The Jews say . . ."[28]

In an unusual display of subservience, he positions the Jews and their corroborative witness over his own authority:

> Certainly, if you are incredulous, read the Greek and Latin books and compare them with these little works, and wherever you will see among them to differ, ask any one of the Hebrews, in whom you might place better faith, and if he confirms ours, I think that you will not consider him a diviner, as he has similarly divined in the very same place with me.[29]

This is an amazing reshaping of Christian supersessionism. Jerome highlights the fact that his study of Hebrew was accomplished through Jewish tutors. He did not teach himself the language. The price of such knowledge was steep, since he mentions that the teachers he hired were of the highest quality: "I remember I paid not a little money to understand this scroll for an instructor

---

24. *Prologue to the Pentateuch* 17; *Biblia Sacra* 3. See also *Prologue to Paralipomenon* 21; *Biblia Sacra* 546.

25. *Prologue to Ezra* 31; *Biblia Sacra* 638; see also *Prologue to Psalms* [second] 28; *Biblia Sacra* 768.

26. *Prologue to Kings* 55; *Biblia Sacra* 365.

27. *Prologue to Pentateuch* 43; *Biblia Sacra* 4.

28. *Prologue to Pentateuch* 21; *Biblia Sacra* 3.

29. *Prologue to Kings* 69–73; *Biblia Sacra* 365–66.

from Lydda who among the Hebrews was thought to have first rank."[30] Jerome even found personal solace from one of his Jewish instructors: "Indeed, a Hebrew was encouraging me, and he was often repeating to me by his language, 'Persistent work conquers all.'"[31] These prologues witness to a Christian who senses his debt and his gratitude to the Jews for their Hebrew truth. Although his actual Latin translations do not betray a consistent adherence to rabbinic exegesis,[32] his debt to the Jews remains transparent.

Jerome's Commentaries

Jerome's commentaries on the Hebrew prophets constitute "the greatest achievement of Jerome's career as a biblical scholar."[33] Spanning the last fifteen years of his life, these detailed works reveal Jerome's dependence on Jewish interpretations. For example, his commentary on Ecclesiastes contains twenty explicit statements attributing his information to Jewish sources.[34] This is highly significant, because while the text was regarded as fixed and reaching back to biblical authors, the interpretations were communicated to Jerome by those very Jews who had rejected the Christian message and contain material from non-Christian rabbinic sources. The Hebrew traditions preserve what Jerome considers the literal and historical senses (*iuxta litteram; iuxta historiam*). Jerome values these as the foundation upon which the truly Christian interpretation, known as the allegorical and spiritual (*iuxta allegoriam, spiritaliter*), can be fashioned.[35] As Elizabeth Clark notes, "according to the Fathers, the allegedly 'literal' reading by 'heretics' and Jews fails to acknowledge the moral or spiritual dimensions of *all* Scripture and does so with nefarious intent."[36] Jerome embraces such nefarious interpretations as crucial to proper Christian readings. Instead of resorting to spiritual interpretations to "save the text" from the Jews, Jerome rejects this Christian exegetical tradition and sets himself up as the

---

30. Prologue to Job 20–21; *Biblia Sacra* 731.

31. Prologue to Daniel 16; *Biblia Sacra* 1341.

32. Cameron argues that Jerome's Latin translations do not evidence the same sort of rabbinic influence as in his commentaries ("Rabbinic Vulgate?").

33. Williams, *Monk and the Book*, 66.

34. Ibid., 82. For an example, see Kraus, "Christian, Jews, and Pagans in Dialogue."

35. He also uses *iuxta tropologiam*, which refers to a figurative reading, seemingly synonymous with the other two terms (Williams, *Monk and the Book*, 115).

36. Clark, *Reading Renunciation*, 79.

one who can successfully recover those "carnal" readings shared with the Jews, and then assemble the christological structure appropriately. He joins the two interpretive approaches together, as the one naturally progresses to the other: "I have united the history of the Hebrews with the tropology of our own [interpreters], so that I might build upon rock and not upon sand, and thus lay a stable foundation."[37] His exegetical work is always based on a close reading of the Hebrew text as well as the traditional Jewish interpretation. He then follows with the Christian allegorical interpretation, at times grounded in the Septuagint.[38] Jerome tantalizes his readers with Jewish mysteries that remain hidden from all Christians except himself: "I formerly resolved to make available to Latin listeners the secrets of Hebrew learning and the hidden knowledge of the teachers of the synagogue."[39]

To begin with, Jerome considered the Hebrew language, which he himself had learned at great cost, to be the original tongue from which all others develop.[40] With such a high view of the Jews' own language, it is not surprising that he wishes to rescue as much Hebrew truth from their language and tradition as is possible for Christian use. For example, when he attempts to explain the Jewish feasts in Zechariah 8:19, Jerome laments the poor Christian interpretations of the passage and finds truth in the Jewish sources: "We are compelled therefore to return to the Hebrews, and to see the knowledge of truth rather from the wellspring than from the rivulets."[41] Using such an analogy, Jerome considers the authority of Jewish interpreters very close to that of the Hebrew biblical text. Although he never accepts such interpretations uncritically, when juxtaposed with Christian interpretations, Jerome at times gives priority to their consideration and to their adoption. Kamesar observes: "It may be, therefore, that in using the same language to describe both the Hebrew text and rabbinic exegesis, Jerome is alluding in this passage not only to the privileged position which he affords the latter, but also to the intimate connection between the two."[42] What is more, Newman has discovered that "in rare cases, Jerome goes

---

37. *Commentary on Zechariah*, prologue 37–39 (CCSL 76A:748). English translation from Williams, *Monk and the Book*, 117. She notes the allusion to the parable of the house built on the rock.

38. Williams, *Monk and the Book*, 120.

39. *Commentary on Zechariah* 6:9–15 (CCSL 76A:796).

40. *Commentary on Zephaniah* 3:18 (CCSL 76A:708).

41. *Commentary on Zechariah* 8:19 (CCSL 76A:820).

42. Kamesar, *Jerome, Greek Scholarship, and the Hebrew Bible*, 182.

so far as to uncover hidden Christian meaning in the aggada itself, and not merely in the Biblical text."[43] This aggada includes post-biblical history as well as the events from the time of Jerome.[44] Thus Jerome purposefully accepts non-biblical texts handed down by non-Christian Jewish rabbis that supposedly contain spiritual truth for Christians. Jerome's Hebrew learning came not only from culling information from the Hebrew texts he had borrowed, but directly from living Jewish teachers. Graves notes that Jerome claims to have had at least five such teachers, in addition to the first instructor (a Jewish convert to Christianity) who taught him the Hebrew language.[45] He defends his comments on the sacred texts by appealing to the living Jew as an unassailable source of scriptural authority, for example: "As the Hebrew used to say me to me."[46] Megan Williams notes an important difference: "Consistently, Jerome portrayed his access to Jewish exegesis as obtained from living Jewish teachers, never from books."[47] One might think that Jerome would appeal to written texts produced by Jews rather than Jewish teachers so as to avoid contamination from such personal contact. But Jerome once again moves against the dominant culture of Christian supersessionism and follows his own agenda of searching out Hebrew truth wherever it might be found.

In Jerome's commentaries and in his Latin translation from the Hebrew Scriptures, he interjects countless rabbinic traditions, a "practically unlimited stock."[48] Several times Jerome mentions the names of older rabbis who were revered among the Jews, such as Rabbi Akiba, whose interpretations are presented as a viable option for Christians.[49] However, Jerome's usual approach is to avoid such direct citations of his Jewish sources, even hiding the fact that he is borrowing Jewish interpretations at all. Benjamin Kedar notes that much of Jerome's uncredited citations are uncovered only by "detective

43. Newman, "Jerome and the Jews," 8.
44. Ibid., 9.
45. Graves, *Jerome's Hebrew Philology*, 88 n. 50.
46. *Commentary on Ecclesiastes* 1.14 (CCSL 72:260).
47. Williams, *Monk and the Book*, 222.
48. Kedar, "Latin Translations," 331. For a bibliographic survey of the general topic of comparative studies of Jewish and Christian exegetical traditions see Baskin, "Rabbinic-Patristic Exegetical Contacts in Late Antiquity"; and Kamesar, "Church Fathers and Rabbinic Midrash."
49. *Commentary on Ecclesiastes* 4:13–16 (CCSL 72:288); Jerome mentions Shammai, Hillel, Johanan ben Zakkai and Meir in his *Commentary on Isaiah* 8:14 (CCSL 73:116), and Akiba, Simeon ben Gamaliel, and Hillel in *Ep.* 121.10 (CSEL 56:41–50).

work."⁵⁰ Kedar's own investigation uncovers many instances in which Jerome subtly introduces Jewish translations and midrashic interpretations that he offers as preferred Christian interpretations. Two examples will suffice. Jerome does not translate Numbers 9:2 so that the red heifer should be "perfect," as the Hebrew word would signify and as he usually translates the word. Rather he renders it as "fully grown," which is just what the *Targum Pseudo-Jonathan* and Ibn Ezra state. Again, in Isaiah 28:20, Jerome rewords "the bed is too short to stretch oneself on it" to "the bed is so narrow that one or the other must fall out." This translation is rooted in the Midrash and the Talmud, and his reason for using this is explained in his commentary.⁵¹ Marc Hirshman notes Jerome's care in distinguishing between the Jewish fables which the New Testament condemns⁵² and the Jewish midrashic traditions that Jerome trusts and from which he forms the basis for his historical interpretation: "I view this as a courageous stance, in quite splendid contrast to the view by Augustine ... where he had compared the Jew to a blind man holding up a light for others but unable to see himself."⁵³ Braverman's conclusion, based on his analysis of Jerome's commentary on Daniel, seems to be representative of the entirety of Jerome's work: "Jerome has cited far more Jewish traditions than any other Church Father or Josephus."⁵⁴ In an extensive treatment of Jerome's commentary on Jeremiah, Graves presents evidence that Jerome borrowed Jewish interpretations directly rather than merely copying them from other Christian interpreters, as some scholars have alleged.⁵⁵ "The value placed by Jerome on the literal sense of the Hebrew sometimes led him to correct the well-intentioned but uninformed spiritual readings of his fellow Christians."⁵⁶

We find suggestive evidence that Jerome very likely attended Jewish synagogue services. When describing such services, his comments sound like the observations of one in attendance: "The preachers persuade the people that what they invent is true, and when, in theatrical fashion, they have invited applause ... they frown and make weighed and balanced addresses, and usurp the authority of the rulers."⁵⁷ Comments about frowning faces

---

50. See his "Jewish Traditions in the Writings of Jerome" and "Latin Translations."
51. Kedar, "Jewish Traditions in the Writings of Jerome," 427.
52. Such as Titus 1:14, "... pay no attention to Jewish myths ..."
53. Hirshman, *Rivalry of Genius*, 106.
54. Braverman, *Jerome's Commentary on Daniel*, 135.
55. See Graves, *Jerome's Hebrew Philology*, 197, for his summary and conclusion.
56. Graves lists three passages found in Jerome's *Commentary on Jeremiah*, xlii.
57. *Commentary on Ezekiel* 34:31 (CCSL 75:490); see also *Commentary on Isaiah* 58:2

and applauding hands surely sound as if Jerome is actually present inside a synagogue and observing such reactions from those near him. His presence in a Jewish worship service would be highly irregular for a fourth-century Christian monk, to say the least. In the same time frame of the fourth century, Chrysostom was forbidding Christians in Constantinople, especially women, from celebrating festivals in Jewish homes, attending synagogue services, and adopting Jewish customs.[58] In spite of ecclesiastical opposition, Jerome's inquisitive mind took him far beyond the Hebrew Scriptures and propelled him across the border maintained by Jerome's accusers.

Finally, in *Hebrew Questions on Genesis* Jerome offers the Christian world a unique work, and in light of its significance two scholars have devoted recent studies to this work. Adam Kamesar argues that Jerome writes with two purposes: "to justify a return to the Hebrew text, and to put forward his own system for interpreting that text."[59] According to Kamesar, Jerome used this platform to defend his sympathetic approach to the Jewish text and tradition in his other commentaries and translations, against his detractors in the Christian tradition.[60] C. T. R. Hayward provides a fresh translation and his own commentary in which he observes that "almost every comment which Jerome makes owes something to Jewish teachings."[61] He discovers significant parallels in this book to the Midrash Rabbah, the Targums, and the two Talmuds.[62] Hayward claims that the purpose of this work is "nothing less than an attempt to justify his dealings with Judaism and the Jews, when the ecclesiastical and civil authorities were intent on pushing that nation to the margins of Christian society."[63] Once again, here is additional evidence that Jerome is unabashed in his quest for Hebrew truth.[64]

(CCSL 73A:660).

58. Wilken, *John Chrysostom and the Jews*, 66–94. Chrysostom admits that his sermons against the Jews had the opposite effect by "making people curious and attracting even more people to Jewish ways" (75).

59. Kamesar, *Jerome, Greek Scholarship, and the Hebrew Bible*, 191. It was not written to defend his Latin translation, since this book was finished in 393, before he translated the Pentateuch, from 398 to 406.

60. Ibid., 80.

61. Hayward, *Saint Jerome's Hebrew Questions on Genesis*, 7 n. 15.

62. Ibid., 19–23.

63. Ibid., 14.

64. For a fascinating example of Jerome's indebtedness to rabbinic scholarship and his subtle Christianizing of their content, see R. Hayward, "Saint Jerome, Jewish Learning."

In summary, Jerome consistently affirms his stated desire to seek out truth from Jewish sources, be they the ancient language of the Jews, the texts of Old Testament books, the interpretations of Jewish rabbis, the influence of Jewish tutors, or the atmosphere of Jewish synagogue services. Jerome stands out for his appreciative valuing of Jews and their oral and written traditions in ways that separate him from the majority of the writings of other Christians.

JEROME'S DEROGATORY DISCOURSE AGAINST JEWS

In light of the foregoing discussion, one might suspect that Jerome is an unqualified philo-Semite. After all, from every genre of Jerome's extant texts, he extols the virtues of Hebrew truth and exemplifies dialogue with Jews. That presentation was somewhat one-sided, however, as the following selections will demonstrate. In the same body of texts referenced above, Jerome speaks in ways that seem to diminish or even contradict his positive sentiments.

Jerome's Letters

In his correspondence Jerome states his suspicion that a second-century Jewish translator has tampered with the meaning of the Hebrew and discovers such in his research: "I have been comparing Aquila's version of the Old Testament with the scrolls of the Hebrew, to see if from hatred to Christ the synagogue has changed the text; and—to speak frankly to a friend—I have found several variations which confirm our faith."[65] In a discussion about Jews lamenting their dead, Jerome says that they "make their superstition complete, they follow a foolish custom of the Pharisees, and eat lentils, to show, it would seem, for what poor fare they have lost their birthright."[66] Here Jerome speaks the classic language of supersessionism—the Jews are forsaken by God. Further, he decries that the religion of the synagogue offers nothing but dead ceremonies.[67] In response to the criticism of his hiring a Jewish teacher, Jerome's anti-Jewish rhetoric is unambiguous: "If it is expedient to hate any men and to loathe any race, I have a strange dislike

---

65. *Ep.* 32.1 (CSEL 54:252).
66. *Ep.* 39.4 (CSEL 54:302).
67. *Ep.* 74.4 (CSEL 55:26).

to those of the circumcision. For up to the present day they persecute our Lord Jesus Christ in the synagogues of Satan."[68]

In addition, Jerome could not conceive of any infusion of the Jewish custom of circumcision, Sabbath keeping, or dietary laws into Christianity, whether practiced by Jews or Gentiles. In correspondence with Augustine, Jerome expresses his disagreement with the practice of permitting Jewish Christians to perform Jewish customs, for such converts are "thereby professing their new faith without renouncing the old . . . in wishing to be both Jews and Christians, they are neither Jews nor Christians.."[69] For Jerome, Christians cannot not hold onto both religions since the new has subsumed the old, thus he fears that if these hybrid Christians "are allowed to observe in the churches of Christ what they practiced in the synagogues of Satan—I speak my mind—they will not become Christians but will make us Jews."[70] Jerome believes the pull toward the old religion to be so strong that even Gentile Christians would apostatize back to the "synagogues of Satan," a reference to the book of Revelation. He exaggerates the threat of Jewish influence on Christians while, at the same time, writing as one who successfully navigates that very area and enjoys protection from pernicious Jewish influence. He accuses Jews of omitting or tampering with the wording in the Greek translations of the Hebrew Scriptures, and he assures Christians that he himself is a reliable guide back so "that Latin-speakers might know what was really in the Hebrew text."[71] One questions how Jerome could trust his own Jewish teachers any more than the untrustworthy Jews who tampered with the wording. He never mentions how he knows the difference, but his posture is designed to elicit trust from his readers as to their infallible guide to Judaica.

In the same letter to Augustine he further constructs his mission as a discerner of Jewish character, even those Jews in North Africa, whom Jerome considers to be liars or less educated than those of Palestine: "But if your Jews, as you claim, whether out of spite or ignorance, said that the Hebrew edition contained the same as the Greek and Latin editions, it is clear

---

68. *Ep.* 84.3 (CSEL 55:123).

69. *Ep.* 112.13 (CSEL 55:382); White, *Correspondence*, 125–26.

70. Ibid. In a follow up letter, Augustine clarifies his misunderstood position as identical to Jerome's: "I never considered that Christian converts from Judaism should nowadays perform those ancient rites, whatever their feelings and intentions, or that they should in any way be allowed to do so" (Augustine's *Ep.* 82.15 [CSEL 34:366]; White, *Correspondence*, 158–59).

71. *Ep.* 112.20 (CSEL 55:390–91); White, *Correspondence*, 135.

that they are either ignorant of Hebrew literature or that they deliberately lied."[72] Here Jerome's supersessionism is marked by the possessive pronoun: "your Jews" and the implied "my Jews." In language that sounds much like that of a slave owner, Jerome refers to the Jewish people as part of the Christians' assets, to be used as needed in whatever lands they reside, even when their trustworthiness is suspect. Jerome was conversant with Jewish traditions, many of which he incorporated into his commentaries. However, in a letter written to a lady who posed exegetical questions to him, Jerome relates one Jewish tradition meant to illicit revulsion. He informs her:

> Many of them are so foul that I would blush to repeat them. Yet I will mention one example for the sake of shaming a enemy nation: the heads of the synagogues are charged with the following disgusting task, that in order to determine whether the blood of a virgin or a menstruant is pure or impure, if they cannot make the distinction by eye, they test it by tasting.[73]

The veracity of the tradition is irrelevant here, but the tenor of Jerome's opinion stands against the view he expresses elsewhere. Perhaps this is designed to provoke sympathy for Jerome as one who wisely interprets all things Jewish. In this letter he consigns an end to the Jewish religion: the "whole cult of Jewish observances was destroyed and they offer all manner of sacrifice not to God but to fleeing angels and unclean spirits."[74] Finally, he denigrates the Jewish custom of repeating the words of Scripture rather than putting them into practice.[75] This survey of Jerome's correspondence over a period of thirty years reveals a consistent attitude of denigration to Jews and Judaism of the fourth century, yet his tone is not as severe as Chrysostom or others in the *Adversus Judaeos* tradition. In fact, the number of his letters with negative sentiments is just half that of those with positive ones.

Jerome's Translation Prologues

There are the four instances of Jerome's negative attitude toward the Jews in his prologues to the Vulgate. They are noticeably lesser in number (less

---

72. *Ep.* 112.22 (CSEL 55:393); White, *Correspondence*, 137.
73. *Ep.* 121.10 (CSEL 56:48); Williams, *Monk and the Book*, 225.
74. *Ep.* 121.10 (CSEL 56:50).
75. *Ep.* 127.4 (CSEL 56:148).

"Back to the Hebrew Truth"

than one half) than those mentioned earlier with a positive tone. Jerome argues with Jews who, in turn, "accuse every word."[76] The details of such debate between Jerome and Jewish teachers are not known, but he does make reference to his interaction. It also reveals Jerome in dialogue with living Jews. For example: "I heard a certain one of the teachers of the Jews, when he derided the history of Susanna and said it to have been forged by an unknown Greek...."[77] Informing his patrons, Paula and Eustochium, of the reason for his learning Hebrew, Jerome claims to have "exerted myself in the learning of foreign languages for this: so the Jews might not jump all day on the errors of the Scriptures in his church."[78] This backhanded attack against the Jews also reveals his sense of Jewish presence and the attendant legitimacy of the opposition. In a more pointed criticism, he regards the Greek translations made by Aquila, Symmachus, and Theodotion to have "hidden many mysteries of the Savior by sly translation" since they are "Judaizing heretics."[79]

Jerome's Commentaries

These exegetical works contain similar restatements of distaste for and distrust of Jews. This is not an exhaustive catalog from Jerome's commentaries, but they are some of the more representative of the worst comments. He suggests that Jews have tampered with an Old Testament text (Deut 27:26) to remove a favorable Christian interpretation, and wonders whether the Septuagint added a particular phrase or that "the ancient manuscripts of the Jews contained a different reading than they do now . . . someone added 'by God' to both the Hebrew manuscripts and our own so as to shame us for believing in Christ."[80] It is puzzling that Jerome suspects that some Jews might tamper with the text, while other Jews he trusts actually preserve the text. In a preface to one of his works he urges the reader to ignore the "belching and nausea" of the Jews.[81] He says that Jewish interpreters "conceal the truth with lies" in passages that predict the coming of Christ.[82] He

---

76. *Prologue to Psalms* [Second] 35; *Biblia Sacra* 769.
77. *Prologue to Ezekiel* 23–25; *Biblia Sacra* 1266.
78. *Prologue to Isaiah* 30; *Biblia Sacra* 1096.
79. *Prologue to Job* 43–44; *Biblia Sacra* 732.
80. *Commentary on Galatians*, 143.
81. *Book on Hebrew Names*, preface (CCSL 72:60).
82. *Commentary on Zechariah* 2:8 (CCSL 76A:767).

calls Jewish prayers the "grunting of pigs and braying of asses"[83] and decries the Jewish hope of a return to the ancient homeland as a "carnal" interpretation.[84] He repeatedly calls the stories of the Jews "nonsense"[85] and the proclivity of Jews to reproduce is compared to that of little worms.[86] The Jews are said to be continually crucifying Christ.[87] Jerome refers several times to the curse against the heretics ("Birkat Ha Minim") that was supposedly prayed in the synagogue and interprets it as a Jewish curse against Christians.[88] Such vituperation is common among Jerome's contemporaries and antecedent commentators. What does stand out is that Jerome nowhere retracts the many positive sentiments toward Jews.

JEROME'S AMBIVALENT APPROACH TO JEWISH TRUTH

Two images have emerged of this early Christian monk: the Jerome whose quest in life drives him "back to the Hebrew truth" for divine revelation, and the Jerome who not only dismisses the Jewish religion as obsolete but inveighs against the Jews as deceivers and enemies. This discourse of opposites permeates Jerome's writings. No other writer in the first three centuries of the Christian church expresses such intimate contact with Jews while voicing a complete distaste for them. He hungers for the Hebrew truth and finds it only in submission to his Jewish teachers, but he ridicules those very teachers as distasteful and blind to deeper spiritual truths. To gain a fair portrait of Jerome, both attitudes must be observed and then evaluated to better understand this complex man.

Scholars agree about this dichotomy in Jerome. One writer describes the situation: "A deep ambivalence remains at the core of Jerome's enterprise–sweetness and bitterness, desire and fear–that marks mastery of Christian scholarship with the danger of the Jewish frontier from which it has been extracted."[89] Another author suspects that Jerome has "a split

---

83. *Commentary on Amos* 5:23 (CCSL 76:295).

84. *Commentary on Hosea* 3:4 (CCSL 76:37).

85. *Commentary on Isaiah* 15:4 (CCSL 73:177); *Commentary on Micah* 2:5 (CCSL 76:442).

86. *Commentary on Isaiah* 50:4–7 (CCSL 73A:553–54).

87. *Commentary on Matthew* 27:48 (CCSL 77:275).

88. *Commentary on Isaiah* 5:19 (CCSL 73A:76); ibid., 49:7 (CCSL 73A:538); and *Commentary on Amos* 1:11 (CCSL 76:227).

89. Jacobs, *Remains of the Jews*, 83.

personality" and a "dual loyalty" to both the Hebrew Old Testament and the Christian message, which produced his "ambivalent attitude towards the Jewish exegesis of the Bible."[90] In setting out to discover Jerome's motivation for going back to the Hebrew truth, yet another admits that "Jerome himself expresses views in contradiction to those I have attributed to him" and suggests that "Jerome expresses conflicting views depending upon his audience."[91] Another describes Jerome's attitude toward Jewish interpretations as "profoundly ambivalent" and "walking a tightrope."[92] Still another describes Jerome's love for Christian allegory coupled with his deep attachment to the Hebrew historical interpretation an "apparent contradiction." She further describes Jerome's attitudes toward his Jewish teachers as "paradoxical"[93] as well as "profoundly ambivalent."[94]

Several scholars go beyond mere description and attempt to resolve such ambivalences. Megan Hale Williams draws the conclusion that Jerome's ambivalence can be attributed to his desire for monastic achievement and authority. His choice of the Hebrew text "was by no means a simple recognition of scientific fact. Rather, it was an idiosyncratic insight, which allowed Jerome to construct for himself a unique position as an authority on the scriptures."[95] She further argues that due to his own dedication to monasticism, Jerome ridiculed any notion of "carnal" life in the eschaton as incommensurable with Christian ideals: "Jerome's particular version of the Jew, that is, served both to facilitate his appropriation of Jewish learning and, by contrast, to legitimate his entire way of life."[96] These insights are valuable in assessing Jerome's construction of his monastic identity, but they do not advance the discussion beyond his ascetic motivation to the larger issues within Christian supersessionism.

Benjamin Kedar offers his conclusion, stating that Jerome "built the most important bridge between the classic Jewish culture and Western Europe." Yet he goes on to suggest: "*Nolens volens* [whether willing or not]

---

90. Kedar, "Jewish Traditions in the Writings of Jerome," 420.

91. Kamin, "Theological Significance of the *Hebraica Veritas*," 250. She continues with, "I can offer no explanation of this contradiction" (251).

92. Newman, "Jerome and the Jews," 8, 10.

93. Williams, *Monk and the Book*, 129, 223. "Jerome's representation of his Jewish teachers, then, is as contradictory as his use of the exegetical materials he attributes to Jews" (226).

94. Williams, "Lessons from Jerome's Jewish Teachers," 67.

95. Williams, *Monk and the Book*, 71.

96. Williams, "Lessons from Jerome's Jewish Teachers," 85.

he did it; but then, history is full of such ironic twists."[97] This is too casual an interpretation of Jerome's motivations. It seems rather that he is quite willing and purposeful to move into the forbidden area of Hebrew truth and even defends himself on that point. The evidence suggests that Jerome displays the candor of one intent on introducing Jewish biblical interpretations into Christian tradition.

RESOLUTION OF JEROME'S APPROACH TO JEWISH TRUTH

Jerome's two dissonant voices are undeniable, but to cast him as merely inconsistent, or suffering from a split personality, or as defining his asceticism are inadequate efforts to understand the complexity of his person and the significance of his life's ambition. It is only when these divergent attitudes are placed within the larger framework of Christian supersessionism that we can begin to grasp how integral and even necessary they are to Jerome's personality. My solution attempts to explain Jerome's ambivalent approach to the Hebrew truth by recognizing that both aspects are a necessary part of a Christian supersessionist whose goal is the radical transformation of Christian identity. In order for him to achieve such a result, Jerome plays the role of three persons that only in tension with each other form the entire person of the ambivalent Christian supersessionist. He is at once an iconoclast, shattering the received tradition of shunning the Jews; he is a traditionalist, maintaining the received tradition of rejecting the Jews; and he is a broker, purchasing and purifying Jewish treasures for Christian use.

Jerome as Iconoclast

Jerome's overarching contribution to the Christian church lies in his charting a new course of Christian identity by resurrecting the ancient roots of the Christian faith. As Alison Salvesen considers Origen to be the one responsible for the "Hebraization of the Christian Bible,"[98] so I consider Jerome to be the one responsible for the Hebraization of the Christian interpretive tradition. He regularly seeks out contacts with Jewish teachers throughout his long life, from his early days in the desert of Chalcis

---

97. Kedar, "Jewish Traditions in the Writings of Jerome," 430.
98. Salvesen, "Convergence of the Ways?," 242.

learning Hebrew,[99] to his time in Rome,[100] and to Bethlehem, where he regularly hires Jews to assist in his work.[101] This is uncharacteristic of Christian monks and church leaders, whose most vocal personalities urge Christians to avoid associating with Jews and the synagogue.

Jerome shifts the balance of fourth-century Christian supersessionism by his overt quotations of and approval of ancient and contemporary Jewish interpretations attained through his personal contact with Jews inside and outside of the synagogue. By the fourth century, Christians had amassed their own body of commentaries on the Old and New Testaments. Jerome has the foresight to realize that Jewish exegesis was largely absent from those Christian exegetical resources. He takes it upon himself to admit the poverty of Christian exegesis and reach across party lines "back to the Hebrew truth." Jerome's inclusion of Jewish sources must also be seen in the context of his inclusion of classical Roman sources as well.[102] Such a background in Roman rhetoric actually forms the categories of exegesis. He studies in Rome while in his teens under the famous teacher Donatus. Graves argues that such Roman training provided Jerome with the categories of literary interpretation that he evinces in his commentaries on biblical texts.[103] This training gives Jerome the methodology to incorporate his quest for Hebrew truth into a coherent system. Jerome blends Roman erudition with Hebrew scholarship and his own Christian interpretation to produce his unique exegesis. Its iconoclastic threat is seen in the writings of one who despised Jerome's Jewish-oriented influence in the Christian church.

Rufinus of Aquila, leader of a monastery on the Mount of Olives and early friend-turned-enemy of Jerome, chides Jerome for an interpretation of Scripture that bears the marks of Jewish roots: "Perhaps it is one obtained from some of your Jews, which is now to be promulgated as a new law for the church, so that we may learn their ways."[104] Rufinus criticizes not only Jerome's use of a Jewish interpretation, but he further censures him for a personal relationship with Jews, implying that such close contact has poisoned whatever is left of Jerome's Christian judgment. Rufinus sees Jerome's

---

99. *Ep.* 125.12 (CSEL 56:131).

100. *Ep.* 36.1 (CSEL 54:268).

101. *Ep.* 84.3 (CSEL 55:123).

102. As noted particularly by Kraus, "Christian, Jews, and Pagans," 213–19.

103. Graves, *Jerome's Hebrew Philology*, 13–75. He describes the four parts: reading aloud, explanation, textual criticism, and literary judgment.

104. *Apology Against Jerome* 1.7 (PL 21:546C).

association with them as compromising his Christian integrity by elevating Jewish teachings as Christian dogma. Although Jerome has a certain control over them ("your Jews"), Rufinus fears that such behavior will blur the traditional boundary between these opposing religions.

In the same text another aspect of Jerome's affirmative stance toward Jews is sarcastically revealed by Rufinus. He berates Jerome for hiring a Jew whom Jerome had named Baranina:[105]

> It is of Barabbas whom, unlike me, he took as his teacher from the Synagogue.... From that other friend of yours, Barabbas, whom you chose out of the synagogue rather than Christ, you learned to hope for a resurrection not in power but in frailty, to love the letter which kills and hate the spirit which gives life, and other more secret things, which, if occasion so require, shall afterwards in due time be brought to light.[106]

In a stinging and sarcastic pun, Rufinus turns Jerome's Jewish teacher into the guilty rebel who was released instead of Christ. Jerome is further positioned as one of the traitorous Jews who said "Give us Barrabas." Rufinus thus considers Jerome to have become one with the Jews. No more pejorative language could be assigned to Jerome than to be labeled as a friend of the Jews—those who have polluted Jerome's mind with sinister secrets unfit for Christian consumption. Rufinus chides Jerome for "making a new translation under the influence of the Jews"[107] and laments that his old friend has turned away—the one who was "most dear to me before you were taken captive by the Jews."[108] In the eyes of Rufinus, his old friend Jerome, ostensibly a former hater of Jews like the rest of supersessionist Christendom, has now become a slave of the intoxicating power of the enemy. This sense of betrayal was voiced not only by Rufinus but also by unnamed others against whom Jerome repeatedly defends himself in his writings, especially his prologues to the translations of the Old Testament. Thus these voices support my contention that Jerome was perceived to have broken the bounds of Christian separation from Judaism. These contemporaries saw it, objected to it, and caused Jerome to defend his reputation against these detractors.

---

105. Previously named by Jerome in his *Ep.* 84.3.
106. *Apology Against Jerome* 2.12 (PL 21:595B).
107. Ibid., 2.32 (PL 21:611B).
108. Ibid., 2.37 (PL 21:615C).

"Back to the Hebrew Truth"

Jerome responds to this criticism by justifying his actions, not by denying them. He sets himself up as a careful sifter of truth from error, just as he read Origen with a critical eye: "I did not say that he was my master; but I wanted to verify my study of Sacred Scripture to prove that I had read Origen just as I had heard it also from the Jew."[109] In Jerome's eyes, to have a Jew as a master is far different than to use a Jew as a servant. Jerome gives a further defense against his own supposed Judaizing—the purpose of his translation is for a Christian defense against the Jews: "So that, if they [Jews] are ever in an argument with Christians, they may not have an avenue of escape, but may be struck down in the main with their own weapon."[110] An additional defense lies in Jerome merely following the example of other Christian writers: "Origen himself, and Clement and Eusebius, and a host of others, whenever they discuss things from Scripture and wish to prove what they say, usually write as follows: 'A Hebrew told me this'; and 'I heard it from a Hebrew'; and 'This is the view of the Hebrews.'"[111] Jerome considers himself in good company and wonders why Rufinus should single him out as a collaborator with Jews while leaving Rufinus' ideal theologian, Origen, free from such accusation. A final rebuttal to this charge is offered: "Shall I not be permitted to inform the Latins in the work of my commentaries of what I have learned from the Hebrews? . . . I would now show you how profitable it is . . . in waiting at the doors of great teachers, and in learning the art from the artists."[112] Just as one without skill submits to the authority and expertise of the skilled, so Jerome admits that he learns in deference to his Jewish teachers—a radical reversal of supersessionism's posture of superiority and replacement.

Jerome's gradual conversion to Hebrew truth produced a progression in his hermeneutic from a purely spiritual one to one grounded in the historical and literal sense first. His evolution can be plainly seen in his first commentary on Obadiah (written in 375, before he learned Hebrew), which he later found embarrassing due to its fanciful and unfounded spiritual exegesis and outright criticism of literal exegesis.[113] There are no extant copies of this commentary, which Jerome claimed to have burned due its deficiency in histori-

---

109. *Apology Against Rufinus* 1.13 (CCSL 79:12). English translations are from *St. Jerome: Dogmatic and Polemical Works*.
110. Ibid., 3.25 (CCSL 79:97).
111. Ibid., 1.13 (CCSL 79:12).
112. Ibid, 1.20 (CCSL 79:20).
113. Kelly, "Bible and the Latin Fathers," 50.

cal exegesis.[114] Twenty-two years later Jerome produced such a commentary on Obadiah in line with his customary model: begin with the Hebrew text for the historical exegesis and only then build upon it the spiritual or tropological exegesis. This model serves as the standard for all his exegetical works.

Jerome's loyalty to his Christian tradition is frequently tested by a conflict between the Hebrew text and the Septuagint. By regularly rejecting the Christian interpretation in favor of the Jewish, Jerome creates a new Christian tradition that is a hybrid of Jewish and christological viewpoints. He grounded such positions on his loyalty to the Hebrew text: "It is the more remarkable then, in view of his fervent belief and unshakeable convictions, that Jerome admitted, nay kept insisting that . . . any Christological interpretation was admissible only to the extent that it was philologically justifiable."[115] Here is but one example of his integrity to the Hebrew text that conflicts with the hallowed Septuagint, which reads, "[God] proclaims his Christ to humanity" (Amos 4:13). Because the Hebrew text Jerome was referencing inserted one letter into what the Old Greek translated "Christ," Jerome omitted the messianic translation and rendered it according to the Hebrew text, "[God] proclaims his thoughts to humanity."[116] Such a passion for Hebrew drove him to revise a traditionally christological translation that would have supported his position against the Jews. Jerome's willingness to expand the horizons of Christian hermeneutic is grounded in what Andrew Jacobs calls his "linguistic archaeology" that centered his exposition on the Hebrew text and tradition.[117] Resisting traditional Christian exegesis became a part of Jerome's reputation as an iconoclast.

Jerome as Traditionalist

A second necessary element in Jerome's complex person is his traditional language of Christian replacement of the very Jews whom his language also extols. This element of his rhetoric keeps Jerome firmly planted within the Christian tradition, in spite of his philo-Semitic actions. After all that has been said about Jerome's love for Hebrew truth, he remains committed to the reality that Christians have superseded the Jews. As Karen Torjesen says:

114. Kelly, *Jerome: His Life, Writings and Controversies*, 45.
115. Kedar, "Latin Translations," 329–30.
116. The LXX reads ἀπαγγέλλων εἰς ἀνθρώπους τὸν χριστὸν αὐτοῦ. The Hebrew reads וּמַגִּיד לְאָדָם מַה־שֵּׂחוֹ (ibid., 316).
117. Jacobs, *Remains of the Jews*, 80.

> Christian exegesis of Jewish Scripture did more than establish the meaning of the text, it also established power relations, it was, in fact, a power struggle over patrimony, a bitter struggle over a contested will, it was a struggle over who would inherit the Father himself, the promises and the central place in history.[118]

Here is the heart of Jerome's two faces—both in tension as a necessary outcome of Christian supersessionism. Due to Jerome's perception of Christian exclusivity, he displaces the ancient people of Israel while he is simultaneously drawn to appreciate them. In order for supersession to function, those two movements must be in flux, each one holding the other in suspension. Although Jerome has changed the relation of the church to its supersessionism, rendering it less harsh and more valuing of the Jews, the fundamental notion of displacement remains. The more he ingests, the greater his need for the rhetoric of rejection.

Jerome's supersessionistic tone reflects the verbal edginess of fourth-century Romans. As favorable a view of Hebrew truth as Jerome boasts, his words never let his readers forget that he regards Jews as a rejected people and their religion as obsolete and even pernicious. At the same time, it must be remembered that Jerome lived in the context of a Roman society where sarcasm had been considered a standard rhetorical device for generations. David Wiesen explores Jerome's writings and discovers sarcasm against many in his day—the clergy, women, heretics, pagans, his personal enemies, and finally against Jews: "As a naturally harsh and caustic personality and as a scholar thoroughly acquainted with the methods of ridicule employed by the pagans, Jerome was extremely fond of using satire to expose and castigate the faults he could perceive in men and morals."[119] The Jews are not the only target of Jerome's tongue-lashing ridicule. Be that as it may, the label of sarcasm must not be permitted to lessen the negative impact of Jerome's attitude to the Jews. He uses it often to sharpen the arguments of Christian replacement.

Of special interest are the insults that Jerome levels against those he calls "Judaizers." One might think that Jerome would embrace such a label that would describe his own fondness for Hebrew truth—but the opposite is true. Newman defines "Judaizing" in Jerome's writings as "the conscious and sympathetic adoption by Gentile Christians of certain practices or doctrines readily identified as Jewish, or the participation of Gentile Christians in

---

118. Torjesen, "Rhetoric of the Literal Sense," 640.
119. Wiesen, *St. Jerome as a Satirist*, 19.

religious ceremonies carried out by Jews."[120] In particular, Jerome castigates both Jewish and Christian interpretations that predict a future reign of God on earth for Jews and Gentiles.[121] Graves concludes that Jerome approves of the Jewish literal interpretation for events in the past (*iuxta historiam* and *ad litteram*), but when that same sense is applied to a future millennial fulfillment by Christians Jerome considers it "Judaizing."[122] Jerome is careful to distinguish between the Jews who hold such views and these Judaizers who are numbered among the faithful Christians. Jerome calls such people "our Judaizers" in his more irenic moments, or the more strident label "half-Jews."[123] In one passage he even calls several well-known Christians "heretics."[124] Kinzig demonstrates that the impetus in Jerome's day behind such Christian Judaizing was none other than Apollinaris, Jerome's former teacher.[125] While Jerome does push the church closer to Jewish traditions, the christological interpretations override the historical and Judaizing interpretations of his fellow Judaizing Christians. Kinzig's observation summarizes the situation:

> The Greater Church consistently attacked and suppressed those Christian exegetical traditions which interpreted the New Testament in the light of the Hebrew Bible or the Septuagint and not vice versa, as it became practice in the majority Church. There is, therefore, not just Christian opposition to the Jews; the formation of Christian orthodoxy also entailed the suppression of philo-Semitic tendencies *within the Church*. Christian anti-Judaism is, at the same time, Christian anti-Christianism.[126]

---

120. Newman, "Jerome's Judaizers," 424.

121. Williams, "Lessons from Jerome's Jewish Teachers," 80. Jerome writes about the "fable of a thousand years, in which they say that Christ will reign in the flesh" (*Ep.* 120.2 [CSEL 55:480]).

122. Graves, "'Judaizing' Christian Interpretations of the Prophets as Seen by Saint Jerome," 142–56. Regarding Jerome's caustic tone toward such millenarians, Scheck believes that Jerome has created a "bogeyman" and that Jerome "describes it only in a distorted depiction that has no historical representatives" (*Commentary on Isaiah*, 50).

123. A thorough list of such terms is provided by O'Connell, *Eschatology of Saint Jerome*, 66.

124. Graves, "'Judaizing' Christian Interpretations of the Prophets," 153 n. 31. In his commentaries on Isaiah and Ezekiel, Jerome names these as Irenaeus, Papias, Tertullian, Victorinus of Pettau, Lactantius, and Apollinaris (ibid., 156 n. 40).

125. Kinzig, "Jewish and 'Judaizing' Eschatologies in Jerome." He argues that this theology can actually be traced back to the earliest days of the church.

126. Ibid., 427.

But why would Jerome be so harsh against those who have borrowed from the Jews in a similar way that he himself did? Rufinus accuses Jerome of Judaizing and Jerome denies it, in contradiction to the evidence of his own support for Hebrew truth. Newman's proposal, with which I concur, suggests that Jerome unfairly caricaturizes his millenarian opponents as Judaizers in order to deflect criticism that was directed at him: "The irony—and perhaps part of the underlying logic—of Jerome's frequent attacks against alleged Judaizers is that in principle no orthodox Christian of his day was more vulnerable than he to the charge of Judaizing."[127] Jerome's harsh language against Judaizers may very likely be a smokescreen to cover his own reputation, hypocritically accusing millennial interpreters of the sin of Jew-loving while he himself continues his pursuit "back to the Hebrew truth." Jerome also lives in the middle space, much like the Judaizers, a place filled with imbalance and contradiction, yet he refuses to identify himself with the label or with others who do the same. In his mind, he remains the standard to which all other Christians must measure their Judaizing. Since he refuses to adopt Jewish customs of worship, Jerome shuns the self-description "Judaizer," reserving the use of the term for his pejorative discourses. Although he avoids adopting Jewish customs in his Christian practice, he embraces Jewish traditions in his Christian hermeneutics. He remains a supersessionist, although a slightly reformed one.

Jerome as Gatekeeper

Jerome's life is riddled with contradictions. He heralded Christian virtues but displayed venomous hatred to his enemies, even his former brothers in the monastic community. He faults the use of rhetoric by heretics, but uses his own arsenal of rhetoric against his opponents. He even boasts of his humility. He faults the Septuagint in many ways, yet continues to expound it as expressing Christian truth.[128] Is this the mark of a man in confusion, with a split personality, or is he simply unexplainable? Or might Jerome's polarities be a part of his self-construction?

Mark Vessey insightfully argues that Jerome constructs his own persona from the model of Origen, riding on the reputation of Origen in order to build his own in the Latin-speaking world.[129] Enlarging on that thesis,

---

127. Newman, "Jerome's Judaizers," 444.
128. As summarized by Kedar, "Latin Translations," 319.
129. Vessey presents a strong case that Jerome constructs his own identity from

Karen Torjesen contrasts the nature of Jerome's rhetorical self-defense with that of Origen's: "The rhetorical language by which each exegete seeks to establish his authority reveals what was persuasive at a particular moment in the history of the church."[130] She argues that Jerome casts himself as a scholar who brings his knowledge to bear in imparting Jewish historical interpretations to the church, while Origen painted himself as a prophet who unveiled hidden mysteries only by divine enablement. Origen's construct of supernatural authority was necessary in the early days of the Christian church, with its brief history. However, within the span of two centuries, Christian interpretive tradition had taken hold in the form of multiple commentaries on Old Testament books. Jerome therefore has no need to promote himself as a divine prophet as did Origen. Rather, his form of self-promotion comes in contrasting hues that blend together to craft a portrait of the supreme intermediary of Hebrew truth to the Christian church.

Jerome's self-constructed authority as mediator of truth from Jews to Christians is exemplified in his careful use of two different terms for those of the Jewish race.[131] Jerome consistently calls those from whom he draws edifying insights "Hebrews," while those whom he condemns are given the name "Jews." Nowhere does he explain the use of these terms, but it would seem that Jerome chooses the ancient and less sullied term "Hebrews" when he describes those who preserve the truth that he considers is from God. In Christian texts the term "Jews" had been assigned to the disobedient and rejected people. Jerome continues to use it in this derogatory way.

Since Jerome argues for what he calls the "Hebrew" truth, it is not surprising that he would use that same term to describe the ancient prophets who wrote the sacred texts. What comes as a surprise is that he uses this label for contemporary Jews living in Palestine. Jerome at times refers to his teachers as "my Hebrews."[132] It would seem to contradict his stance against contemporary "Jews," but he names living non-Christian Jews with the same appellation as their ancestors from biblical times. Other Christian writers excoriate all living Jews as rejected; Jerome rescues some and considers them

---

the acknowledged strengths of Origen in his article, "Jerome's Origen: The Making of a Christian Literary Persona." For a broader analysis of the impact of reading on the construction of Christian identity and Jerome's influence in the fourth century, see also Chin, *Grammar and Christianity in the Late Roman World*, 76–102, 155–69.

130. Torjesen, "Rhetoric of the Literal Sense," 642.

131. This is discussed by Brown, *Vir Trilinguis*, 167–74.

132. For example, *Commentary on Isaiah* 13:10 (CCSL 73:163) and *Commentary on Ecclesiastes* 1:14 (CCSL 72:260).

his forebearers. In another example Jerome discusses charity for the poor in Jerusalem, who are taken care of by both Christians and Jews:

> This custom continues in Judea to the present day, not only among us, but also among the Hebrews, so that they who meditate in the law of the Lord, day and night, and have no father upon earth except the Lord alone, may be cherished by the aid of the synagogues and of the whole world; that there may be equality—not that some may be refreshed while others are in distress, but that the abundance of some may support the need of others.[133]

In this rare instance Jerome lends legitimacy to places of Jewish synagogues and their social efforts. When other Christian leaders are calling on the destruction of synagogues, Jerome honors their practice in tandem with the Christian church. Again, Jerome lends credence to the giving of alms to the poor—poor Jews and Samaritans as well as poor Christians: "We do not deny that doles should be distributed to all poor people, even to Jews and Samaritans, if the means will allow. But the Apostle teaches that alms should be given to all, indeed, especially, however, to those who are of the household of faith."[134] Although Jerome consistently uses the term "Jews" to refer to the rejected people, in rare occurrences he uses it for those who deserve charity. If a comment calls for a condemnation of the same people, the term becomes "Jews" whether they are contemporary or found in the pages of the Old or New Testament. This pejorative term, rarely used in the singular, embodied the growing anti-Jewish feeling expressed by Christian writers.[135] In this subtle, linguistic move, Jerome proves to be a broker over the text and people of the Bible by creating two categories of the same people. Those he considers to be honorable are "Hebrews," while those unworthy of such respect are "Jews." His use of language empowers him to discern between the retrieval of worth and the condemnation of evil. Through this subtle distinction, Jerome projects his authority onto sacred and contemporary history as the divider and discerner of Palestine's ancient people.

Finally, the self-portrait Jerome composes is complex and ambivalent. The bridge that Jerome constructs between his role as innovator and traditionalist is that of a broker. As mediator between extremes of Jewish

---

133. *Against Vigilantius* 13 (PL 23:365C).

134. Ibid., 14 (PL 23:366).

135. Brown notes what he considers to be an exception when Jerome pairs Jews and Christians against the heathen. Jerome makes no derogatory remarks about Jews in this context (*Vir Trilinguis*, 169, quoting Jerome's *Commentary on Malachi* 4).

appreciation and degradation as well as between Jewish sources of truth and Christian readers, Jerome positions himself unlike anyone in the fourth century. If Jerome casts himself "to the public in the mask of Origen [and] had a head-start on his rivals,"[136] then by the time he disassociates himself from Origen, Jerome has crafted his distinctive persona without fear of rivals. His position as broker goes unchallenged, a fact that is reinforced by Jerome's entry for himself in his *On Illustrious Men*.[137] The extent of his own biography is greater than any contemporary writer and is almost as long as that of Origen. This example of self-promotion indicates that "he was announcing himself as the primary latter-day bearer of the patristic torch."[138] It is therefore not surprising that Jerome does not seem to have trained other monks to continue the exegetical work that was left unfinished at his death—he simply engages monks as scribes working under his authority. He never founds a movement to continue pursuit of Jewish relations about which he has written; those works are preserved as instruction from an authoritative church teacher. He set himself as the Christian clearinghouse, the sanctified filter, taking on the role of a pope over digested Hebrew doctrine procured for the good of the Christian church. The man who almost became the pope[139] made his mark on the church. His works have been more widely read than the works of any pope. His individuality marks his entire work and, unfortunately, ends it as well. Jerome's influence as *the* Christian Hebraist lasted well into the Middle Ages. For a thousand years his work was relied upon as the voice of "Hebrew truth," until the Hebrew language emerged once again into Christian scholarly communities.[140] Only when Jerome is understood as a complex mixture of an iconoclastic Christian Hebraist, a traditional Christian supersessionist, and the authoritative dispenser of Hebrew truth for the Christian church can we begin to comprehend his impact and utilize it in order to explore possibilities for productive interaction between Christians and Jews.

136. Vessey, 144.
137. *On Illustrious Men*, 77–79, 167–168.
138. Cain, *The Letters of Jerome*, 3.
139. Rebenich, *Jerome*, 31–40.
140. See Kugel, *How to Read the Bible*, 24–26.

Chapter 4

"Bethlehem . . . Now Ours"
Jerome's Ambivalent Remapping of Jewish Land

WRITING TO PAULINUS, PRIEST and friend, Jerome compares the days of Roman idolatry in Aelia Capitolina, Jerusalem's Roman name, to that of nearby Bethlehem: "Even Bethlehem, now ours, that most venerable spot in the whole world . . . was overshadowed by a grove of Tammuz, that is of Adonis."[1] Bethlehem, the city where David was born as well as Jesus, lately occupied by pagan Rome, had witnessed a transformation. In Jerome's day the hegemony of Byzantine Rome had extended its Christian influence over the little town. As a Christian monk, Jerome considered Bethlehem as his own, or rather, as belonging to the land now ruled by Christians, who had inherited it from the pagan Romans and who, in turn, had displaced the Jews. Traditionally, the Jews claimed that their God had granted them land via Abraham and his descendants. They considered Palestine their own, naming it "our land,"[2] a land considered sacred due to the divine presence dwelling among them in the temple. Their land became sacred space and became known as the "holy land,"[3] even when it fell under the hegemony of other empires. In the fourth century the Jews faced competition over the right to possess their land as holy territory. The Christian church, recently linked with imperial power, began to replicate the Jewish tradition of a holy land in the very same location as the Jewish land, thus displacing the Jews from their ancient homeland and inaugurating a new map of Christian sacred space.

---

1. *Ep.* 58.3 (CSEL 54:532).
2. Ps 85:9, 12; Mic 5:5–6; 1 Macc 5:48.
3. Zech 2:12; Wis 12:3; 2 Macc 1:7.

As we have seen, Jerome disrupted ecclesiastical traditions by his forthright appropriation of the Jewish biblical text along with contemporary rabbinic interpretations. In addition to these two groundbreaking displacements that propelled Jerome's shaping of Christian tradition toward Jewish expressions, Jerome introduces a third, not as radical as a new Old Testament text and a fresh approach to Christian hermeneutics, but just as profound: he elevates the value of pilgrimage to the holy land to the level of a requirement for Christians, and he redirects the devotion afforded Jerusalem to Bethlehem. His appropriation of Jewish text and hermeneutic combined with the reconfiguration of Christian sacred space yields an imposing and novel version of Christian supersessionism. I will begin by presenting the development and significance of Christian pilgrimage as a background for Jerome's personal pilgrimage to the holy land. I will then describe his invitations to other Christians to make their own pilgrimages to Palestine. Finally, I will attempt to unravel the discordant strands of Jerome's writings regarding the sanctity of Christianity's holy city: its identification and its character. I will argue that Jerome displaces the Jewish veneration of the holy land with a Christian notion that involves a complex mixture of veneration for both the earthly and heavenly Jerusalems while subtly displacing the former's position with that of Bethlehem, "now ours."

JEROME'S RELOCATION: PILGRIMAGE AND SETTLEMENT IN BETHLEHEM

The background for Jerome's personal odyssey of Christian pilgrimage begins in about 360 in Rome, where he received training in a classical education and was baptized. From there he headed north to Trier, where he prepared for civil service. Although the details are uncertain, it seems that there Jerome became attracted to the ascetic movement, moved back to his hometown of Aquilea, and joined a small circle of young men who quickly sought a deeper experience of ascetic life elsewhere. In 373 Jerome arrived in the eastern city of Antioch, and a few years later he joined a community of hermits for eighteen months in the nearby desert of Chalcis.[4] This first experience of the ascetic life proved distasteful to Jerome when, after sickness and trouble with an Arian monk, he abandoned the desert and returned to Antioch, eventually receiving ordination as a priest. Still unsettled, he traveled to Constantinople, where he studied under Gregory

4. Chronology is based on the work of Williams, *Monk and the Book*, 267–301.

of Nazianzus, and then to Rome in 382, where he was employed by Pope Damasus. There he made the acquaintance of several women who in due course became his patrons as well as a source of ecclesiastical gossip. Jerome felt pressured to leave Rome due to libelous accusations about these female relationships and set off for Palestine, arriving late in 385. It is at this juncture that Jerome makes his first journey in the Christian holy land along with Paula from Rome, who followed him separately. This initial pilgrimage to Palestine's holy sites forms the basis for his permanent settlement, his founding of a monastery in Bethlehem, and the setting for his ambitious writing career. Before an analysis of Jerome's travels within Palestine, it is important to rehearse the origins and development of Christian pilgrimage in the fourth century.

Christian Pilgrimage

Christians were interested in pilgrimage to Palestine long before Constantine's promotion of holy places in the early fourth century.[5] The first Christian mentioned as journeying to Bible lands is Melito, bishop of Sardis, who in the late second century "went East and came to the place where these things were preached and done" in order to investigate the books in the Hebrew canon. The second is Alexander of Cappadocia, whose purpose was said to be "in consequence of a vow and for the sake of information in regard to its places."[6] These two journeys state their motivation as a need for knowledge or for religious devotion.[7] In the third century Origen wrote about his investigative visits to sacred sites in Palestine, such as Bethany beyond the Jordan, where John baptized; Gergesa, where the swine were cast out; Hebron's tomb of the Patriarchs; Ashkelon's wells dug by Abraham; and Bethlehem, where he was shown the cave where Jesus was born.[8] His travels while he resided in Palestine seem marked by his gathering of data over a wide area of the biblical landscape, and there is no hint of acts of devotion. In Origen's time two others spoke of their visits to Palestine

---

5. Hunt, "Were There Christian Pilgrims before Constantine?"

6. Eusebius, *Church History* 4.26.14 for Melito; 6.11.2 for Alexander.

7. Hunt demonstrates that the quest for historical verification "need not be devoid of religious significance" ("Were There Christian Pilgrims before Constantine?," 38). A more skeptical opinion overall is offered by Taylor, *Christians and the Holy Places*.

8. Origen, *Contra Celcus* 1, 51. For other references to Origen's travels see Hunt, *Holy Land Pilgrimage*, 92–93.

and the consequential impressions left upon them: Pionius, a martyr in Smyrna, defended his faith based on his visit: "Once on a journey I travelled all through Palestine and . . . I saw the land which to this day bears witness to the wrath of God."[9] Firmilianus, a bishop in Cappadocia, travelled "to Palestine to visit the holy places."[10] Eusebius recorded in the early fourth century that in his time, before the construction of Christian churches, "believers in Christ all congregate from all parts of the world [in Jerusalem so that] they may learn both about the city being taken and devastated as the prophets foretold, and that they may worship at the Mount of Olives opposite to the city."[11] What began as a stream in the second and third centuries became a flood after Constantine's mother, Helena, visited Palestine in 324 to authorize construction of churches associated with holy places—a radical concept, since up to this time "true worship had no relation to any particular place. Until the fourth century Christians inhabited a spatial universe spiritually largely undifferentiated."[12] Helena was able to locate these holy places from their supposed historical roots by "a pre-existing tradition of the location of key moments in the scriptural record, albeit only occasionally and dimly documented."[13]

Several texts from the Constantinian era and immediately afterward reveal the extent of pilgrimage in this new era. Eusebius composed a travel guide listing biblical sites entitled *Onomasticon*, which Jerome would later translate into Latin for Western Christian readers and pilgrims. The first detailed itinerary of a Christian pilgrim comes from a traveler from Bordeaux in Gaul.[14] He recorded his journey to Palestine in 333 in intricate detail, but without personal reflections. A second journal of early Christian pilgrimage was written by Egeria, a nun from Spain who traveled to Egypt and Palestine.[15] Her diary records inspiring visits to Jewish and Christian holy places. John Wilkinson notes that in the records of both of these pilgrims, visits to Old Testament sites outnumber the New Testament ones by

---

9. *Martyrdom of Pionius and His Companions* 4.18, in Musurillo, *Acts of the Christian Martyrs*, 140.

10. Jerome, *On Illustrious Men* LIV, 5.

11. Eusebius, *Demonstratio Evangelica* 6.18.23.

12. Markus, *End of Ancient Christianity*, 141.

13. Hunt, "Were There Christian Pilgrims before Constantine?," 39.

14. Hunt provides a map with the routes of several early pilgrimages (*Holy Land Pilgrimage*, 52).

15. See *Egeria's Travels*.

"BETHLEHEM ... NOW OURS"

an average of 60–40 percent.[16] The typical itinerary of pilgrims included the major turning points of Christian history and prophecy, beginning with Old Testament locations and concluding with the life and death of Christ.[17] Such a ratio indicates that the Christian church had appropriated the Jewish Scriptures as its own. In the same manner that the Christian church had claimed the text of Jewish Scripture, so too the church adopted Jewish geography of the places described in those texts. Text and place converged as two realities in conversation with each other. Ora Limor insightfully observes: "The map of holy places constitutes a polemical text, and like any polemical text it aims at justifying the particular truth of its authors–in this case, Christian claims to ownership over the sacred space–and to refute the arguments of the rival claimant, that is, the Jews."[18]

This leads to the question of the origin of Christian pilgrimage. While it was undoubtedly influenced by Greco-Roman patterns[19] (which are common to most religions[20]), I will direct the focus onto the early and close association of Christians with Jews that produced shared customs of pilgrimage. Ora Limor's assessment highlights the unique nature of Christian pilgrimage: "Even though Christian pilgrimage was inspired by both Jewish pilgrimage to the Second Temple and by pagan travelling to historical and religious sites, it should be considered a new phenomenon and dealt with as such."[21] I will narrow the discussion from the larger Greco-Roman world in order to demonstrate that the similarities between Jews and Christians in contemporaneous practices indicate a relationship of influence with cur-

---

16. John Wilkinson, "Jewish Holy Places and the Origins of Christian Pilgrimage," 44–45. He also lists the tombs of Jewish saints mentioned in Jewish literature of the Second Temple Period and correlates it with such tombs visited by the Bordeaux Pilgrim, Egeria, and Jerome, all displaying significant overlap with the Jewish sources (49).

17. Maraval provides a general listing of sites visited by fourth- to sixth-century pilgrims in canonical order in "Bible as a Guide for Early Christian Pilgrim" 382–87.

18. Limor, "'Holy Journey': Pilgrimage and Christian Sacred Landscape," 351.

19. For example, Dillon, *Pilgrims and Pilgrimage in Ancient Greece*. Taylor says, "Constantine brought to Christianity a pagan notion of the sanctity of things and places" (*Christians and the Holy Places*, 308). This notion is also found in the Jewish Scriptures. Not all scholars agree; Maribel Dietz opts for an agnostic approach: "The actual historical origins of religious travel in the complex world of the late antique Mediterranean basin remain largely unknown" ("Itinerant Spirituality and the Late Antique Origins of Christian Pilgrimage," 126).

20. See Holm, *Sacred Place* for the concept in Buddhism, Hinduism, Islam, Sikhism, and Chinese and Japanese religions.

21. Limor, "'Holy Journey,'" 327.

rents flowing in both directions between Jews and Christians.[22] One must explain the curious fact that Christian pilgrimage grew into a major influence in the church in spite of the absence of any command for it in the New Testament. I believe that the idea was derived from the Jewish practice and serves as a classic example of Christian appropriation of Jewish tradition. Rather than an invention of the third-century Christian church, pilgrimage was apparently a diminutive element of early Christianity as inheritors of the Jewish Scriptures as it continued to mimic the Jewish religion with which it interacted. In the fourth century it took on its own identity as its popularity flourished with the access granted by Constantine.

The background to Jewish pilgrimage lies in the Torah's legislation that the Israelites were required to travel to the central sanctuary (first at Shiloh, then Jerusalem) three times each year for the festivals of Passover, Weeks, and Booths,[23] forming the custom as a habitual part of Jewish existence. Broadening and universalizing the concept, the Hebrew prophets speak of an eschatological inclusion of the Gentile nations in pilgrimage to Jerusalem.[24] In addition to corporate pilgrimage to Jerusalem, Jewish individuals honored righteous people at their tombs. Jesus referred to those who "build the tombs of the prophets and decorate the graves of the righteous" (Matt 23:29; Luke 11:47–48). Herod the Great constructed for his Jewish subjects an elaborate enclosure for the tombs of Abraham, Isaac, Jacob, and their wives at Hebron. Second Temple Judaism actively honored its deceased who had exemplified pious living.[25]

Temple-based pilgrimages drastically changed after the temple's destruction by the Romans, forcing Jewish sages to reformulate, not eliminate, pilgrimage in the new conditions of exile. As a result, Jewish pilgrims continued to visit Jerusalem to grieve over the temple's destruction and to pray for its restoration. Jerome records his witness of Jewish pilgrims congregated on the Mount of Olives: "This miserable flock herds together at the spot where rose the cross of our Lord, at the very scene of His glorious

---

22. Such crosscurrents between Jews and Christians are extensive; see Becker and Reed, eds., *Ways that Never Parted*.

23. Exod 23:14–17; Deut 16:16. The story of the church's origin is placed in Jerusalem during the Jewish feast of Weeks or Pentecost (Acts 2).

24. Isa 2:1–4; 56:6–8; 66:18–24; Mic 4:1–4; Zech 8:20–23; 14:16–21.

25. Wilkinson, "Jewish Holy Places," 48–50. Schwartz suggests that Jews were countercultural in their remembering the deceased for their godly benefaction, even though Josephus's downplaying of monumental structures is contradicted by the archaeological record ("Memory in Josephus and the Culture of the Jews in the First Century," 185–94).

"Bethlehem ... Now Ours"

resurrection. The standard of the cross glitters upon the Mount of Olives, while this miserable race weeps over the ruins of its Temple."[26] Among the archaeological evidence for Jewish pilgrims to the temple mount is an inscription carved into a block of the Herodian wall surrounding the temple mount. The inscribed words express hope for a rebuilt temple and a restored nation.[27] Since the writing is carved on the wall above the level of the Byzantine street, archaeologists suggest the date of the inscription is at the time of Julian's reign or somewhat later. The latter possibility coincides with the discovery of glass vessels inscribed with menorahs that closely resemble bottles made with Christian symbols. Such evidence indicates the presence of Jewish and Christian pilgrims in the city of Jerusalem in numbers sufficient to elicit the manufacture and sale of souvenirs.[28] As Christians continued to observe and interact Jews, even to the point of competition, they produced rival practices that were designed to displace Jewish traditions of sacred space. The primary example of these mirrored traditions is the Church of the Holy Sepulcher, constructed by Constantine, and thereafter described by Eusebius as a temple.[29]

In addition, the date of the annual ceremony to commemorate the dedication of the church (the *Encaenia*) fell on the date of the dedication of Solomon's temple. The celebration

> bore uncanny echoes of Hanukkah or the Feast of Lights which marked the rededication of the Temple under the Maccabees in the second century BCE.... Both the Encaenia and Hanukkah occupied the same space of a totalizing discourse that reinscribed a biblical past on a more recent one.[30]

The church added New Testament justification for the festival, citing the eight days between Christ's two resurrection appearances as the reason for its length.[31] For Christians bent on mimicking their Jewish contemporaries out of the a desire to contest and conquer the rival, the two sources, the

---

26. *Commentary on Zephaniah* 1:15–16 (CCSL 76A:674).

27. The inscription quotes Isaiah 66:14: "When you see this, your heart will rejoice and you will flourish like grass," which is preceded in Isaiah with the words "you will be comforted over Jerusalem" (66:13).

28. Tsafrir, "Jewish Pilgrimage in the Roman and Byzantine Periods," 375.

29. *Life of Constantine* 3.33, 36, 45. For other parallels see Kuehnel, "Jewish Symbolism of the Temple and the Tabernacle."

30. Sivan, *Palestine in Late Antiquity*, 197.

31. Hunt, *Holy Land Pilgrimage*, 110.

Old and New Testaments, ensured a solid foundation for the tradition and a comfortable reception among the worshippers. The church memorialized the rock where Christ was crucified, and Origen linked the same spot as the place of Adam's burial: "Concerning the place of the skull, it came to me that Hebrews hand down [the tradition that] the body of Adam has been buried there."[32] Other Christian writers repeated and embellished this link with Hebrew tradition and related it to Paul's christological view of the old and new Adam.[33] While the veracity of Origen's claim is beside the point, these attempts to remove the novelty of the recently established "Christianity" indicate the church's need to justify its claims by leaning on the Jews for their support. However, Jewish tradition teaches that the rock on the temple mount, not Golgotha, is the foundation stone. Such competing claims continue in this transfer of traditions from the Jewish Mount Moriah to the Christian Mount Calvary: the garden of Eden typified the place of the crucifixion in a garden near Jesus' tomb,[34] Isaac's sacrifice was shifted to Golgotha, and even Solomon's ring was displayed in the church that had been used to help in constructing the first temple (according to Jewish tradition[35]). To summarize, Christians relocated the center of sacred space from the temple mount to the Church of the Holy Sepulcher.

The rabbinic conception of sacred space began with the Holy of Holies and extended outward in concentric circles to include the temple, Jerusalem, Israel, and the world.[36] Similarly, the Christian notion centered holiness at the rock of Golgotha with radiated holiness extending outward to the holy land and beyond to the rest of the world. These ripples of holiness radiated from Jerusalem through the land of Palestine and included all the Jewish sites mentioned in the Old Testament in addition to many New Testament sites. Some Christian holy sites overlapped with Jewish places of sanctity, the juxtaposition of such Old and New Testament sites revealing a pattern of what Sabine MacCormack describes as "overlapping layers of

---

32. *Commentary in Matthew* 27:32–33, quoted by Taylor, *Christians and the Holy Places*, 124.

33. Epiphanius says that Adam's skull was discovered there. Out of the many writers who mention this tradition, there are three who link it with a Hebrew tradition (Taylor, *Christians and the Holy Places*, 127–28).

34. So Cyril of Jerusalem, cited by Walker, *Holy City, Holy Places*, 262.

35. In *b. Gittin* 7.68a, cited by Taylor, *Christians and the Holy Places*, 131.

36. This reflected the biblical concept of holiness extending outward from the ark, to the tent, the enclosure, the camp, and then to the outside world. See Kunin, "Judaism," 117–19.

sacred history."[37] For example, the spot where John baptized Jesus on the bank of the Jordan River is the same place where Jewish tradition places the crossing of the Israelites into the land, and it is next to the place of Elisha's entry to heaven. Also, the tomb of David is close by the cave of Christ's birth in Bethlehem, and the Constantinian church at Mamre honors the preincarnate visit of Jesus to Abraham.[38] In addition, the Mount of Olives is situated directly across from Jerusalem's temple mount and became a hive of Christian presence. Taking their cue from Ezekiel's description of God's glory moving from the temple onto the Mount of Olives,

> this new sacred site receives its identity not only from scriptural events but, no less important, from not being the other "earthly Jerusalem." ... The relocation of Divine Presence and patronship is reenacted as a supersessionalist mythologeme in the ritual behavior of the pilgrims who imitate the "glory of the Lord," as their own trajectory moves from the old to the new.[39]

In addition to the Christian appropriation of the holy land centering in Jerusalem, Christians maintained the Jewish tradition of visiting the tombs of righteous men and women. Second Temple Judaism honored the tombs of the patriarchs in Hebron and the tombs of David, Solomon, and Hezekiah in Jerusalem.[40] The pre-Christian Jewish practice informed the evolution early Jewish Christians, who apparently continued the custom of visiting tombs since "from the very outset of the new faith, they took the Jewish habit of pilgrimage for granted."[41] Christian pilgrims began to lay claim on Jewish tombs of Old Testament personalities for the church, as shown by records of visits to the tombs of St. Rachel and St. Abraham: "All through the fourth and fifth centuries, Jewish 'saintly' tombs were being discovered and appropriated by the Church."[42] For example, Jerome confirms the standing custom: "Everywhere we venerate the tombs of the

---

37. MacCormack, "Loca Sancta," 25.
38. Taylor, *Christians and the Holy Places*, 105. She adds, "The identification of this place [the Hebrews' crossing point] with the baptism of John, however, must have been made by local Christians.... The Jews were not pointing out the site because of its Christian significance; but because of its importance in Jewish tradition; the Christians then made the identification that it was here that John baptized."
39. Levinson, "There Is No Place Like Home," 111. See Ezek 11:22–23.
40. Ibid., 322.
41. Wilkinson, "Visits to Jewish Tombs by Early Christians," 464.
42. Taylor, *Christians and the Holy Places*, 325.

martyrs; we apply their holy ashes to our eyes; we even touch them, if we may, with our lips,"[43] and Jerome's friend Paula "made pilgrimages to the tombs of Joshua the son of Nun and Eleazar the son of Aaron."[44]

Christian veneration eventually went beyond what Jews practiced, including prayers for intersession and the treasuring of relics. Robert Markus argues that the fourth-century flood of holy places stemmed from the post-Constantinian church's desire to reclaim its persecuted past by identifying with tombs of martyrs to incorporate the "sense of the past, and the need to experience it as present. Place became sacred as the past became localised in the present."[45] MacCormack links the Christian practice to the Jewish custom: "The interpretation of Scripture, initially by Jews and then also by Christians, favored the formation of a sacred topography of the Holy Land."[46] Combining the veneration of tombs with worship at holy places produced a new atlas of Palestine superimposed over the Jewish labels.

Finally, Christian pilgrimage is necessarily linked with Christian monasticism in the holy land. Christian monks scattered throughout Palestine served as hosts providing shelter for pilgrims and as guides and interpreters of holy sites. Local monks became the commentators of the new Christian map: "The accelerating Christian 'takeover' of the Holy Land resulted in both the appropriation of the Jewish sacred map of the region and the proliferation of different, and sometimes conflicting, traditions in the name of its new masters."[47] Christian traditions were reinforced by monks who used Eusebius's *Onomasticon* (including Jerome's later edition in Latin) as their travel guide. Monasticism and pilgrimage, each one satisfying the need of the other, synergistically produced Christian topography within the Jewish homeland.[48]

In the sixth century, Christians emblazoned their supersessionistic geography upon the holy land in what archaeologists call the "Madaba Map." Located on the floor of a church in Jordan, the large mosaic depicts cities, churches, and holy places with graphic realism. Everything on the map is Christian, with absolutely no references to anything Jewish, most notably the temple mount. It is the largest contiguous area inside the city

43. *Ep.* 46.8 (CSEL 54:338).
44. *Ep.* 108.13 (CSEL 55:332).
45. Markus, "How on Earth Could Places Become Holy?," 271.
46. MacCormack, "Loca Sancta," 20.
47. Hunt, "Itinerary of Egeria," 49.
48. Sivan, "Pilgrimage, Monasticism, and the Emergence of Christian Palestine."

walls and its absence from the map highlights Christian supersession of the Jewish temple in favor of the Christian replacement, the Holy Sepulcher Church. It is "the most public expression of Christian land theology in antiquity ... an illuminated concretization of the religious concept of the 'Holy Land.'"[49] The major feature of the map is its central positioning of Jerusalem depicted by an elliptical shape. Sivan suggests that this is yet another attempt by Christians to imitate the Jews: "Its shape, an oval, was strikingly reminiscent of the rabbinic *omphalos* [navel] which designated the centrality of the city in the universe."[50] This mimicking of Jewish beliefs, rooted in the earlier construction of the Church of the Holy Sepulcher as the new Christian temple, recalls the rabbinic tradition:

> As the navel is set in the centre of the human body, so is the land of Israel the navel of the world ... situated in the centre of the world, and Jerusalem in the centre of the land of Israel, and the sanctuary in the centre of Jerusalem, and the holy place in the centre of the sanctuary, and the ark in the centre of the holy place, and the Foundation Stone before the holy place, because from it the world was founded.[51]

Into such a world of inherited and overlapping traditions entered Jerome.

Jerome's Pilgrimage and Settlement

In late 385, Jerome embarks on a ship carrying passengers to the Roman district of Palestine, a land laden with deep significance for Jerome and for fourth-century Christians. On the journey he composes a letter to defend his reputation against the slander being spread about his relationship with his female friends, describing his destination in both figurative and literal terms:

> I write this in haste, dear Lady Asella, as I go on board, overwhelmed with grief and tears; yet I thank my God that I am counted worthy of the world's hatred. Pray for me that, after Babylon, I may see Jerusalem once more; that Joshua, the son of Josedech, may have dominion over me, and not Nebuchadnezzar, that Ezra, whose name means helper, may come and restore me to my own country.[52]

49. Demsky, "Holy City and Holy Land as Viewed by Jews and Christians," 290.

50. Sivan, *Palestine in Late Antiquity,* 256–57.

51. *Midrash Tanchuma, Parashat Kedoshim* 10; also in the Talmud, *b. Yoma* 54a–b. These traditions reflect Ezek 5:5; 38:12; *Jub.* 8:19; 1 *En.* 26:1.

52. *Ep.* 45.6 (CSEL 54:327).

Jerome mixes a double layer of meaning with the geographical and biblical terms: "Babylon" is Rome, the city he is leaving; "Jerusalem" refers to the holy land; and the three personalities carry their own typology of good (Joshua, Ezra) and evil (Nebuchadnezzar). The names chosen by Jerome are found in the narrative of the Jewish return from Babylon, and he expresses his yearning to go home, to his "own country." Jerome, in his typical supersessionistic stance, assumes the role of an ancient Israelite returning from Babylonian captivity to his Judean homeland. Strangely, it is a country in which he had never resided, yet he voices his true identity and citizenship as if it was his native land. Apparently he had traveled there in his imagination, and now his body is catching up to his heart. His desire to "see Jerusalem" does not refer to the heavenly Jerusalem, a term used early by Christians to mean one's eternal destiny, but to the earthly city.[53] Jerome's plan from the beginning was a one-way venture, a permanent settlement and not a pilgrimage.[54] In a later document he summarizes his initial impressions and early devotion to Bethlehem:

> I entered Jerusalem in the middle of a very bitter winter. I saw many marvels; and the wonders that I had previously heard about through reports, I verified with the judgment of my very own eyes. From there I proceeded to Egypt . . . I hurried to return to my Bethlehem where I poured perfume upon the manger and the crib of the Savior.[55]

In a retrospective description penned some twenty years after his arrival in Bethlehem, Jerome unveils his patron Paula's motivations for settling there—she wished to live in Jesus' divinely selected birthplace:

> I too, miserable sinner though I am, have been accounted worthy to kiss the manger in which the Lord cried as a babe, and to pray in the cave in which the travailing virgin gave birth to the infant Lord. 'This is my rest' [quoting Psalm 132:14] for it is my Lord's native place; 'here will I dwell' for this spot has my Savior chosen.[56]

---

53. He had earlier written from the desert of Chalcis to his fellow monk Florentius in Jerusalem about his desire to eventually visit Jerusalem (*Ep.* 5.1 [CSEL 54:21]). He also wrote about a trip that never came to fruition: "Many years ago, when for the kingdom of heaven's sake I had cut myself off from home, parents, sister, relations, and—harder still—from the dainty food to which I had been accustomed; and when I was on my way to Jerusalem to wage my warfare . . ." (*Ep.* 22.30 [CSEL 54:189]).

54. Bitton-Ashkelony uses the term "emigration" in *Encountering the Sacred*, 67.

55. *Apology Against Rufinus* 3.22 (CCSL 79:94).

56. *Ep.* 108.10 (CSEL 55:318).

"BETHLEHEM . . . NOW OURS"

In quoting a psalm that extols God's choice to dwell in the temple of Jerusalem, Jerome reconfigures the meaning to suit his own shared experience with Paula, shifting the holy place from Jerusalem to Bethlehem. It is, in his own words, "my deep-seated love for the holy places" that draws him to and keeps him in Bethlehem.[57] Jerome's personal relocation consisted of a journey of about fifteen years begun in the year 385. Once he settles his soul in Bethlehem for the next thirty-five years until his death, he begins his lifelong task of remapping Palestine according to his own dictates.

JEROME'S REMAPPING THE HOLY LAND: FROM JEWISH TO CHRISTIAN PALESTINE

Once settled in Bethlehem, Jerome established a monastic community to house monks, to host pilgrims, and to serve as the administrative center for his publishing ventures. His large body of letters written during this time functions as a window to his multifaceted personality. Jerome's first journey to Palestine is vividly presented in a letter written in retrospect of his initial pilgrimage to the holy land with Paula some twenty years earlier.[58] As one of Jerome's longest letters, its immediate purpose is to paint a portrait of Paula, his closest female friend and patron, who had recently died, and thus to console her daughter Eustochium as well as his wider readership. The letter begins with their traveling parties embarking on separate journeys to the holy land, their rendezvousing at Antioch, and their continuing journey together southward into Palestine. The letter vividly portrays Paula's reactions to the sacred sites they visit together before they decide to settle in Bethlehem and found twin monastic communities. The letter describes their journey in three stages: first, they begin in Antioch and head south to Jerusalem and Bethlehem; second, they travel from Bethlehem to the hill country of Judah and the Negev; and third, they set out from Bethlehem and head north to Samaria and Galilee. I have chosen certain details in the letter that convey Jerome's image of the holy land through Paula's eyes, since in this letter he never personalizes his own impressions—they always come to the reader through Paula's viewpoint, whose traveling entourage, including

---

57. *Ep.* 77.8 (CSEL 55:46).
58. Their trip occurred in 385; *Ep.* 108 was written in 404. For a detailed examination of this document, see Cain, *Jerome's Epitaph on Paula*.

Jerome, learns many geographical details from local Jewish guides that the they hire,[59] and from from local Christian monks as well.[60]

I begin with Jerome's description of Paula's journey within the land of the Bible: "She entered Elijah's town on the shore at Zarephath and therein adored her Lord and Saviour."[61] The reader is prompted to recall the christological typology in the narrative of Elijah that issued from Paula's worship. One of Jerome's techniques throughout this letter is his collapsing of historical time and centering on christological moments. This sort of time displacement is a mark of pilgrimage literature, and it has the effect of reinforcing the difference between the reader and the one described in the text—the pilgrim is the one who is closer to the past.[62] As the journey continues, he describes those places with Jewish backgrounds as decaying or already in ruins, while those marked by Christ's presence or by contemporary Christians are thriving.[63] For instance, he writes that Megiddo is connected with Josiah's death, Dor is in ruins, while Caesarea houses a church; Antipatris is "a small town half in ruins" while Lydda, "now become Diospolis, a place made famous by the raising again of Dorcas and the restoration to health of Aeneas"; the former Emmaus is now Nicopolis and has a church, but the cities founded by Solomon were "subsequently destroyed by several devastating wars."[64] The pattern seems obvious and the point is clear: Christian presence rejuvenates what Jewish presence has destroyed. Jerome explores their visit to Gibeah, where a large number of Benjamites were saved from death so "that in after days Paul might be called a Benjamite."[65] Jerome reads sacred history backwards, elevating the apostle Paul's status while diminishing that of the Jewish tribe of Benjamin, whose sole reason for surviving the battle was to generate the great apostle to the Gentiles. Jerome's rhetorical strategy reinforces his replacement theology.

---

59. *Prologue to Paralipomenon* from LXX (PL 29:402). Jerome mentions, "The town of Nain was pointed out to her" (*Ep.* 108.13 [CSEL 55:322]). A Jewish guide showed Jerome the location of Nahum's hometown (*Commentary on Nahum*, prologue [PL 25:1232]).

60. Weingarten sees the letter as "a carefully contrived rhetorical product, and by no means always reliable as evidence of the *realia* of fourth century Palestine" (*Saint's Saints*, 193). She provides a helpful map of their journey on p. 271.

61. *Ep.* 108.8 (CSEL 55:313).

62. See Frank, *Memory of the Eyes*, 54–55.

63. Weingarten lists some of the sites in contrasting pairs (*Saint's Saints*, 238–39).

64. Ibid.

65. Ibid.

"Bethlehem ... Now Ours"

The itinerary continues south to Jerusalem and the Church of the Holy Sepulcher. Jerome's language is marked by metaphors of the senses to portray Paula's emotions at sacred spots and filled with vivid words of appetite and passion:

> She *kissed* the stone which the angel had rolled away from the door of the sepulcher. Indeed so *ardent* was her faith that she even *licked with her mouth* the very spot on which the Lord's body had lain, like one *thirsty* for the river which he has *longed for*. What *tears* she shed there, what *groans* she uttered, and what *grief* she poured forth, all Jerusalem knows.[66]

Paula is presented as one unashamedly passionate for pilgrimage, and the reader is subtly invited to imitate her. Jerome reflects his contempt for the Jewish city of Jerusalem's accursed state of destruction:

> Going out thence she made the ascent of Zion ... "The Lord loves the gates of Zion more than all the dwellings of Jacob" [Ps 87:2]. He does not mean the gates which we see today in dust and ashes; the gates he means are those against which hell prevails not and through which the multitude of those who believe in Christ enter in.[67]

Jerome sees little value in the Old Testament city of Jerusalem. However, the fourth-century city was certainly not in the dilapidated condition he constructs for his readers. For Jerome the significance of Jerusalem lies in its spiritual counterpart of a heavenly city "of those who believe in Christ."

The tone of Jerome's geographic descriptions now turn in another direction with Paula's arrival at Bethlehem and is laced with twice the detail he gives for Jerusalem.[68] Jerome develops Paula's visionary experience, a vital feature in all pilgrimage accounts:[69]

> She came to Bethlehem and entered into the cave where the Savior was born. Here, when she *looked* upon the inn ... when she *looked* upon these things I say, she protested in my hearing that she could *behold* with the *eyes* of faith the infant Lord wrapped in swaddling clothes and crying in the manger.... She declared that she could *see* the slaughtered innocents.[70]

---

66. *Ep.* 108.9 (CSEL 55:315); emphasis added.
67. Ibid.
68. Stemberger, *Jews and Christians in the Holy Land*, 102.
69. In addition to Frank, *Memory of the Eyes*, see her article, "Pilgrim's Gaze in the Age before Icons."
70. *Ep.* 108.10 (CSEL 55:316); emphasis added.

In another location he highlights the realm of vision beyond the dimension normal to most: "She *saw* demons screaming under different tortures before the tombs of the saints."[71]

Throughout the letter's itinerary Jerome conflates the Jewish Old Testament locations with their prophetic New Testament significance, effectively equalizing the testaments. For example, he writes that Bethlehem's fields were where "Jacob fed his flocks" and also where the shepherds heard the angels announce Jesus' birth; the Ethiopian eunuch "read the Old Testament [and] found the fountain of the gospel"; the spies brought back grapes that proved "the fertility of the land and a type of" Christ; Abraham's oak marks the spot where the patriarch "saw Christ's day and was glad"; Othniel's land with gushing springs "typify the redemption . . . in the waters of baptism"; the morning rays of sun over the Jordan River "recalled to mind the rising of the sun of righteousness"; the river also was divided by Elijah and Elisha and also "cleansed by [Jesus'] baptism waters which the deluge had polluted and the destruction of mankind had defiled." Reaching back to Noah's flood, Jerome's span of sacred history commences in pre-Israelite times and consummates with Jesus' arrival. His Christian remapping of the Jewish holy land can be no clearer than in these two examples: "She gazed at the twelve stones brought out of the bed of Jordan to be symbols of those twelve foundations on which are written the names of the twelve apostles,"[72] and Jerome's pointing out the city of Moresheth, which was "in old days famed for the tomb of the prophet Micah, and now for its church."[73] This sort of redrawing of the sacred map uses an eraser over the old labels, but they never totally disappear. The new letters are written over the image of the old. Andrew Jacobs describes this conceptualization of the Christian holy land: "The Jewish 'other' was at once expelled and internalized, erased and appropriated, the signifier of Christian difference that could never be totally eradicated but must always leave traces for the imperial Christian to master."[74] However, Jerome deems one site unworthy of remapping and instead berates Judaism with a clever etymological attack by recalling that Paula "did not care to go to Kirjath-Sepher" since the

---

71. *Ep.* 108.13 (CSEL 55:323); emphasis added. Limor observes that, in comparing the itineraries of Egeria and Paula, "the liturgical aspect of the Holy Places, which is so important in Egeria's account, is entirely absent from that of Paula . . . [whose] visit is a purely textual experience, limited to seeing the place and reflecting on its significance" ("Reading Sacred Space," 9).

72. *Ep.* 108.10–12 (CSEL 55:316–21).

73. *Ep.* 108.14 (CSEL 55:324).

74. Jacobs, *Remains of the Jews*, 142.

meaning of the name is "the village of letters." She despised "the letter that kills [because] she had found the Spirit that gives life."[75] A city not worth a visit is likened to a religion similarly unworthy.

Jerome and Paula continue to follow a multilayered itinerary that includes both Jewish and Christian holy sites. The ongoing theme of supersession pervades the letter, so that the Mount of Olives is said to be where the Jews burned a red heifer and where "the Cherubim after leaving the temple founded the church of the Lord."[76] Similarly, Jacob's well becomes a story of replacement, for the woman of Samaria, "forsaking her five husbands by whom are intended the five books of Moses ... found the true Messiah."[77] Jerome's sacred geography also involves the creation of holy space by Jesus' presence: "The lake of Tiberias [is] sanctified by his voyages upon it."[78] The final leg of their journey took them to Egypt but only to those places where Jesus and his family had visited—what Jerome calls the "holy places"[79]— and several of the monastic communities. After spending some time there, Paula could stay no longer since she was "drawn away by a still greater passion for the holy places" in Palestine. "She returned so rapidly that you would have thought her a bird" and quickly decided to "dwell permanently in holy Bethlehem."[80] The magnetic attraction of Bethlehem proves irresistible to Paula and Jerome alike, a theme that I will explore later.

Jerome's lengthy letter sheds light on his construction of the Christian holy land. He reads the text of the Old and New Testaments onto the map of the text's geography, producing yet another text: "For a believer, sacred space is a text, to be interpreted and deciphered, just like the Holy Scriptures and in parallel to them."[81] Once these twin texts merge into one, Jerome's version of Christian supersessionism is empowered to persuade others to embrace that text through pilgrimage.

---

75. *Ep.* 108.11 (CSEL 55:319).
76. *Ep.* 108.12 (CSEL 55:320).
77. *Ep.* 108.13 (CSEL 55:322).
78. Ibid. (CSEL 55:323).
79. *Ep.* 108.14 (CSEL 55:325).
80. Ibid.
81. Limor, "'Holy Journey': Pilgrimage and Christian Sacred Landscape," 324.

Invitations to Pilgrimage

Jerome encouraged others to make pilgrimage to the holy land, as demonstrated in some of his other letters. The first and most compelling appeal is written to Marcella in 386, ostensibly from her Roman friends Paula and Eustochium, who have established a monastery in Bethlehem, but many scholars consider Jerome to be the true author.[82] The purpose of the letter is to convince Marcella that the holy land is worthy of her pilgrimage and not under God's curse as she apparently believed. The letter begins with a call to imitate Abraham, who left his home country for the promised land, a theme that is found in four other letters.[83] Jerome then moves to the heart of the Christian holy land, Jerusalem, as he adulates its spiritual virtues, first as the city of Melchizedek, a type of Christ, to David's capital city, and to Mary, "who made her way to the hill country" of Judea.[84] He records the tradition that the Church of the Holy Sepulcher marks the spot where Adam lived, died, and was buried, so that the second Adam's blood might cleanse the first Adam. Jerome's imagination soars to new christological heights as he lists the three names of the city (Jebus, Salem, Jerusalem) and their Hebrew meanings, which "prove the doctrine of the Trinity" and also illustrate, by the meanings of their names, the progressive pilgrimage of the godly in three "slow stages" from suffering to peace to the final vision of peace.[85] Finally, Jerome elevates the city of Jerusalem to geographical supremacy: "As Judea is exalted above all other provinces, so is this city exalted above all Judea."[86] He reflects the recent Christian tradition of the sanctity of earthly Jerusalem as the navel of the earth: "Jerusalem is located in the middle of the world, showing that she is the navel of the earth."[87] Jerome supports this fourth-century superesessionist geography, but he will eventually subvert it for Bethlehem. For "Jerome's Christian Jerusalem is, then, no longer the cursed land of previous Christian authors, but must

---

82. Smith argues for Paula as the author ("'My Lord's Native Land,'" 14). For a survey of the literature on both sides of the debate, see Cain, *Letters of Jerome*, 68–71, 95–98; and Bitton-Ashkelony, *Encountering the Sacred*, 71 n. 35.

83. *Ep.* 58.3; 71.2; 108.31; 125.20.

84. *Ep.* 46.2 (CSEL 54:331).

85. *Ep.* 46.3 (CSEL 54:332).

86. Ibid.

87. *Commentary on Ezekiel* 2.5.5 (CCSL 75).

be regarded as the most precious soil inasmuch as the blood of Christ had been poured into it."[88]

However, Jerome then delves into a question he perceives Marcella would ask: If God judged the Jews by destroying their city and its temple, why does Jerusalem still hold spiritual meaning? He answers by rehearsing the classic mantra of supersessionism: "All the spiritual importance of Judea and its old intimacy with God were transferred by the apostles to the nations."[89] Foreseeing that he might be outmaneuvered by the logic of supersessionism with its total dismissal of the earthly Jerusalem, he counters by cleverly distinguishing between "the people who sinned and not the place."[90] Certainly the city and its temple were destroyed, but the "lapse of time has but invested it with fresh grandeur."[91] He says that glory of the Jews' temple has been transferred to Jesus' tomb, even as predicted by a Jewish prophet: "Long before this sepulcher was hewn out by Joseph, its glory was foretold in Isaiah's prediction, 'his rest shall be glorious,' (Isaiah 11:10) meaning that the place of the Lord's burial should be held in universal honor."[92] He calls his reasoning "an easy solution" to the problem she presents, namely that the city of Jerusalem, once the object of God's wrath because of its sinful people, absorbed God's judgment in the past and has experienced a renewal to its former splendor centered in the ongoing presence of Jesus: "As often as we enter [the sepulcher] we see the savior in his grave clothes, and if we linger we see again the angel sitting at his feet."[93] The present-tense verbs accentuate Jerome's understanding of holy space, namely that to the enlightened believer Jesus' presence continues in a perpetual moment of time. For this reason, "the Lord's sepulcher [is] worthy of veneration."[94]

The implications of such intrinsic holiness move Jerome to a deeper level of personal connection with Jerusalem. Pilgrimage to this sacred place, claims Jerome, is not optional "since the evangelists and all the Scriptures speak of Jerusalem as the holy city, and since the psalmist commands us to

---

88. Perrone, "'Mystery of Judaea' (Jerome, *Ep.* 46)," 233.
89. *Ep.* 46.4 (CSEL 54:333).
90. *Ep.* 46.5 (CSEL 54:334).
91. Ibid.
92. Ibid.
93. Ibid.
94. Ibid.

worship the Lord 'at his footstool' (Psa. 132:7)."[95] Jerome's unique contribution to the Christian church's notion of pilgrimage is that he considers it to be mandatory, as Bitton-Ashkelony observes: "Scholars seem to have missed the language of obligation used by Jerome and, therefore, the significance and uniqueness of this claim. To the best of my knowledge, there is no parallel in the writings of other Christian thinkers of his day; it was straightforward innovation."[96] This sort of novelty is not out of character with the monk who also argues for a wholly new Old Testament text and a historical hermeneutic based on Hebrew interpretations. In this instance, his personal pilgrimage acts as a mandatory template for his fellow Christians—suggestion is transformed into obligation. As we have seen in previous chapters, Jerome elevates his authority as a gifted discerner of Hebrew text and interpretation and also as one who is to be trusted by his Christian readers. His air of authority is seen here by his unilateral declaration of pilgrimage as a necessary part of Christian devotion.

After cataloguing several other reasons why Christians must visit Jerusalem, Jerome concludes that many other Christian leaders have made such a pilgrimage to adore Christ "in the very spot where the gospel first flashed from the gallows. . . . Can we suppose a Christian's education complete who has not visited the Christian Athens? . . . We merely assert in the strongest manner that those who stand first throughout the world are here gathered side by side."[97] In his unflinching way, Jerome contradicts Tertullian's geographic binaries ("What indeed has Athens to do with Jerusalem?"[98]) by creating a singularity. Using multiple avenues of persuasion, from Scripture to example to command to intimidation, Jerome applies his variety of rhetorical pressure to convince Marcella, and all of his eventual readers, that Jerusalem absolutely must be visited. Jerome garnishes his portrait of the holy city to the point of being irresistible: perfect unity exists among Christians in Jerusalem ("there is no arrogance, no disdain of self-restraint; all strive after humility"[99]) as well as perfect sanctification ("no one judges another lest he be judged of the Lord. Backbiting, so common in

---

95. *Ep.* 46.7 (CSEL 54:338).

96. Bitton-Ashkelony, *Encountering the Sacred*, 76.

97. *Ep.* 46.9-10 (CSEL 54:339-340).

98. *De praescriptione*, 7. Tertullian wrote these words c. 205, before Jerusalem's conversion into a Christian city.

99. *Ep.* 46.10 (CSEL 54:340).

"BETHLEHEM... NOW OURS"

other parts, is wholly unknown here. Sensuality and excess are far removed from us"[100]). It sounds like heaven has come to earth.

What greater picture of paradise could there be than this? Jerome will answer that in an amazing feat of one-upsmanship. Jerome usurps the supremacy just conferred on Jerusalem and presents an astonishing conclusion: Bethlehem is holier than Jerusalem! He portrays his own town self-effacingly, using Jerusalem as a foil. What Jerusalem gains in glory it loses in wealth and worldliness; Bethlehem with its cave of Christ quietly exceeds Jerusalem by its rich poverty:

> Words are inadequate to speak its praise. Where are the spacious porticoes? Where are the gilded ceilings? Where are the mansions furnished by the miserable toil of doomed wretches? Where are the costly halls raised by untitled opulence for man's vile body to walk in? Where are the roofs that intercept the sky, as if anything could be finer than the expanse of heaven?[101]

Rather than comparing the holiness of Bethlehem to that of Jerusalem, which he had earlier praised, he uses the temple of Jupiter on the Palatine Hill Rome: "This spot is holier, I think, than that Tarpeian rock which has shown itself displeasing to God by the frequency with which it has been struck by lightning"[102] This curious comparison is left unexplained, but it demands clarification for those far removed from the fourth century. I suggest that Jerome is drawing a parallel between Jupiter, the chief god of the Roman pantheon, whose temple adorned the Tarpeian rock,[103] and the humble cave of Christ, the god of the Christians. By ignoring Jerusalem in this comparison, he dismisses its holiness as secondary. He places Rome and Bethlehem on equal footing as homes of the god(s). In this way Jerome readjusts the center of the holy land a mere five miles south but a world away from where Christian tradition has located it. Topping off the picture of paradise in Bethlehem, Jerome sees his city as the kingdom already come, as Eden's bliss duplicated and the Old Testament prophets' dreams realized in the fourth century:

> In the cottage of Christ all is simple and rustic: and except for the chanting of psalms there is complete silence. Wherever one turns

---

100. Ibid.
101. *Ep.* 46.11 (CSEL 54:341).
102. Ibid.
103. Stamper, *Architecture of Roman Temples*, 11–17.

the laborer at his plough sings alleluia, the toiling mower cheers himself with psalms, and the vine-dresser while he prunes his vine sings one of the lays of David. These are the songs of the country; these, in popular phrase, its love poems: these the shepherd whistles; these the tiller uses to aid his toil.[104]

In a grand finale of arrogant humility, Jerome invites Marcella to join him on a pilgrimage to all the holy sites in Palestine and then make their way "back to our cave."[105]

In four other letters Jerome touches on the subject of pilgrimage. First, writing in 393, Jerome invites Desiderius in Rome to visit Bethlehem. His appeal is blunt and forceful as he repeats his innovative definition of pilgrimage as an obligatory part of the Christian faith. Notice that Jerome here places Bethlehem and Jerusalem on equal footing, where divine "traces" bring the holy past into the holy present: "It is still your duty [or "part of faith"] as a believer to worship on the spot where the Lord's feet once stood and to see for yourselves the still fresh traces of His birth, His cross, and His passion."[106] Jerome's softer side is revealed in a letter to Castrutius, written in 397, whose physical blindness caused others to cut his pilgrimage short. Jerome commends his friend's intent to perform pilgrimage as a substitute for the act itself: "You would have actually accomplished your purpose, had not our brethren with affectionate care held you back. I thank you all the same and regard it as a kindness shown. For in the case of friends one must accept the will for the deed."[107] In 398 Jerome writes to Lucinius in Spain, who had expressed some desire to visit Bethlehem. Once again Jerome uses the Abrahamic model to call his friend to Bethlehem. The tone begins with an imperative and ends with an invitation: "You too must leave your home as he did. . . . You can see for yourself why I mention these things; without expressly saying it I am inviting you to take up your abode at the holy places."[108] Finally, in 399 Jerome writes to Abigaum, a priest in Spain, asking him to encourage a widow named Theodora to persevere in her pilgrimage.

---

104. *Ep.* 46.12 (CSEL 54:342).

105. *Ep.* 46.13 (CSEL 54:344). For more analysis of Marcella's identity and zealous Christian devotion, including her learning of Hebrew, see Graves, "Biblical Scholarship of a Fourth-Century Woman Marcella of Rome."

106. *Ep.* 47.2 (CSEL 54:346).

107. *Ep.* 68.1 (CSEL 54:675).

108. *Ep.* 71.2, 4 (CSEL 55:2).

The rhetoric of replacement echoes in Jerome's casting her in the role of an ancient Israelite on her own personal exodus from Egypt:

> Tell her that she must not grow weary of the path upon which she has entered, and that she can only reach the Holy Land by toiling through the wilderness. Warn her against supposing that the work of virtue is perfected when she has made her exodus from Egypt. Remind her that she must pass through snares innumerable to arrive at Mount Nebo and the River Jordan, that she must receive circumcision anew at Gilgal, that Jericho must fall before her, overthrown by the blasts of priestly trumpets, that Adoni-zedec must be slain, that Ai and Hazor, once fairest of cities, must both fall.[109]

Her pilgrimage is intended to reenact the conquest of the land from the Canaanites as a Christian soldier going to war against the unnamed but still fierce inhabitants of the land. In these four letters there is no talk of the heavenly Jerusalem, of the New Jerusalem, or of a spiritualized future. Jerome invites, even commands, the potential pilgrims to enjoy the rewards immediately attainable upon stepping on the soil of Palestine. His overarching presupposition, that the Christian church is the true Israel, is localized onto a concrete reality by stating that no other land but the Jewish holy land will do, for it has been sanctified by the God of Israel and the messiah of Israel. Now sufficiently reclaimed by the Christian church, Jerome's permanent home becomes an obligatory stop on the journey to heaven.

Cataloging the Holy Land

In addition to Jerome's personal invitation to pilgrimage, his pen also becomes the cartographer's tool. In the year 390 Jerome embarks upon the creation of a trilogy designed to provide encyclopedic resources of Hebrew knowledge to his Christian readers: the *Book of Hebrew Names* listed all the biblical proper names and their supposed Hebrew etymology; the *Book of Hebrew Places* translates and updates Eusebius's work entitled *Onomasticon*, a gazetteer of biblical sites written between 313 and 325; and the *Hebrew Questions on Genesis* sets out to justify his translation and commentary method of retrieving truth from Jewish sources. The *Book of Hebrew Places* prepares Christian monks to remap the Christian holy land for visiting pilgrims. Jerome's Latin work is a revised edition of Eusebius's Greek text

---

109. *Ep.* 76.3 (CSEL 55:36).

that alphabetically lists sites in Palestine associated with biblical references. Eusebius was the first to systematically appropriate the land of the Bible:

> By conceiving of the land of the Bible as a geographical territory in which Christians have an interest and in which Christian sites are mentioned along with ancient Israelite sites, Eusebius had begun to envision Palestine not as a Roman province but as a land whose character and identity were formed by biblical *and* Christian history.[110]

He wrote before the inauguration of the concept of a Christian holy land, and "Eusebius does not indicate that any sites should be venerated as sacred by Christians."[111] In Jerome's time the conditions had changed. The *Book of Hebrew Places* would now become a tool for Christian monks and pilgrims to further enhance their grasp on the holy land.

Jerome's preface to Eusebius's work explains how his edition differs from the original. He sets himself up as more than a translator, "leaving aside those things that do not seem to be worth remembering, and changing several."[112] Once again, Jerome presents himself as a trustworthy guide who bridges the past to inform the present. Within the translation, the significant differences include updated information about churches built since Eusebius's day, local details shared with him by Jewish guides, and corrections of the first edition. Worth noting is the entry for Jerusalem. Both write about Jerusalem beginning with the Jebusite inhabitants, then David's conquest and creation of "the mother-city of the whole province of Judaea." Only Jerome adds that it was home of Solomon's temple, and neither says anything further about its destructions or its prominence in Jesus' death or its enhancement as a Christian city.[113] In the entry for Bethlehem Jerome states: "The city of David in the lot of the tribe of Judah, in which our Lord and Savior was born, six miles from Aelia to the south," in contrast to Eusebius, who merely states the Old Testament data. Jerome adds further detail about the tower of Ader, where "in prophecy the shepherds became aware of the nativity of the Lord."[114] His agenda to elevate Bethlehem as the most holy city in the holy land, especially over Jerusalem, is unobtrusively tucked away in an alphabetical listing of place names.

110. Wilken, *Land Called Holy*, 100.
111. Taylor, "Introduction," 1.
112. "Preface of Jerome," in Eusebius, *Onomasticon*, 11.
113. Ibid., 61.
114. Ibid., 31.

"Bethlehem... Now Ours"

Susan Weingarten carefully compares the linguistic differences between Eusebius's Greek original and Jerome's Latin translation.[115] She confirms that Jerome accurately translates the work and updated names and descriptions in light of fourth-century conditions. Eusebius comments on thirty occasions that a site "was pointed out" to him by someone else, most probably a local guide. In his translation Jerome adds the Latin word "it was shown" an additional thirty-three times as an indicator of his eyewitness appraisal of the land.[116] His knowledge of the land originated from natives, some undoubtedly Jewish, who lived near enough to the spot to possess accurate information. Jews are depicted in this work, as in many other Christian texts, as those who hold the key to truth but are blind to its meaning. Although they are cursed for rejecting the Christ, they are trusted to transfer information about sacred texts or sacred space and at the same time disclose trusted information about Christian geography: "Jews were regarded as the authority not only with respect to sites of the Old Testament, but also with respect to sites and relics of the New Testament."[117] Jerome positions himself as the bridge between the Hebrew truth and the Christian truth seekers.

Jerome mediates the knowledge, filtered through his Christian grid, to his readers. This position is remarkably similar to his mediating the Hebrew text to Latin Bible readers and his transferring Jewish interpretations to Christian readers of his commentaries. Jerome constructs a persona of himself as translator, interpreter, and now geographer for the Christian church. This confluence discloses the intimate connection between text, hermeneutic, and sacred space as they were articulated and transformed by a single individual.

---

115. Weingarten, *Saint's Saints*, 251–63.

116. Ibid., 258. Jerome's personal acquaintance with the sites came during his early pilgrimage with Paula as described in *Ep.* 108.

117. Limor, "Christian Sacred Space and the Jew," 57–58. Her article demonstrates the authority of Jewish knowledge in stories relating to the discovery of the true cross, St. Stephen's bones, Jesus' mantle, the virgin's robe, Jesus' shroud, the foundation stone, and King David's tomb.

JEROME'S REMAPPING THE HOLY CITY: FROM JERUSALEM TO BETHLEHEM

Up to this point in my consideration of Jerome's remapping of the holy land, his views have been fairly consistent with most Christian writers of the fourth century. I have hinted earlier in this chapter about one tenet that sets him apart from the rest. Just as Jerome departed from Christian tradition over the Hebrew text of the Old Testament and over the Jews as a viable source of Christian interpretation, so he pioneers a new sacred space by promoting Bethlehem's sanctity over Jerusalem's. He does so in two ways: first, he strategically deemphasizes pilgrimage to Jerusalem in favor of Bethlehem, and second, he replaces the eschatological sanctity accorded the earthly Jerusalem with that due the heavenly Jerusalem.

Replacement of Jerusalem's Present Sanctity

Jerome downplays the holiness of the city of Jerusalem after first holding the traditional Christian view of its supremacy. I have evaluated his letters in which he encourages his friends to make pilgrimage to the holy land and to include Jerusalem's holy places in their itinerary. The posture of preference toward an earthly Jerusalem was a recent development in Christian theology, but one that Jerome promoted in the late fourth century. Earlier in the second century, Christian exegetes Tertullian and Origen had written rejoinders against the prevailing Jewish opinions that envisioned a restoration of the Jews to their ancient homeland. They endeavored to erase Jewish aspirations of a restored future by interpreting the prophecies that speak of such things as pointing to the Christians' eternal destiny in the heavenly Jerusalem rather than an earthly Jerusalem. As Rome had erased Jewish presence from Jerusalem by expelling those Jews who survived their failed rebellion in 135 and renamed the city Aelia Capitolina, so Christians hermeneutically expelled the Jews from their claim on their prophets' words. Origen based this approach on the New Testament's resignfication of Jerusalem into a spiritual entity.[118] Thus a theological tradition commenced that focused eschatological hopes on the next world, a spiritually minded vision of eternal bliss. However, an enormous shift occurred when Con-

---

118. "The Jerusalem that is above" (Gal 4:26) and "the heavenly Jerusalem" (Heb 12:22); for Origen's hermeneutic and debates with Jews, see Wilken, *Land Called Holy*, 65–72.

stantine, recently converted to Christianity, introduced an unknown aspect of religious thought to Christianity: the memorialization of sacred space. "Formerly Christians had spoken of virtuous men and women as holy, of the holy church of holy Scriptures. Now holiness is attributed to a place."[119] This effected a modification of Christian theology that further nuanced the meaning of Jerusalem, a change that is most evident in Eusebius. His writings before Constantine's inauguration of a Christian holy land present the promised Jerusalem as the Christian's heavenly abode. After the Constantinian legislation promoting Christianity, Eusebius created space (quite literally) for an earthly Jerusalem—not fashioned after the Jewish model of temple cult and priestly leaders, but with Christian bishops reigning from their churches in the spiritual yet physical kingdom of Christ on earth. Eusebius recorded Constantine's great accomplishments in the holy land by suggesting that they fulfill Old Testament prophecies: "It may be that this was that second and new Jerusalem spoken of in the predictions of the prophets, concerning which such abundant testimony is given in the divinely inspired records."[120] What he considered as a possibility he changed to a reality in his commentary on Isaiah, in which he "uses the triumphant imagery of Isaiah about the messianic age to describe the reign of the new Christian emperor, an interpretation that was unimaginable in Origen's day."[121]

The Christian world of the late fourth century had been transformed from its earlier centuries of persecution and eschatological hopes. A newly fashioned, realized eschatology wrote such hopes onto the map of fourth-century Palestine, rewriting the sacred geography of the Jews and the pagan geography of the Romans:

> After the discovery of the tomb of Christ under Constantine, the building of basilicas in the holy places of Palestine and the development of pilgrimage to them on an unprecedented scale—the dominant spiritualizing approach expounded at that time by as [an] important exponent of the Origenian tradition as Eusebius of Caesarea—were no longer tenable. It had to be tempered, or even transformed, in the face of the new reality of a Christian "Holy City" in a "Holy Land."[122]

---

119. Wilken, *Land Called Holy*, 89.
120. *Life of Constantine* 3.33.
121. Wilken, *Land Called Holy*, 79.
122. Perrone, "'Mystery of Judaea' (Jerome, *Ep.* 46)," 228.

Jerome inherited those transformed notions of the benefits of the earthly Jerusalem, however, he will revert back to the pre-Constantinian position after the year 394. I will examine the evidence of his progressive distaste for Jerusalem, offer a reason for the modification, and suggest why he chooses Bethlehem in place of Jerusalem.

First, Jerome shifts his interpretations of scriptural texts about Jerusalem, in particular, considering the significance of Adam and the rock of Calvary. In a letter written in 386 he repeats the tradition that Adam is buried in Jerusalem:

> Tradition has it that in this city, nay, more, on this very spot, Adam lived and died. The place where our Lord was crucified is called Calvary, because the skull of the primitive man was buried there. So it came to pass that the second Adam, that is the blood of Christ, as it dropped from the cross, washed away the sins of the buried prototype, the first Adam.[123]

Somewhat later, circa 386–88, he leaves the reader to ascertain the verity of the tradition but gently disagrees with it himself:

> I know that I have heard someone preaching about this passage in church. As a theatrical marvel he presented a model never before seen by the people so that it was pleasing. He said of this testimony, that it is said that Adam was buried at Calvary where the Lord was crucified. The place was called Calvary [i.e. skull], therefore, because the head of the ancient man was buried there. At the time when the Lord was crucified, therefore, he was hanging over Adam's grave and this prophecy was fulfilled which says, "Awake," Adam, "who are asleep and arise from the dead," and not as we read that is, "Christ will rise like the sun on you," but, that is, "Christ will touch you." That was because, of course, by the touch of his blood and hanging body Adam would be made alive and would arise.... Whether these things are true or not I leave to the reader's decision. They were certainly pleasing at the time they were spoken among the people who received them with applause and by stamping their feet. I mention one thing which I know: that understanding does not fit with the interpretation and coherence of this passage.[124]

---

123. *Ep.* 46.3 (CSEL 54:332).

124. *Commentary on Ephesians* 5:14 (PL 26:559). English translation is from *Commentaries of Origen and Jerome on St. Paul's Epistle to the Ephesians*, 224.

About ten years later, in 398, he reviews the interpretation given above and rejects it, listing several arguments against it:

> This interpretation is attractive and soothing to the ear of the people, but it is not true.... But if anyone should wish to contend that the reason the Lord was crucified there was so that his blood might trickle down on Adam's tomb, we shall ask him why other thieves were also crucified in the same place.... But in the book of Joshua the son of Nave we read that Adam was buried near Hebron and Arba.[125]

Between the years 388 and 398 his view gradually changes into a firm stance against an entrenched Christian tradition, a new position. This stance is strikingly similar to Jerome's demolition of the myth of the Septuagint's divine inspiration and his return to the Hebrew text as the source of truth.

Another example of an interpretational reversal concerns the actual place where resurrected people appeared: "After his resurrection they came out of the tombs and entered the holy city and appeared to many" (Matt 27:53). Writing in 386, well before the Origenist affair, Jerome derides those who interpret this as happening in the heavenly Jerusalem: "We must not interpret this passage straight off, as many people absurdly do, of the heavenly Jerusalem: the apparition there of the bodies of the saints could be no sign to men of the Lord's rising."[126] Yet in 396 he embraces that interpretation: "Therefore at His rising again 'many bodies of the saints which slept arose, and were seen in the heavenly Jerusalem.'"[127] A more mediating posture is discernable in 398, in which Jerome offers two interpretations without stating his preference: "Now we should understand the holy city in which they were seen when they were being resurrected either as the heavenly Jerusalem, or this earthly one which was previously holy."[128] Perhaps he states the first option as what he would wish in light of his growing anti-Jerusalem stance, but he includes the second with the designation of "holy" in the past.

Second, I consider a startling letter, written in 395, in which Jerome reverses his position on pilgrimage and his favorable sentiment toward

---

125. *Commentary on Matthew* 27:33 (CCSL 77:270). English translation is from *Commentary on Matthew*, 315–16. Jerome refers to his Vulgate translation of Josh 14:15.

126. *Ep.* 46.7 (CSEL 54:338).

127. *Ep.* 60.3 (CSEL 54:551).

128. *Commentary on Matthew* 27:52–53 (CCSL 77:276). English translation is from *Commentary on Matthew*, 321.

Jerusalem. With content that reflects an epistle written by Gregory of Nyssa in about 384,[129] this letter is written to Paulinus of Nola, who wishes to become a monk in the holy land but is soundly rebuffed. Jerome had written him a year earlier urging him to sell all and come to Bethlehem (*Ep.* 53, dated 394). Jerome uses several arguments "against the sanctity of the earthly Jerusalem, which he had flatly rejected in *Letter 46* . . . to prove his new stance—indeed, [it is] an acrobatic act."[130] Jerome discourages his friend first by disparaging the benefits of coming to Jerusalem, the earthly city, in favor of the heavenly city:

> What is praiseworthy is not to have been at Jerusalem but to have lived a good life while there. The city which we are to praise and to seek is not that which has slain the prophets and shed the blood of Christ, but that which is made glad by the streams of the river, which is set upon a mountain and so cannot be hid, which the apostle declares to be a mother of the saints, and in which he rejoices to have his citizenship with the righteous.[131]

Jerome thus removes the geographical markers of sacred space: "Each believer is judged not by his residence in this place or in that but according to the merits of his faith. The true worshippers worship the Father neither at Jerusalem nor on Mount Gerizim; for 'God is a spirit, and they that worship Him must worship Him in spirit and in truth.'"[132]

Jerome now subtly downplays the spirituality of those living in Jerusalem by raising the bar to include only those who "bear their several crosses, who day by day rise again with Christ, and who thus show themselves worthy of an abode so holy."[133] Apparently, those worthies are few, and one suspects that this is Jerome's attempt to belittle the spiritual characters of those already living in Jerusalem. Jerome once again universalizes the presence of God: "Access to the courts of heaven is as easy from Britain as it is from Jerusalem; for 'the kingdom of God is within you.'"[134] He continues to deemphasize Jerusalem by pointing out that other holy people never visited

---

129. In brief, Gregory's *Ep.* 2 argues that pilgrimage to Jerusalem is needless and potentially harmful, since no place possesses more or less of God's presence than his own Cappadocia and because Jerusalem is full of sinful temptations and physical danger.

130. Bitton-Ashkelony, *Encountering the Sacred*, 91.

131. *Ep.* 58.2 (CSEL 54:529–30).

132. *Ep.* 58.3 (CSEL 54:530).

133. Ibid.

134. *Ep.* 58.3 (CSEL 54:531).

there, and even the monk Hilarion,[135] who lived in Palestine, only visited Jerusalem for one day so as not "to appear to confine God within local limits."[136] Jerome bolsters his argument by reminding Paulinus about the statues of Roman gods erected on the spot of the crucifixion and resurrection, as well as the grove of Adonis and worship of Venus at the holy places of Bethlehem. Such idolatrous pollution never drove Christians from their faith since the veracity of their faith is not linked to a holy place.

How should we understand Jerome's seemingly contradictory statements on pilgrimage and Jerusalem? Some scholars propose that Jerome reflects two positions—one of the official church, the other of popular religion.[137] They see a perpetual ambivalence in Jerome, who simultaneously holds two opposite views of Christian pilgrimage. The point of view reflecting the church represents the anti-Jerusalem stance, while the "expression of popular piety" comes out in his other letters that encourage pilgrimage. However, these views both fail since they lack an appreciation of the historical purview of Jerome and the Origenist controversy that caused a temporary reversal of Jerome's views.

I agree with the scholars who suggest that the reason for Jerome's increasing aversion to pilgrimage in Jerusalem was the personal and theological disputes with Rufinus and Melania the Elder, whose monasteries headquartered on the Mount of Olives were aligned with Bishop John in Jerusalem, all of whom were the subject of scrutiny over their defense of the teachings of Origen.[138] Epiphanius of Salamis, exposer of heresies and native of Palestine, led the attack against Origen's disciples, enlisting Jerome's support against Bishop John, Rufinus, and Melania the Elder, who defended Origen's theology.[139] Earlier, an ecclesiastical bond between a triad of churches had been formed based on the Constantinian basilicas constructed in Jerusalem, on the Mount of Olives, and in Bethlehem; now Bethlehem stood alone.[140] Bishop John excommunicated Jerome in re-

---

135. Jerome composed *The Life of Hilarion* c. 390 and presented him as the first ascetic who was born and lived in Palestine.

136. *Ep.* 58.3 (CSEL 54:531).

137. Bitton-Ashkelony, *Encountering the Sacred*, 85–88, discusses the works of J. Prawer, F. Carman, and R. Markus.

138. Stemberger, *Jews and Christians in the Holy Land*, 102; Perrone, 234; Bitton-Ashkelony, 97; and Newman, "Between Jerusalem and Bethlehem," 220, who cites earlier scholarship.

139. See Clark, *Origenist Controversy*, 11–42.

140. Walker, 184–194.

taliation for his stance on the Origenist controversy, barring him from the Church of the Holy Sepulcher as well as from churches in Bethlehem and not permitting him to bury in consecrated ground. He did allow Jerome to stay in his cell and worship at his monastery's church. It is not surprising that Jerome's affection for Jerusalem became tainted with bitterness and anger during these years, a drama he unfolds in *Against John of Jerusalem*, composed in early 397. Thus, I suggest that in his letter to Paulinus, Jerome advises against coming to Jerusalem in order to prevent this friend from becoming an enemy, as Paulinus's other friends in Jerusalem, Rufinus and Melania, were now Jerome's enemies: "He therefore had no choice but to minimize the religious significance of the sacred topography and the importance of visiting the holy places—even though he had taken an opposite view when attempting earlier to convince Marcella to follow him [Letter 46]."[141] However, after his three-year excommunication came to an end, Jerome does resume his former posture of recommending pilgrimage, and in an about-face he avoids assaults on Jerusalem.[142]

From the time of the Origenist controversy, Jerome's new center of earthly sanctity becomes Bethlehem. This should not be a surprise, since hints of this move are evident in his earlier letters. In a previously unexplored point in his correspondence in 395, Jerome places Bethlehem in high esteem, regarding it as a fulfillment of a psalm: "Even Bethlehem, now ours, that most venerable spot in the whole world of which the psalmist sings, 'The truth has sprung out of the earth.'"[143] Jerome's innovative interpretation runs counter to that of Cyril of Jerusalem (d. 386), who interprets it as a prophecy of Jesus' resurrection in Jerusalem.[144]

Finally, it might be asked why Jerome settled in Bethlehem originally, since no explanation is ever offered. One might suspect that, in view of Jerome's conflicts with Rufinus, he wants to put distance between the two of them. However, this hostility between them occurred later in their relationship. Alternatively, Jacobs suggests: "Perhaps Jerome and Paula imagined their monastic settlement as an extension of the new Christianized Jerusalem."[145] Andrew Cain argues that "Jerome attached profound spiritual significance to Bethlehem for another, more personal reason," namely, because of his

---

141. Bitton-Ashkelony, 90.
142. *Eps.* 68, 71, 76, 108, 122, 139, 145.
143. *Ep.* 58.3 (CSEL 54:532).
144. Walker, 182, n. 43. Eusebius interprets it as referring to the entire world.
145. *Remains of the Jews*, 164–165.

desire to press for the sainthood of his close friend Paula, who was buried in Bethlehem.[146] However, I find Kelly's proposal more satisfying in light of Jerome's personality: "Jerome had no wish to be a disciple, overshadowed by a much more experienced pioneer like Rufinus, while Paula instinctively felt the wisdom of placing a certain distance between herself and the devout but imperious Melania."[147] In addition, Hunt suggests that Jerome established a rivalry in light of the parallels between them, such as their "western foundations, with 'twin' monasteries for men and women, opening their doors to the stream of visitors to the Holy Land."[148] Other similarities include the prior pagan idols where both cities' churches stand and a unique connection with Christ's earthly life. At least two monastic communities existed in Bethlehem before Jerome's arrival: John Cassian records his stay at one such lodging on his way to Egypt, and Palladius lived for one year at Posidonius's monastery. But we hear nothing about these communities from Jerome. It would seem that, in light of Jerome's eccentric and iconoclastic personality, what appeals to him is a location close to the center of Christian sanctity but without the competition. He would rather enjoy being in the spotlight on a smaller stage than sharing a larger stage with his rivals.

Replacement of Jerusalem's Eschatological Sanctity

Alongside the transfer of Jerusalem's sacred space status to the city of Bethlehem, Jerome transfers the eschatological sanctity of Jerusalem from the earthly to the heavenly city. This growing outlook can be seen in a sermon delivered a few years after the Origenist controversy. Jerome's homily comes on the anniversary of the Church of the Holy Sepulcher's dedication and surprisingly includes no mention of the church itself. He elevates spiritual realities over holy places, demoting Jerusalem in favor of the spiritual value of the cross being found "in England, in India, in the entire world. Happy

---

146. "Jerome fixed Bethlehem, and more specifically Paula's tomb beneath the Church of the Nativity, as the geographical focal point of her nascent cult.... Thus, he promoted Bethlehem as the major Christian cult center and even more ambitiously as the spiritual (and scholarly) center of gravity of the universal church" (Cain, "Jerome's *Epitaphium Paulae*," 139). See Cain's detailed commentary on Jerome's work about his devoted female companion, *Jerome's Epitaph on Paula*.

147. Kelly, 128. Compare his comments about the contact between Jerome and Rufinus before their parting (136).

148. Hunt, *Holy Land Pilgrimage*, 174.

is he who carries in his bosom the Cross, the Resurrection, the place of Christ's nativity and the place of his ascension."[149]

I suspect another reason behind Jerome's growing aversion for the Christian idolizing of Jerusalem may have been his deep disgust at similar Jewish restoration eschatology, whose tenets Jerome had battled for years. Origen argued against the Jewish hopes for a rebuilt Jerusalem as well as against Christians whom he called "chiliasts," since they believed in a future thousand-year kingdom. Eusebius continued Origen's line of reasoning against the Jews, except that his notion of Jerusalem underwent a radical change after the Constantinian revolution: "Eusebius was the first to discern the profound shift in devotion that was taking place in his day and to lay the foundations for a Christian idea of the holy land."[150] Jerome resumes the polemic begun by Origen against contemporary Jews and fellow Christians who, like Origen's chiliasts, were labeled "Judaizers."[151] While Jerome participates in the veneration of the earthly Jerusalem, his mood changes after 394 and his theology shifts: Jerusalem's earthly sanctity is transferred to Bethlehem; Jerusalem's sanctity moves from the earthly to the heavenly Jerusalem.

Another factor in Jerome's stance against Judaizing might have come from the recent attempt of Emperor Julian, nephew of Constantine who despised his uncle's Christianity, to revive the religion of Judaism's sacrificial cult.[152] Julian proposed in 363, a mere fifty years after the legalization of Christianity, to rebuild the Jewish temple in Jerusalem so that Jews would be able to emulate the Romans in sacrificial worship. The threat was addressed by Gregory of Nazianzus, who formerly had studied the Bible together with Julian. With firsthand knowledge, Gregory states that Julian attempted to prove to the Jews from their Scriptures that it was now time for them "to return to their native land, to rebuild the Temple and to set up the rule of their ancestral ways."[153] The Jews were said to have requested of Julian: "'Restore to us the City, rebuild the Temple, and the Altar, and we shall offer sacrifices as in the days of old.' Julian [responded], 'I shall endeavor with the utmost zeal

---

149. *Homily on Psalm XCV* (CCSL 78:154–155); cited in Newman, "Between Jerusalem and Bethlehem," 221–22.

150. Wilken, *Land Called Holy,* 81.

151. For examples of Jerome's anti-Jewish rhetoric, see his *Commentary on Micah* 4:11–13; 5:7–14; 7:8–13; and *Commentary on Zephaniah* 2:12–15 (cited by Kelly, *Jerome,* 164).

152. See Sivan, *Palestine in Late Antiquity,* 204–10; and Stemberger, *Jews and Christians in the Holy Land,* 198–216, for a bibliography of ancient citations and recent studies.

153. From Gregory of Nazianzus, *Oratio V,* 3, in Avi-Yonah, *Jews of Palestine,* 193.

to set up the Temple of the Most High God.'"[154] The construction began but came to an abrupt halt when an earthquake and fire broke out on the temple mount, which for the Christians signaled divine displeasure at this challenge to Christian supremacy. Julian's untimely death on the battlefield with Persia brought an abrupt end to the project. This brief interruption in Christian ascendency revealed the fragility of the church's power. The very intimation of reversing the progress of Christian supersession caused an uproar of fear and protest among Christian writers, including Gregory of Nazianzus, Ephrem Syrus, Rufinus, Socrates, Sozomen, Philostorius, Theodoret, and Chrysostom: "Their vehemence suggests that the possibility of resurrecting the holiest monument of Judaism on the holiest site to Jews was seen to undermine the bind of power that informed the Christian discourse of Jerusalem."[155] For centuries the Christian church had used the temple's desolation to prove Christian supersession, basing their claim on the words of Jesus, "Not one stone [of the temple] here will be left on another; every one will be thrown down" (Matt 24:2). The church's authority was at risk of being overturned if the temple should reappear. A mere twenty-three years after Julian's abortive attempt to reverse Christian supersession, Jerome settles in Bethlehem. No doubt the memory still lingered and the fear still remained. Perhaps Julian's promise entailed more than a rebuilt Jewish temple, namely, the possibility of a repatriated Jewish people and a displaced Christian population.[156] Such conjecture remains unverifiable, but the large body of textual sources from the Christian side discloses a great fear of displacement and humiliation.[157] Hunt believes that this propelled the church into a tighter grip on the holy city of Jerusalem: "The failure of Julian's challenge can only have enhanced the position of the 'new Jerusalem', and further encouraged the concentration of Christian pilgrims visiting what were now indisputably *their* holy places."[158] But for Jerome, I believe it had the opposite effect: it further sours Jerome on Jerusalem. Rather than encouraging Jerome to promote Jerusalem's holy places, it drives him to deflect that authority onto Bethlehem.

---

154. Ibid., 191.

155. Sivan, *Palestine in Late Antiquity*, 207.

156. Avi-Yonah, *Jews of Palestine*, 192.

157. Stemberger lists the Christian texts that mention Julian: Ephrem's Syriac hymns, Gregory of Nazianzus' speeches, John Chrysostom's sermons, and a letter by Ambrose. "There is not a single authenticated Jewish source to set against the plethora of Christian texts" (*Jews and Christians in the Holy Land*, 203).

158. Hunt, *Holy Land Pilgrimage*, 157.

One of Jerome's letters devastatingly condemns the earthly city of Jerusalem and the Jewish people for their irreversible sin and the resultant curse. In 414, some five years before his death, Jerome responds to Dardanus's question, "What is the promised land?"[159] The letter reveals Jerome's mature and studied stance on this question. He begins by denying that Christians are ever promised an earthly territory; rather, they are promised the eternal life with God as the fulfillment of the promises originally formulated using terms such as "the land" of the Jews. He discovers this spiritual land already mentioned in the Old Testament, citing David's desire to "see the goodness of the Lord in the land of the living" (Ps 27:13), a land that David did not yet occupy even though his kingdom extended beyond the borders of Israel. Jerome concludes that there must be another land of which David speaks, thus this perception "draws us toward a spiritual understanding."[160] As Robert Wilken summarizes: "In Christian parlance the land of promise was a celestial country established by God, a place more splendid than any to be found on this earth, a land that awaited the saints after death."[161] Further, Jerome points out Jesus' promise that the gentle would inherit the earth (or "possess the land"), clearly speaking of something beyond what gentle people possess in this life. By yoking these verses, Jerome equates "the promised land" with "the land of the living" and with Jesus' mention of "the land," utilizing the semantics of Christian supersessionism. Jerome is careful to begin in the Old Testament, rather than in the New. By anchoring his spiritualized land in David rather than in Jesus, he retroactively anticipates his own Christian interpretation generations before Christians existed, implying that the original Jewish view of the promised land *is* the Christian view. In Jerome's eyes David becomes a supersessionist for the Christian cause.

Jerome continues to dismantle the Jewish notion of the promised land by claiming that the Old Testament Jews "were not inhabitants [of the land] but itinerants and sojourners," while the indigenous inhabitants were sinners.[162] Jerome is referring to Jewish heroes honored in Hebrews 11 who were seeking the heavenly Jerusalem, the very same city envisioned for Christians. Jerome equates these competing ideas of physical and spiritual land: "This land ... has now been made the promised land for us by

---

159. *Ep.* 129.1 (CSEL 56:162). English translation kindly provided by Dr. Bernard Prusak, Villanova University, 2009.

160. *Ep.* 129.1 (CSEL 56:163).

161. Wilken, *Land Called Holy*, 128.

162. *Ep.* 129.3 (CSEL 56:167).

the passion and resurrection of Christ" and cannot be compared to that previously possessed by the Jews.[163] That land is quite small geographically ("It is embarrassing to say the width of the promised land") but still considered an object of boast by contemporary Jews. Even if they might claim the larger dimension from what was promised by Moses, that land was never fully conquered due to the sin of idolatry resulting in the loss of everything promised to the Jews. Instead, Jerome characteristically contradicts himself: "In the gospel the kingdom of heaven is promised to me, of which there is entirely no mention in the Old Testament."[164] Jerome summarizes his argument against a literal interpretation and in favor of a metaphorical or spiritual reading: Jews "prefer the narrowness of the synagogue to the breadth of the church.... They show us a promised land flowing with milk and honey [instead of] that metaphor [which] indicates an abundance of all things ... the land of the living."[165] The metaphor becomes his gateway into "breadth" and "abundance," words that speak of geography and sacred space. Jerome's relocation of Jerusalem is complete.

He concludes this letter by excoriating the Jews for their many crimes of idolatry resulting in their slavery and the destruction of their temple. He lays the blame for their suffering on their rejection of Christ and on their self-incriminating words identifying themselves and their children as Christ-killers: "You now have what you chose; you will be slaves of Caesar until the end of the world."[166] Thus Jerome's final answer to the question consigns the Jewish view of the promised land to the same punishment assigned to the people who hold it. An earthly land associated with the Jews, now or in the future as potentially feasible with another emperor like Julian, had no place in Jerome's map of the holy land.

RESOLUTION OF JEROME'S APPROACH TO JEWISH LAND

"This glory [of holiness] our poor Bethlehem possesses, since it does not have gold and jewels but bread—the bread that was born in it."[167] Here,

---

163. *Ep.* 129.4 (CSEL 56:169).

164. *Ep.* 129.5 (CSEL 56:172).

165. *Ep.* 129.6 (CSEL 56:173). In commenting on the prophets, Jerome's spiritual interpretation is evident: "... except in the holy land, which is explained by the church ..." (*Commentary on Zechariah* 2:10 [CCSL 76A:768]).

166. *Ep.* 129.7 (CSEL 56:175).

167. *Commentary on Jeremiah* 19:10 (CCSL 74:186); English translation is from

in an unfinished work written at the end of his life, Jerome expresses his sacred geography. He always compares earthly Bethlehem, as the center of his world, to earthly Jerusalem, the center of the Christian world. He regards his city as poor and holy, and theirs as wealthy; his city has Jesus as the bread of life, Jerusalem has nothing to compare. But Jerusalem had not always been configured this way by Jerome, who characteristically travels a road marked by switchbacks and dead ends to arrive at his geographical conclusion. How does the choice of Bethlehem echo Jerome's Christian supersessionism of Jewish text and exegesis? It seems that Jerome would have confirmed Jerusalem as the Christian capital of the holy land, as others before him had established. However, just as Jerome redefined the limits of Christian text and exegesis, so he does in regarding sacred geography.

Jerome's early vision of pilgrimage cited Jerusalem as his goal: "Nowhere in the works written before his immigration to Palestine does Jerome indicate his intention to settle in Bethlehem or display particular fascination with the nativity of Jesus."[168] His orientation to Bethlehem rather than Jerusalem probably comes as a result of his growing dissatisfaction due to the Origenist controversy. He had lived in Rome and settled in Bethlehem, bypassing nearby Jerusalem. "Nothing cemented Jerome's association with Rome like his leaving it... Bethlehem... became indeed a new Rome."[169] The congruence of the three cities forms a triad of comparison and contrast. Rome, capital of the old empire and seat of its most powerful bishop, grows distasteful to Jerome when his reputation suffers a brutal attack.[170] Jerusalem, likewise, falls out of Jerome's favor when its leaders assail his credibility. The two cities are strikingly similar: "Constantine and his successors were, in essence, erecting an alternative Christian capital for their empire in Jerusalem, a site from which imperial authority could emanate in proper religious dress."[171] For Jerome, Rome in the East (Jerusalem) is too much like Rome in the West. Bethlehem surpasses both cities as a more venerable capital: "Let Rome have in you what a more sacred [Latin "august"] city than Rome, I mean Bethlehem, has in

---

Jerome's *Commentary on Jeremiah*, 119.

168. Newman, "Between Jerusalem and Bethlehem," 224.

169. Vessey, "Jerome and the *Jeromanesque*," 232.

170. "Although he lived for more than thirty years after his enforced departure from the city in 385, many of his subsequent decisions and judgments either reinforced, adapted, or consciously reacted against the experience and convictions of those years in Rome" (Rousseau, *Ascetics, Authority, and the Church*, 108).

171. Jacobs, *Remains of the Jews*, 145.

"Bethlehem ... Now Ours"

her."[172] Unscarred by wars, unpolluted by disobedient inhabitants or a ruined temple, so unlike the Rome of the West and of the East, pristine Bethlehem suites Jerome admirably. His allegiance focuses rather on the ruler of earth and heaven, whose birthplace is now Jerome's abode.[173]

In addition, Bethlehem's history is rooted in the Israelite king David, whose ancestral story is narrated in the book of Ruth. Israel's preeminent king was born and raised in Bethlehem.[174] An Israelite prophet predicted that a future king would emerge from a small clan in Bethlehem.[175] Jerome, no doubt well aware of the Jewish associations and christological import of the town, seizes an important opportunity to appropriate and transform the Jewish village into his Christian hometown. Whenever Jerome mentions Bethlehem, he imbues it with its rich Jewish past and its connection to royalty. Thus Jerome crafts a new sacred topography, similar to that of Christian tradition, but different owing to his flair for originality and his taste for Hebrew truth. While Old Testament prophets foretell a future for the city of Jerusalem, the basis of which becomes the "heavenly Jerusalem" and "New Jerusalem" of the New Testament, the prophets of both testaments say nothing about the city of Bethlehem—there is no "heavenly Bethlehem." With only an ecclesiastical present and no eschatological future, Bethlehem sits undisturbed, except for Jerome's belligerent presence. He remaps his own identity over the city of a Jewish king and of the nativity of the Christians' king, birthing his own enterprise from his cave. His goal is to inscribe Christian identity over the land of the Jews, claiming it all for the church: "The Christian maps of the 'holy land' of the fourth and fifth centuries were mental, textual, architectural, and ritual."[176] All four of these maps are present in Jerome, with "holy Bethlehem" as his center.[177] That humble city is associated with two notable figures—David and Jesus. Perhaps Jerome considered himself a worthy successor.

172. *Ep.* 54.13 (CSEL 54:481). Also in Jerome's prologue to his translation of Didymus, *On the Holy Spirit* and prologue to *Commentary on Ecclesiastes* as cited in Newman, "Between Jerusalem and Bethlehem," 226, n. 21.

173. Weingarten notes that Jerome uses Christian satire to contrast Bethlehem as rival to Rome (*Saint's Saints*, 234–35).

174. 1 Sam 17–20.

175. Mic 5:2.

176. Smith, "'My Lord's Native Land,'" 31.

177. The phrase is not found Scripture but is used in *Ep.* 108.14 (CSEL 55:325); *Ep.* 143.2 (CSEL 56:293); *Commentary on Ezekiel*, preface to book 3 (CCSL 75:91); *Commentary on Amos*, preface (CCSL 76: 211); *Commentary on Daniel* 2:2 (CCSL 75A:784); *Tractate on Psalm 95* (CCSL 78:154–55).

Chapter 5

"Ask the Jews!"
Transforming Jerome's Supersessionism into a Basis for Christian-Jewish Relations

BY THE FOURTH CENTURY, Christian identity had cemented its claim as the new Israel, a position that Jerome inherited and propagated. The body of Christian literature familiar to Jerome had rooted its Christian identity in outright opposition to the Jews. This *Adversus Judaeos* tradition wielded its rhetorical theology of contempt and thereby defined difference and distance between Jews and Christians. Jews who refused the Christian message were considered cursed, objects of God's judgment, and forever disconnected from the God of Israel.[1] The essence of Christian supersessionism is succinctly expressed by Soulen: "After Christ came . . . the special role of the Jewish people came to an end and its place was taken by the church, the new Israel."[2] Christians in the fourth century had inherited this tradition of replacement from earlier centuries, and Christian writers who inscribed Christianity's dominance simultaneously erased Judaism's legitimacy: "The church is a 'new Israel' in such fashion that there can be no other, thus removing Judaism from God's saving plan."[3]

Jerome's fingerprint on Christian supersessionism is marked by the manner in which he reshaped the church's relation to the Jews and their role as a transmitter of divine truth. The preceding chapters have presented his iconoclastic and ambivalent moves in relation to the Jewish people and their sacred texts that inadvertently reduced the distance between himself and the Jews in three interrelated phenomena: he redirected the church's

1. Ruether, *Faith and Fratricide*, 94.
2. Soulen, *God of Israel and Christian Theology*, 1–2.
3. Braaten and Jenson, "Introduction," viii.

Old Testament text away from the Septuagint and back to the Hebrew text; he promoted Jewish exegetical authority by embedding rabbinic traditions into his exegetical works; and he reoriented the perception of the former Jewish holy land from a Jerusalem-centered sacred geography to a one built upon a combination of an earthly Bethlehem and a heavenly Jerusalem. By traveling into such uncharted territory, Jerome unintentionally raised the Christian church's indebtedness to the Jews, thereby elevating their legitimacy. Jerome repeatedly invited his readers to engage in conversation with Jews in order to test the validity of his translations: "Ask the Jews!"[4] This may be the closest Jerome comes to calling other Christians into discussion with Jews. He invites discussion of the validity of his Hebrew renderings, but he never wavers on theological issues that maintained strict separation of Christians from Jews. He never calls for rapprochement. While his words about Jews consistently deny an affable alliance with those whom he viewed as enemies of Christ, the impact of his strategic changes can serve to challenge our contemporary Christian awareness of the Jewish text, the Jewish people and their exegetical traditions, and the Jewish land with its native inhabitants. In the convergence of these three elements I find useful paradigms for insights into contemporary Christian and Jewish interaction.

Jerome's monastic calling to Bethlehem commenced when he was about forty years of age, blossomed into a vast literary output influenced by the "Hebrew truth," and continued at a whirlwind pace until his death thirty-five years later. In the years since Jerome's death and up to the mid-twentieth century, the Christian church consistently viewed itself as Israel's replacement, the new and final people of God, thus rendering the Jewish people obsolete in the divine economy. This entrenched viewpoint was exposed by events in the middle of the twentieth century, the most traumatic of which was the Holocaust.[5] Since that horrific event, Christian theology has undergone a massive reappraisal in light of the brutality of a

---

4. This challenge is issued by Jerome in the following texts (noted by Kamesar, *Jerome, Greek Scholarship*, 61, n. 78): *Prologue to Pentateuch* 43 (*Biblia Sacra* 4); *Prologue to Kings* 70–71 (*Biblia Sacra* 365 366); *Prologue to Ezra* 31 (*Biblia Sacra* 638); *Prologue to Psalms according to Hebrew* 28 (*Biblia Sacra* 768); *Ep.* 112.30 (CSEL 55:391); and *Commentary on Ezekiel* 10:33 (CCSL 75:475). Jerome's words read literally, "Ask the Hebrews," using the ancient name of the Jewish people for contemporary Jews whom Jerome considered trustworthy.

5. I use the traditional term rather than the Hebrew word "Shoah," although the latter term (meaning "calamity, devastation") is more accurate and sensitive to Jewish suffering than the word "holocaust," a term used in the Septuagint for the sacrifice of an animal as a "burnt offering" (for example, Exod 29:25).

planned and almost successful genocide of the Jewish people in the heart of Christian Europe. Since the Holocaust, the Christian church has generated a variety of attempts to reconfigure its identity in relation to the Jewish people and religion.

In this chapter I will examine Jerome's three interrelated, bold moves toward the Jews—text, exegesis, and land—searching out models for dialogue and theological approaches to reduce the distance between Christians and Jews imposed by traditional Christian supersessionism. I will then pursue that trajectory into the twenty-first century and explore developments and possibilities of ongoing interreligious relations. Jerome refused to accept the status quo of Christian and Jewish relations in late ancient Christian culture, and as a result, he influenced that tradition in its apprehension of Jews as conduits of divine truth for Christian formulation. Looking back more than fifteen hundred years, we can read Jerome as one who explored and expanded the borders of Christian indebtedness to the Jews. The twenty-first century inherits pivotal historical events from the previous century, the conjunction and interaction of which provides a catalyst for change among contemporary historians and theologians.

WHAT IS THE CHRISTIAN OLD TESTAMENT SCRIPTURE?

"The Hebrew truth must be set forth."[6]

In the wake of the fall of Jerusalem and the failure of the Jewish revolts, Christians and Jews made rival claims on the Jewish Scriptures. Those texts formed a crucial inheritance for both groups as they sought to form their identities. In the second century Justin claimed to recount his dialogue with the Jewish Trypho, in which he contested the Jewish Scriptures: "David sang them, as Isaiah announced them as good news, as Zechariah proclaimed them, and Moses wrote them. Aren't you acquainted with them, Trypho? You should be, for they are contained in your Scriptures, or rather not yours, but ours. For we believe and obey them."[7] Rather than affirming that the Scriptures were shared by both Christians and Jews, Justin represented

---

6. Jerome's comment about the Hebrew text of Gen 19:14-15 (Hayward, *Saint Jerome's Hebrew Questions on Genesis*, 51).

7. *Dialogue with Trypho* 29.2. See the discussion of Justin in Buell, *Why This New Race*, 95–115. She notes that "Justin makes use of the double-sided dynamic of ethnoracial discourse in defining Christians the Jews," namely, that Jewish identity is fixed by birth whereas Christians derive their fluid identity by their faith (95).

the Christian posture as one of exclusive ownership as the "true Israel."[8] For Jerome, the issue did not involve the right of Christians to consider the Jewish Scriptures its own–by his time that was a settled conclusion. Rather, Jerome challenged the traditional Christian identification of the Old Testament text with the Greek Septuagint, appealing instead to what he deemed the Hebrew original, a tradition that he reshaped to reduce the distance between his Latin translation and its Jewish source.

Jerome's Ambivalent Textual Shift

As discussed in chapter 2, Jerome progressively shifted his view of the Old Testament away from the Greek Septuagint in favor of the Hebrew text. His writings reveal an agenda of persuasion designed to wean his readers away from the Greek version, which he painted as less divinely inspired than widely assumed by most, and to convince them of the Hebrew version's higher authority. His pursuit of what he considered "Hebrew truth" empowered him to challenge entrenched Christian tradition. Jerome exercised critical readings of his sources and found them lacking, to the extent of laying blame on his own church tradition: "I do not know who was the first author whose lie constructed seventy cells in Alexandria."[9] His linguistic training in three languages probably led to his conviction that only by returning to the source language of the Hebrew Scriptures could Christians have an accurate Latin translation. He repeatedly claimed that the apostles quoted passages found only in the Hebrew and not in the Septuagint. These motivations led Jerome to pursue learning the Hebrew language, hire Jewish teachers, and endeavor to shape the Christian notion of a sacred text as originating with the "Hebrew truth." In conjunction with Jerome's promotion of the Jewish text, he advanced arguments favoring the Jewish canon, a list that omitted certain texts ensconced in Christian tradition.

Jerome broke away from the embedded tradition about the Septuagint. His model serves those who attempt to facilitate relations between the Christian and Jewish communities by reminding them that one must confront any questionable tradition within one's own community. In light

---

8. A phrase used repeated by Justin in his *Dialogue with Trypho*, for example: "We are the true spiritual Israel, and the descendants of Judah, Jacob, Isaac, and Abraham" (11.5). Boyarin points out that "once becoming a Christian became identified with 'entering [the true] Israel,' the whole semantic/social field changed" (*Border Lines*, 73).

9. *Prologue to Pentateuch* 26; *Biblia Sacra* 3.

of his expressed antipathy toward the Jews, as amply documented in his texts, Jerome undoubtedly pursued the Hebrew text without wishing to improve relations with his local Jewish community. Ironically his rhetoric of contempt is betrayed by the reality of his need—he constantly associated with Jews in face-to-face encounters as he learned their language in personal tutelage, asked to borrow their scrolls, discussed what texts might have been available, and trusted their expertise as translators. These actions are recorded by Jerome himself, and one wonders what unrecorded events might shed even more light on his need for and interaction with Jews. Such a relational posture to the Jews, as people who were trustworthy transmitters of the Hebrew text, affirms Jerome's implicit recognition of Jewish legitimacy.[10] His actions perpetuated his desire to remain in close proximity to the Jews, since there was always a need to have a scroll available or a word translated from Hebrew. The relationship was undoubtedly successful: Jerome paid his Jewish teachers for their services, defended himself against allegations of complicity with the Jews, never recorded attempts of proselytism by either parties, and grew ever more determined to disseminate the Hebrew Old Testament by his Latin translation in spite of the opposition from Rufinus, Augustine, and others whose names are never mentioned. I find it significant that Jerome recorded no opposition to his project by his Jewish teachers. While Jerome was generous with his vilification of Jews, never did he accuse them of withholding the texts or resisting his requests to learn from them. From what is recorded, the attitude of the Jews toward Jerome seems to have been one of mutual respect and a desire to communicate their own learning and traditions to a friendly Christian. Jerome's own writings portray a creative example of fourth-century Christian and Jewish discussion, albeit constructed on Jerome's terms and meant to enhance his own standing.

Opposition to Jerome's choice of the Old Testament text arose from two fellow Christians, a distant friend in North Africa and an enemy close at hand on the Mount of Olives, both of whom scrutinized Jerome's stance as too Jewish. This, then, may have been the real source of enmity—not so much that Jerome offered a replacement for the received text, but that he embraced the text of the rejected people. He crossed party lines, and rather than invite the rabbis to defend their own text to his fellow Christians—a move that might have isolated Jerome's voice as too extreme—he himself

---

10. Jacobs, *Remains of the Jews*, 83. Jacobs labels Jerome's position as "academic imperialism," with the stigma attached to it.

invited the rabbis' text into the church. Although he denied the accusation of Judaizing, a stance he strongly condemned in others, the charge carries some weight in that Jerome endeavored to erase established barriers between the two parties. He opened the possibility for a textual common ground for Christians and Jews that had been diminished when Christians appropriated, and the Jews abandoned, the Septuagint as the authentic version of the Scriptures. Jerome tapped into the shared heritage represented by the Hebrew Bible and began to bridge the gap between himself the Jewish people.

Jerome's Trajectory

For Jerome, only one language preserved the original Old Testament text: the *Hebraica veritas*. Influenced by Origen's *Hexapla*, yet without the awareness that the Septuagint represented a different Hebrew vorlage than the Hebrew text before him, Jerome's textual-critical skills led him to the Hebrew as the source text for his Latin translation and for his Old Testament commentaries. His dogged determination to revert to the Hebrew text is now an assumption of contemporary biblical scholarship. As Andrew Cain observes, "As far as Jerome was concerned, any aspiring biblical exegete without a solid grasp of Hebrew has no right presuming to explain Scripture to other Christians, for this would be a case of the blind leading the blind."[11] This legacy of textual investigation will be examined in two contemporary disciplines.

First, Jerome's method of textual analysis formed the foundation of a field that continues to resonate in contemporary biblical scholarship: that of textual criticism of the Hebrew and Greek manuscripts of the Jewish Scriptures. The domain of textual criticism of the Hebrew Bible received an infusion of interest after the discovery of the Dead Sea Scrolls in 1947, when manuscripts of Hebrew texts (biblical and non-biblical) produced textual witnesses one thousand years earlier than any other extant manuscripts. Scholars date these ancient texts generally from the third century B.C.E. to the first century C.E.[12] The initial translation project of the scrolls was dogged by accusations of secrecy and anti-Semitism, until several texts

---

11. Cain, "Jerome's Pauline Commentaries between East and West," 100.

12. Vermes, *Introduction to the Complete Dead Sea Scrolls*, 22–31; VanderKam and Flint, *Meaning of the Dead Sea Scrolls*, 20–33.

trickled out and became available to the public.¹³ After an outcry for reform and the retirement of some of the original translators, the work resumed with transparency and a timetable for publication. Yet those years also witnessed ongoing controversies: the publication of a facsimile edition without official permission, charges of conspiracy, and a costly lawsuit between the translators. Such setbacks prompted the creation of policies designed to promote free access to future discoveries and harmony between scholars in those ventures.¹⁴ Ongoing research concerning the Dead Sea Scrolls includes a number of organizations and educational institutions. One example demonstrates the interfaith cooperation of Jewish and Christian scholars: the Christian-sponsored Dead Sea Scrolls Institute, which exists "to foster serious study and dialogue among biblical scholars and scholars of the Dead Sea Scrolls throughout the world."¹⁵ The information gained from the texts illuminates the complex relation of Second Temple Judaism to both Christianity and rabbinic Judaism. The Dead Sea Scrolls have added an immense amount of information to a formerly sparse field of study, but they have also created an enormous number of questions, particularly the textual history of the Hebrew Bible in relation to the various Hebrew manuscript traditions, as well as the Hebrew text underlying the Septuagint and the later Greek recensions.

Scholars now reconstruct the transmission of Hebrew texts in a way that places Jerome's Hebrew text as one of several ancient Hebrew textual sources, another of which is the source of the Septuagint. What Jerome thought were faulty translations of the Septuagint may in fact be alternate readings of Hebrew texts. This conclusion and a host of others is the result of the beginning of serious study of the Septuagint in the twentieth century.¹⁶ An international effort is underway, the International Organization for Septuagint and Cognate Studies (IOSCS), the purpose of which is "to promote international research in and study of the Septuagint and related

---

13. John Strugnell, editor of the translation team from 1984 to 1990, once described Judaism as "a horrible religion." Strugnell, a Presbyterian turned Roman Catholic, was thereafter replaced by the Jewish scholar Emmanuel Tov (VanderKam and Flint, *Meaning of the Dead Sea Scrolls*, 390).

14. The Society for Biblical Literature and the American Schools of Oriental Research adopted policies in the early 1990s (ibid., 403).

15. https://www.twu.ca/research/institutes-and-centres/university-institutes/dead-sea-scrolls-institute.

16. Swete, *Introduction to the Old Testament in Greek*; Jellicoe, *Septuagint and Modern Study*; Jobes and Silva, *Invitation to the Septuagint*; Law, *When God Spoke Greek*.

texts."[17] Their conferences and publications represent an ecumenical approach without a theological agenda, and include Jewish and Christians scholars from around the world. Septuagint scholar James A. Aitken's work gathers many fellow scholars' work on the individual books of the Septuagint. He proposes that current trends in Septuagint studies, such as the reception and use of Greek versions by Jewish groups in the first few centuries, "could radically change our perception of Jewish-Christian relations and of the parting of the ways."[18]

Second, there is a venture underway to mine Jerome's commentaries for their textual-critical import.[19] For example, after examining Jerome's commentary on Jeremiah, Graves concludes that while Jerome's etymologies suffer from inadequate Hebrew knowledge, "much of Jerome's work on the Hebrew text of Jeremiah at the literal level compares favorably with modern scholarship on the book."[20] Graves recommends that Jerome be consulted for the retrieval of particular readings of ancient textual witnesses: "The interpretation of the Hebrew text found in Jerome (and other ancient sources) should certainly be given no less attention than is given, for example, to the vocalizations found in Medieval Masoretic manuscripts."[21]

An exception to the overall unanimity of an early and authoritative Hebrew text should be mentioned. The Orthodox churches maintain the tradition, established in the earliest Greek-speaking churches of the East, that elevates the Septuagint to a divinely inspired textual authority above the Hebrew: "When this [the Septuagint] differs from the original Hebrew (which happens quite often), Orthodox believe that the changes in the Septuagint were made under the inspiration of the Holy Spirit, and are to be accepted as part of God's continuing revelation."[22] This doctrinal position

---

17. http://ccat.sas.upenn.edu/ioscs.

18. Aitken, *T&T Clark Companion to the Septuagint*, 9.

19. See Graves, *Jerome's Hebrew Philology*, who explains: "Throughout our study, we will consider the ways in which Jerome's approach to the study of the Hebrew Old Testament is similar to, and differs from, that of modern scholarship" (12). See also the work of Kamesar, *Jerome, Greek Scholarship, and the Hebrew Bible*; and Newman, *Jerome and the Jews*."

20. Graves, *Jerome's Hebrew Philology*, 198.

21. Ibid., 199. "It is significant that Jerome apparently made use of a Hebrew text that corresponded closely with the MT of his day and of the later Middle Ages" (Wurthwein, *Text of the Old Testament*, 143).

22. Ware, *Orthodox Church*, 200. The Old Testament in the *Orthodox Study Bible* is based on the Septuagint, the "acceptable Old Testament text" (xi).

is fixed as an inviolable church law, hence all discussion of the Hebrew as a supplemental or rival text is officially precluded.

In conclusion, while traces of an embedded Christian textual supersession still persist in vernacular usage (e.g., the terms "Old Testament" and "New Testament"), contemporary scholarship has overcome the prejudicial tone of late ancient Christianity and pursues Jewish and Christian textual studies with mutual respect and cooperation. While none of the organizations engaged in interreligious textual study has as its goal a theological dialogue, that outcome is being indirectly achieved as a byproduct of the larger endeavor. In the same way, Jerome stands as an ancient resource and example through his rudimentary yet significant textual-critical approach to the Jewish Old Testament, which yielded an unintended dependence on his Jewish teachers. Although his methods were somewhat misguided, his instincts have proved correct. Such an attitude of Christian trust of Jewish sources betrays the deeper and unspoken sentiment of legitimacy, even when other differences seem insurmountable. Contemporary scholarship continues to reduce the linguistic gap between the ancient texts, revealing that the process of textual criticism also enhances the mutual respect among those who share its texts.

HOW SHOULD THE CHURCH INTERPRET THE OLD TESTAMENT?

"That tradition of the Hebrews ... is true."[23]

Jerome's foundational move toward Hebrew truth was textual, embracing the Jewish language, text, and canon that formed the foundation for his Latin translation. Once the text was established, he could then begin a conversation about its meaning. Jerome accomplished that by not only reading the works of earlier Christian authors, whose comments had been based on the Septuagint, but by personally consulting with the Jews, whose text Jerome had now embraced. This distinctly different approach emerging from Jerome's monastic cell embodied conversation between a Christian and a Jew about the interpretation of a text shared by both. The voice of the other, the replaced and suppressed Jew, was temporarily respected and utilized.

---

23. Jerome's comment about a Jewish interpretation of Gen 12:4 (Hayward, *Saint Jerome's Hebrew Questions on Genesis*, 43).

"Ask the Jews!"

The reality of Jerome's rhetoric reveals the fragility of that moment. His explicit anti-Jewish sentiment juxtaposed with the conversation of equals around the text did not hold. Jerome's writings reflect a consistently derogatory positioning of Jews and their religion by use of vitriolic language. However, what is puzzling and exceptional among late ancient Christian writers is Jerome's ambivalent stance regarding the Jews, for they were the object of his scorn and simultaneously the object of his appropriation. It is between these two stances that we can consider Jerome's strategies that incidentally minimized the gap separating fourth-century Christianity and Judaism.

Jerome's Ambivalent Hermeneutical Shift

As discussed in chapters 2 and 3, Jerome's classical training and exegetical research enabled him to deduce that the initial path for illumination in understanding the Old Testament's historical meaning was to be found with the Jews, since divine truth resided in their sacred text coupled with their traditional interpretations. Jerome's shorthand term that encapsulates both text and interpretation was "Hebrew truth." He purposefully based the name of this pursuit on the identity of the biblical Israelites, rather than use "Jewish truth." To have done so would have exposed himself to further ridicule from his detractors, so Jerome customarily used "Jews" as a pejorative description of both biblical and contemporary people of Israel. Ironically, he believed that divine truth could only be obtained from living Jews whose memories and writings preserved the ancient interpretations. This stance is illustrated in how Jerome defends his reason for delaying a response to Pope Damasus' request. Jerome explains that he "was interrupted by a Jew (*Hebraeus*) who had arrived from the synagogue with some Hebrew books that Jerome wanted to borrow. He insisted that Jerome put aside all else for the time being and focus only on copying these texts. Jerome buckled under the pressure and did as he was told."[24] Jerome is devoted to the "Hebrew" friend's delivery of books even over the constraints of the pope. This example demonstrates that Jerome's supersessionism was mingled with ambivalence, namely, the Jews of his day preserved the biblical truth of their Hebrew ancestors. Ironically, Jerome's "Jews" were cursed for their rejection of Christ yet were blessed for their conservation of the "Hebrew" truth. This distinction in Jerome's vocabulary is subtle yet vital, for it reveals

24. Summary of Jerome's *Ep.* 36.1 (CSEL 54:268–69) by Cain, *Letters of Jerome*, 58.

his profound distaste for contemporary Jewish people and their religion, coupled with his need for their unique mediation of the truth. In summary, Jerome, a member of the "new true Israel," sought truth about the "old true Israel" through the "false Israel." Yet he treated the "false Israel" as if it were "old true Israel," incorporating certain traditions into the "new true Israel." This subtle linguistic maneuver effectively legitimized Jewish tradition and the Jewish receptors of that tradition. For Jerome, both person and text were packaged together.

On the surface it appears that Jerome sealed off contact with Jews whose religion, as he described in his commentaries, shared no present standing with Christianity. In reality, Jerome's writings reveal that he must have continued to share common ground through personal contact with Jewish teachers until the end of his life. That amounts to at least forty years of habitual contact with Jewish people, who acted as conduits for Jewish knowledge of the Hebrew text and its accompanying interpretations. He never found sufficient cause to sever all contact with them. Jerome obtained and translated what he considered to be the original Scripture text, regarded as faithfully preserved in contemporary scrolls, only through the indispensable assistance of Jewish teachers whom he trusted to relay ancient and contemporary rabbinic interpretations that he considered just as trustworthy. Jerome inadvertently reduced the distance between the Jews and Christians by assimilating their interpretive exegesis, thereby bringing a sense of legitimacy to his Jewish teachers in spite of his distrust for their religion. Regardless of his intention, Jerome's opening holds promise for twenty-first-century Christian relations with Jews.

Jerome's Trajectory

Those who constructed Christian identity in the fourth century differentiated Christianity from the Judaism of that time, pursuing as much boundary marking and contrast as possible. Jerome's innovative approach to Jews defined his Christianity in a slightly different way than his tradition had taught. His need for them influenced his conception of them. Sadly, in the ensuing centuries, Jerome's rhetoric of anti-Jewish sentiment, rather than his reluctant relationship with Jews, found fertile ground in the Christian church. What for Jerome was a *language* of contempt evolved into a *doctrine* of contempt for later Christians. The extended and tragic history of Christian anti-Judaism reached a focal point in the Nazi Holocaust. Christian complicity in this horror eventually compelled the church to examine the pernicious influence of Christian supersessionism and the church's implicit theological complicity in the Holocaust.

The challenge for contemporary Christians has been to reformulate a theology that corrects the toxic portions of the interpretive tradition, thus precluding another similar tragedy and building understanding between Christians and Jews. Many Christian theological systems have been influenced by the Holocaust, and the spectrum of Christian reactions is mirrored by the variety of Jewish reactions. From moderate to radical approaches, Christians theologians condemn the horrific deeds of the Nazis and reject the theology of hatred, spoken by Jerome in particular, that produced a Christian Europe capable of such evil. The following survey of post-Holocaust Christian proposals is organized on the basis of biblical covenantal structures involving the Jewish people and the Christian church.

One Covenant People (Strong Supersessionism)

When commenting on Paul's phrase "the Israel of God" in Galatians 6:16 ("Peace and mercy to all who follow this rule—to the Israel of God."), Jerome expressed his strong Christian supersessionism:

> In fact he has said "Israel of God" to distinguish it from that Israel that ceased to be God's. For they "claim to be Jews and are not," but they are lying, since they are from the "synagogue of Satan." You should not be surprised if there is a carnal Israel in imitation of spiritual Israel, who have neither "peace" nor "mercy."[25]

By removing Israel's connection with God, Jerome eradicated all divine association with the Jews. This conception of Christian supersessionism still finds contemporary expression in the Christian church. Hymn writer Edward Perronet characterized the Christian church as "Ye chosen seed of Israel's race" in the words of the classic hymn "All Hail the Power of Jesus' Name."[26] Some contemporary Reformed Protestants maintain the longstanding posture of Christian supersessionism, believing that God has completely abrogated the covenant with Israel due to the rejection of Jesus by the Jewish people and has replaced them with the Christian church as sole inheritors of the former covenant. These evangelicals consider the

---

25. *St. Jerome's Commentaries on Galatians, Titus, and Philemon*, 273.
26. *Worship and Service Hymnal*, 111.

Christian church to be the new Israel. They preserve the theological dogma of the early Christian *Adversus Judaeos* tradition, except for the anti-Jewish tone. Some examples may sound similar to words written during Jerome's era. A Reformed Presbyterian states: "This new body of people constitutes the Israel of God,"[27] and a Christian Reformed theologian nuances his argument somewhat, writing that he wishes to present "a sustained argument about the centrality of Jesus ... and ... an implicit argument with Judaism.... Of course, those who hold to the New Testament teaching must take care that neither their teaching nor their rhetoric produces contempt for the Jewish people."[28] Anti-Semitism is thus condemned while theological anti-Judaism is sustained. Their hermeneutic reconfigures the Old Testament promises in a spiritual sense for the Christian church's benefit, bypassing any sort of uniquely Jewish fulfillment. Evangelical systematic theologian Wayne Grudem concludes his discussion of the church as the replacement for the Jews: "What further statement could be needed in order for us to say with assurance that the church has now become the true Israel of God and will receive all the blessings promised to Israel in the Old Testament."[29] Erasing Israel's claim to any future fulfillment of God's promises to them, Grudem clarifies: "There does not seem to be any strong reason to deny that this really is the only fulfillment that God is going to give for these promises."[30] Again, this strong supersessionism is succinctly summarized: "The church, then, as the people of the New Covenant has taken the place of Israel, and national Israel is nothing other than the empty shell from which the pearl has been removed and which has lost its function in the history of redemption."[31]

It comes as no surprise that little mention of interfaith relations exists between these supersessionist Christians and Jews, for with an "empty shell" theology neither party perceives value in such discussion. The only impact that the Holocaust seems to have made on these theologians is to sensitize them to the rhetoric of anti-Semitism. One fellow evangelical observes:

> The wrong perception of Israel and the Jews by Christians ... has produced consequences of horrific proportions during the history

27. Robertson, *Israel of God*, 44.
28. Holwerda, *Jesus and Israel*, 24–25.
29. Grudem, *Systematic Theology*, 863.
30. Ibid., 863 n. 21. He does admit to the possibility of a future salvation of Israel (1099, 1104).
31. Ridderbos, *Paul*, 354–55.

of the Christian Church in all its strands. Such a shameful legacy
… is still prevalent in substantial degrees in many Calvinist, Reformed, and Sovereign Grace environments.[32]

This version of what I call "strong supersessionism" has changed little since Jerome's time, except for differentiating between anti-Jewish theology (which they affirm) and anti-Jewish rhetoric (which they deny). From the Jewish side, nothing is to be gained from dialogue with strong supersessionists: "If one holds that God has exchanged the Jewish people for the church, thus canceling the election of Abraham and his progeny, there is no incentive whatsoever for Jews to formulate a positive theology of Christianity."[33]

The Orthodox Church, professing a pedigree to the earliest apostolic churches, began ecumenical relations with the Jews in the late 1970s sponsored by the World Jewish Congress and the Ecumenical Patriarchate of Constantinople. Gatherings have addressed mutual concerns such as the notions of law and tradition within both traditions and the shared commitment to peace and justice. Dialogue has also included an international conference in 2005 entitled "Peace and Tolerance II," pleading for mutual toleration among the religions of the world.[34] In 2009 Patriarch Bartholomew spoke to Jewish religious leaders at the Park East Synagogue.[35] Building on these initial attempts at dialogue, Patriarch Bartholomew met with the American Jewish Committee in Jerusalem in 2014, recognizing that "a mere 60 years ago, a joint visit of this magnitude would not have been possible."[36] Just where such dialogue might travel is questionable. Because the Orthodox Church elevates its tradition to a high authority, supersessionism's grasp is hard to release, thus "the fundamental problem is not so much that of ingrained prejudice as of the place of *tradition* within Orthodoxy."[37] Such tradition of strong supersessionism, rendered sacrosanct by the Orthodox, maintains a barrier to full ecumenical relations, in contrast to other efforts to be described next.

32. Horner, *Future Israel*, xix.
33. Novak, "From Supersessionism to Parallelism," 95.
34. http://www.ec-patr.org/docdisplay.php?lang=en&id=585&tla=en.
35. https://www.patriarchate.org/-/ecumenical-patriarch-bartholomew-meets-with-jewish-religious-and-lay-leaders?inheritRedirect=true.
36. https://www.apostolicpilgrimage.org/-/address-of-his-all-holiness-ecumenical-patriarch-bartholomew-to-the-american-jewish-committee-may-25-2014.
37. De Lange, "Orthodox Churches in Dialogue with Judaism," 55. "True dialogue lies far in the future and will entail a great effort … on the Christian side" (61).

Two Covenant Peoples (Mild Supersessionism)

Within evangelical Christianity, some theologians present a less traditional form of supersessionism and argue that two covenants are simultaneously in force: one with Jews and the other with Christians. They state that the covenant made with Abraham is eternal and national in its scope, incorporating both present and eschatological fulfillment of earthly Jewish hopes as described in the Jewish Scriptures. Thus, present covenant participation includes the Jews as the specially chosen people, apart from any conversion to Christianity, alongside the Christian church related to God through the Jewish messiah. While both covenantal relationships are ongoing, they do not convey equal benefits.[38] Some of these evangelicals embrace supersessionism's language of replacement and yet include in their eschatology a future conversion of Jews to Christianity: "There is, however, a future for national Israel. They are still the special people of God.... The church is the new Israel.... There is a special future coming for national Israel, however, through large-scale conversion to Christ and entry into the church."[39] While holding to the replacement notion, these theologians join ethnic Jews to the Christian church at the end history.[40]

These evangelical Christians see a major difference in the soteriological dimension of the covenants: Jews as Jews are chosen, yet they are incomplete without the messianic covenant through Jesus Christ. The two covenants produce a dissimilar status, namely, one promises eternal salvation for Christians (including Jewish and Gentile converts) and the other promises Jewish perpetuity and divine presence short of eternal salvation. These theologians justify this twofold model by their exegesis of Romans 9–11, a pivotal text that shapes notions of Jewish identity within the Christian church. For example, New Testament scholar C. E. B. Cranfield argues against strong supersessionism from this Pauline text:

> It is only where the Church persists in refusing to learn this message, where it secretly—perhaps quite unconsciously—believes that its own existence is based on human achievement, and so fails to understand God's mercy to itself, that it is unable to believe in

---

38. For example, see Blaising and Bock, *Progressive Dispensationalism*, 294–97; and the essays in Bock, Kaiser, and Blaising, *Dispensationalism, Israel and the Church*.

39. Erickson, *Christian Theology*, 965–66.

40. Horton nuances his view: "The church does not replace Israel; it fulfills the promise God made to Abraham ... Israel is especially judged now that the reality to which they pointed has arrived" (*Christian Faith*, 730–31).

> God's mercy for still unbelieving Israel, and so entertains the ugly and unscriptural notion that God has cast off His people Israel and simply replaced it by the Christian Church. These three chapters [Romans 9–11] emphatically forbid us to speak of the Church as having once and for all taken the place of the Jewish people.[41]

He admits his own guilt in a footnote: "The assumption that the Church has simply replaced Israel as the people of God is extremely common.... And I confess with shame to having also myself used in print on more than one occasion this language of the replacement of Israel by the Church."[42] Other evangelical authors acknowledge Israel's place in the eschatological future. For example, Kevin Vanhoozer summarizes the end of the narrative structure of Scripture: "The fifth and final act is the eschaton, the consummation of all things, and the consummation of God's relationship with Israel and the church."[43] Thomas Oden affirms the present calling of the Jewish people by God: "The Jews are a special people chosen not by you or me or themselves but God—chosen for a special service in human destiny as God's people, a holy nation set apart."[44] His work on systematic theology presents the consensus view of ancient Christian tradition on Israel as being restored to God as a sign of Jesus' second coming.[45] Gregg Allison holds what he calls a "moderate discontinuity" position that affirms "a future fulfillment of Old Testament prophecies directed at national Israel, including the salvation of many Jewish people and restoration to the land of Israel."[46] Those who hold this position reduce the distance between Jews and Christians by legitimizing a Jewish present because of a guaranteed Jewish future.

This expression of philo-Semitism in the church echoes the theology of Jerome's despised Judaizing Christians. Those maligned Christians expressed similar eschatological hopes for the Jews as do these evangelical theologians. It would be intriguing to discover if those ancient voices also mentioned any sort of legitimacy vis-à-vis their contemporary Jews. Their stance serves as an exception to the spiritualized readings of traditional

---

41. Cranfield, *Commentary on Romans*, 448.
42. Ibid., n. 2.
43. Vanhoozer, *Drama of Doctrine*, 3.
44. Oden, *Rebirth of Orthodoxy*, 110.
45. Oden, *Classic Christianity*, 800–801. His work with Packer, *One Faith*, rejects strong supersessionism while holding to the necessity of faith in Jesus Christ for Jewish people (140–46).
46. Allison, *Sojourners and Strangers*, 88.

supersessionists, like Jerome, whose writings fueled later anti-Semitism for generations. It might have been that these atypical Christians were in dialogue with Jews and consequently were considered an imposing threat by Jerome and other non-chiliast Christians. What we do know is that their eschatology clearly differed from Jerome's in foreseeing a future "eschatological Jerusalem which is not seen as Christian city, but primarily as *Jewish* capital of a restored Israel."[47] A distinct expression of this understanding has developed in some of the European and American evangelical denominations, to which I now turn.

This emphasis on Jewish legitimacy actually developed before the Holocaust's awakening influence on Christian theology. David Rausch's work argues that nineteenth- and twentieth-century evangelical Christians fought anti-Semitism and "were generally more positive toward the Jewish community than were other Christians."[48] Due to their biblical literalism regarding Jewish restoration combined with their opposition to the mainline Christian agenda of triumphalism and supersessionism, they concluded that "anti-Semitism was anti-God."[49] Early fundamentalists in America who were premillennial "considered themselves to have turned their backs on the hostility that had at times characterized the Christian attitude toward Jews and . . . often expressed their regret for the mistreatment Jews had suffered at the hands of Christians."[50] This is a tenet of contemporary premillennialism and dispensationalism, most of whose adherents are committed to some form of philo-Semitism.[51]

Another distinct emphasis that was espoused in Jerome's day by the Nazareans is today echoed by Messianic Jews.[52] Jerome had no time for their fourth-century ancestors: "Since they want to be both Jews and

---

47. Kinzig, "Jewish and 'Judaizing' Eschatologies in Jerome," 425.

48. Rausch, *Fundamentalist-Evangelicals and Anti-Semitism*, 205.

49. Ibid., 206.

50. Ariel, *On Behalf of Israel*, 119. Note the similarities to Augustine's "witness doctrine" in Fredriksen, *Augustine and the Jews*, 290–352. Ariel's more recent book, *An Unusual Relationship: Evangelical Christians and Jews*, nuances the evangelical approaches to philo-Semitism.

51. See the articles in Bock and Glaser, *To the Jew First*. The term "Judeophilia" is used by Lossl, "Shift in Patristic Exegesis," 164.

52. The Nazareans "were Jewish Christians, descendants of the primitive community at Jerusalem . . . apart from adhering strictly to the Jewish Law, they were orthodox in their Christian beliefs" (Kelly, *Bible and the Latin Fathers*, 65).

"Ask the Jews!"

Christians, they are neither Jews nor Christians."[53] Evangelical Christianity does have time and has created space for them. These Jews believe that Jesus is the Jewish messiah and include some level of Torah observance in their version of Jewish Christianity. They generally hold to a conservative interpretation of the New Testament, profess to reject strong supersessionism, and are Christian Zionists.[54] The movement is diverse, and further analysis is beyond the scope of this book.[55] These Messianic Jewish evangelicals have engaged in dialogue with Jews, first in 1970,[56] then again in 1975 when the American Jewish Committee and the Institute of Holy Land Studies cosponsored the first national conference of Jewish and evangelical scholars and religious leaders.[57] Similar encounters seem to have reached a stalemate, perhaps due to the Jewish objections to Christian mission targeted at Jews. A Jewish participant in those early discussions betrays his dissatisfaction with the status quo and imagines a better future when "every individual Jew and evangelical will be encouraged to live out his or her religious commitment to the fullest, drawing on the richness of our unique traditions."[58] Such a vision remains unfulfilled.

Among evangelicals there are signs of Christian sensitivity to Jewish concerns, such as the revision of the New International Version, which regularly translates "the Jews" in John's gospel and in Acts as "the Jewish leaders."[59] Most missionary organizations that have Jewish people as their target are strong opponents of anti-Semitism, strong supporters of the State of Israel and Zionism, and oppose any effort to coercively proselytize Jewish people. For example, Chosen People Ministries' vision and core values include the desire to "proclaim the Gospel to the Jew first and also to the

---

53. *Ep.* 112.13 (CSEL 55:382). For an impressive collection of essays on Jewish believers in Jesus during the first five centuries, see Skarsaune and Hvalvik, eds., *Jewish Believers in Jesus*.

54. Stern, *Messianic Judaism*. Many authors contribute to the helpful work of Rudolph and Willitts, eds., *Introduction to Messianic Judaism*.

55. Kinzer, *Postmissionary Messianic Judaism*, comes very close to the two covenant peoples view discussed below.

56. At the annual meeting of the Evangelical Theological Society in Santa Barbara, California.

57. The papers of the conference are assembled in Tanenbaum, Wilson, and Rudin, eds., *Evangelicals and Jews in Conversation*.

58. Rudin, "Current Evangelical-Jewish Relations," 43.

59. John 1:19; 5:10, 15–16; 7:1, 11; 9:22; 18:14, 28, 36; 19:7, 12, 31, 38; 20:19; Acts 13:50; 21:11; 25:2; 28:17.

Gentile" and to promote "the welfare of the Jewish community."[60] The mission agency Jews for Jesus affirms two covenant peoples: "We believe that Israel exists as a covenant people through whom God continues to accomplish His purposes and that the Church is an elect people in accordance with the New Covenant, comprising both Jews and Gentiles who acknowledge Jesus as Messiah and Redeemer."[61] The Friends of Israel Gospel Ministry considers itself as "a worldwide Christian ministry communicating biblical truth about Israel and the Messiah, while fostering solidarity with the Jewish people."[62]

In spite of such moves in the direction of Jewish appreciation and cooperation with Jews, there is no desire among evangelicals to redefine mission or the exclusivity of Christianity. This outlook is represented in an address presented at the Evangelical Theological Society's annual meeting in 2000 stressing the distance between evangelicals who argue for a national restoration of Israel and those who affirm complete soteriological parity between Jews and Christians through a dual covenant theology.[63] The proposal includes injecting a Jewish orientation into classic systematic theological categories, including "the doctrine of God, anthropology, Christology, ecclesiology, and eschatology."[64] The absence of soteriology is striking, but not surprising since evangelicals do not wish to revise this doctrine and do not wish to make a connection between the exclusive Christian claims and the intrinsic anti-Jewish spirit that has so often been a necessary correlation. These evangelicals reject this inherent connection to anti-Semitism and wish to steer a middle course between traditional supersessionism's ethic of contempt and those who deny Christian exclusivity. This position has been articulated by the World Evangelical Alliance, which issued in 2008 a document entitled "The Berlin Declaration on the Uniqueness of Christ and Jewish Evangelism in Europe Today." While expressing regret for the Holocaust, it states forthrightly this group's priority: "There is a tendency to

60. http://www.chosenpeople.com/main/index.php/about-us.

61. http://jewsforjesus.org/about-jews-for-jesus/who-we-are/statementoffaith.

62. http://www.foi.org.

63. Blaising, "Future of Israel." The best treatment of the inadequacies of dual covenant theology is Vanlaningham, *Christ, the Savior of Israel*.

64. Blaising, "Future of Israel," 443. For example: God "is the God of Israel, and also of the Gentiles" (ibid.); he discusses the "myth of an undifferentiated humanity" (444); the Jewishness of Jesus (445–46); Jewish Christians as a distinct part of the church (446–48); a new creation eschatology with Jews and Gentiles "differentiated in ethnic and communal dimensions" (449).

replace direct gospel outreach with Jewish-Christian dialogue." It concludes with a call for "solidarity with the Jewish people, opposing anti-Semitism" and "the importance of dialogue in promoting mutual understanding and sympathy.... Dialogue and evangelism are not mutually exclusive."[65] In summary, this position of two covenant peoples claims to jettison the worst traits of supersessionism and affirm present Jewish participation alongside the Christian church without losing the exclusivity of the Christian message. I believe that this view is the most faithful expression of the biblical texts and theology concerning the Jewish people. It is not surprising that other Christian theologians regard this movement as nothing more than a rebranded version of Jerome's pre-Holocaust Christianity.[66] It is this revision of supersession that I now consider.

Two Covenant Peoples (No Supersessionism)

A number of Christian theologians have entered a door that Jerome never opened, much less even know of. He never proposed the equal legitimacy of Judaism and Christianity. This tolerant view is represented by a segment of Christian denominations that have reached a consensus concerning the theological status of the Jewish people. Purging all remnants of a supersessionistic reading of the New Testament and church tradition, these theologians state that the Jews stand in an earlier and continuing relationship to the God of Israel, who is the God of Christians as well. This consensus began to emerge separately but with equal potency among Roman Catholics and mainline Protestants in the middle of the twentieth century.

In the 1960s, theologians across the spectrum of Roman Catholic and Protestant denominations began to address the post-Holocaust interfaith tensions. The Roman Catholic Church produced in 1965 the "Declaration on the Relation of the Church to Non-Christian Religions," also called *Nostra Aetate* ("In Our Times"). This watershed document began the arduous task of progressively reversing almost two millennia of Roman Catholic supersessionistic doctrine and practice. The document begins by stressing the church's indebtedness to the Jews and strikingly revokes its tradition of the perpetual Jewish guilt for Christ's death: "What happened in his passion

---

65. http://www.worldevangelicals.org/commissions/tc/berlin.htm. The WEA is comprised of seven regional organizations plus 121 national evangelical alliances. Its executive director, David Parker, has edited *Salvation and the Jewish People*.

66. Lindbeck, "What of the Future?," 363–64.

cannot be blamed upon all the Jews then living, without distinction, nor upon the Jews of today.... Although the church is the new people of God, the Jews should not be presented as repudiated or cursed by God."[67] A by-product of this statement was the creation of the International Catholic-Jewish Liaison Committee in 1970 and the Commission for Religious Relations with the Jews in 1974, whose purposes are to further interfaith dialogue. In 1990 the Catholic Church officially condemned anti-Semitism as a sin, calling for repentance of such deeds in its past.[68] By 2007 a consensus had been reached on four issues summarized by these statements: "At no point in time did God revoke his covenant with Israel"; the church and Judaism are uniquely bound together; dialogue is now possible and ongoing; and the church rejects "the hostility and persecution of Jews by Christians that had continued for centuries."[69] Thus the two covenant position rendered traditional Catholic supersessionism null and void.

In an attempt to further the dismantling of any type of supersessionism, the Roman Catholic Church has issued an important document whose "text is not a magisterial document or doctrinal teaching of the Catholic Church, but is a reflection prepared by the Commission for Religious Relations with the Jews on current theological questions that have developed since the Second Vatican Council."[70] This text reviews the progressive undoing of supersessionism since *Nostra Aetate*: "The Church does not replace the people of God of Israel, since as the community founded on Christ it represents in him the fulfilment of the promises made to Israel. This does not mean that Israel, not having achieved such a fulfilment, can no longer be considered to be the people of God." While "confessing the universal and therefore also exclusive mediation of salvation through Jesus Christ," they propose that this seemingly restricted view is not meant to reject the Jewish people: "It does not in any way follow that the Jews are excluded from God's salvation because they do not believe in Jesus Christ as the Messiah of Israel and the Son of God." Recognizing such seemingly irreconcilable positions, they go on to affirm: "That the Jews are participants in God's salvation is

---

67. From *Nostra Aetate*, in Willebrands, *Church and Jewish People*, 205.
68. Manuel, *Broken Staff*, 319–20.
69. Zenger, "Covenant That Was Never Revoked," 92–93.
70. "'The Gifts and the Calling of God Are Irrevocable' (Rom 11:29): A Reflection on Theological Questions Pertaining to Catholic-Jewish Relations on the Occasion of the 50th Anniversary of 'Nostra Aetate,'" http://www.vatican.va/roman_curia/pontifical_councils/chrstuni/relations-jews-docs/rc_pc_chrstuni_doc_20151210_ebraismo-nostra-aetate_en.html.

theologically unquestionable, but how that can be possible without confessing Christ explicitly, is and remains an unfathomable divine mystery." It is for this reason that "the Catholic Church neither conducts nor supports any specific institutional mission work directed towards Jews." By denying dual covenant theology, which affirms two separate and legitimate covenants, the Catholic Church subsumes Jewish people into an already existing relationship with God that finds fulfillment in the New Covenant. Similar views are explained by the director of the Institute for Jewish-Catholic Relations at Saint Joseph's University.[71]

Protestant theologians have also been prolific instigators of interfaith discussion. They have attempted to identify the varied sources of the church's anti-Judaism, and they have created numerous proposals to remedy the church's praxis. Their research tends to center on the interpretation of specific biblical passages, in contrast to the Roman Catholic position that deals largely with creedal formulations. As to the foundation of Christian anti-Judaism, mainline Protestant theologians disagree as to whether it stems from the New Testament texts themselves or rather from the church's earliest interpreters of that source material. Some scholars attempt to rehabilitate the New Testament by reconstructing the historical context to dispel the supposed anti-Jewish sentiment and "to close the gap between Judaism and Christianity as they are imagined to have been in the first century,"[72] while others lay blame directly on the New Testament texts.[73] Among such scholars there are disagreements, but the discussion continues to progress in spite of internal differences.[74] Several scholars have written systematic theologies "to reconstruct Christian theology in the light of the searching critique to which examination of its anti-Jewish past subjects it."[75] John Gager indicates the immensity of the task and his optimism as one

---

71. Cunningham, *Seeking Shalom*.

72. Fredriksen and Reinhartz, "Introduction," 5. Attempts at mollifying the anti-Jewish notion in Paul's writings include Hall, *Christian Anti-Semitism and Paul's Theology*; and Gager, *Reinventing Paul*.

73. The first to do so was Parkes, *Conflict of the Church and the Synagogue*.

74. For instance, in the matter of Christology, an ongoing challenge is how to maintain a unique view of Jesus and at the same time avoid the superiority entailed by the traditional supersessionistic claims of the church. Bader-Saye critiques Soulen on this point: "Soulen's discussion of Christ's life, death, and resurrection does not require that we attribute to Jesus any more than that he was an extremely faithful Jew" (Bader-Saye, *Church and Israel after Christendom*, 84).

75. Williamson, *Guest in the House of Israel*, vii. See also Van Buren, *Theology of the Jewish Christian Reality*.

whose pioneering work serves as an pattern for other scholars: "Standing against me are not merely twenty centuries of reading Paul as the father of anti-Judaism, but the manifest tensions between the two sets of texts themselves [in Paul's writings that speak in favor of the Jewish law and in opposition to it]. But the tide has begun to turn."[76] Such endeavors by post-Holocaust theologians attempt to admit culpability for the Nazi terror and to progressively eliminate Christian anti-Semitism.

A common thread running through these creative proposals is to deny any Christian mission to Jews. Most Jewish people regard the notion of "missionary activity" as highly objectionable, since it recalls the history of oppressive Christian proselytism coupled with threats of physical violence. In the words of one Jewish historian, "Only by a total renunciation of such mission is the way open to true dialogue."[77] The German Protestant Church began to evaluate its complicity in the Holocaust in 1950, but it was not until 1980 that its Rhineland Synod renounced the Christian church's mission to the Jews.[78] The World Council of Churches, home to many Protestant denominations, achieved this goal over a period of almost forty years, progressing from a 1948 document that proclaimed an ongoing mission to the Jews to the statements in the late 1980s reversing such mission and stressing "the continuing covenant between God, whom Christians know through Jesus of Nazareth, and the Jewish people."[79] The driving force behind the missional imperative is the traditional teaching of the church that the Jews (as well as all people) are deficient in their faith without allegiance to Christ because their covenant was annulled through their rejection of Jesus. Much of the literature on contemporary Christian and Jewish relations affirms the Christian renunciation of the exclusivity inherent in traditional supersessionist theology. This rejection of any hint of the inadequacy of Judaism is a major reversal of an almost two-thousand-year-old tradition:

> Whenever the church's own affirmations depend upon the negation of Judaism and the Jewish people, the church not only undermines its own ethical integrity but also advances an incoherent theological position, namely, that God cannot be trusted to remain faithful to God's promises.... One of the key tasks to

---

76. Gager, *Reinventing Paul*, 10.
77. Wigoder, *Jewish-Christian Relations*, 30.
78. Hockendos, "German Protestant Church."
79. Brockway, *Theology of the Churches*, 185.

"Ask the Jews!"

demand the attention of Christians ... is to neutralize the ideological alignments that have produced the rotten fruit of theological arrogance.[80]

The following examples reveal strategies designed to "neutralize" the harmful elements of Christian supersessionism based on a new understanding of two separate and equal covenants. The Institute for Christian and Jewish Studies was founded in 1987 by a Presbyterian clergyman and its mission is "to build learning communities where religious difference becomes a powerful force for good."[81] This interfaith coalition of laity and clergy offers a variety of educational programs that highlight the distinctiveness of Jewish, Christian, and Muslim traditions and confront misunderstandings that have evolved in the faith communities. Another example is the Evangelical Lutheran Church in America's pursuit of relations in the same spirit of mutual recognition, denying the scriptural basis for supersessionism and regretting its denigration of the Jewish people. The ELCA affirms two covenants, one as an eternal bond with Jews and the other with Christians, forming the basis for recent discussion of major differences between Christians and Jews.[82] Lutheran theologian James Moore has contributed to the dialogue using a Christian midrash to reshape his own theology, offering a "radical revision of Christian theology" incorporating "the twin principles of ambiguity and pluralism" to undo the notion of contempt in order "to safeguard the legitimacy of Judaism."[83] He calls for continual dialogue as the only path toward progress: "Crossing boundaries breaks down boundaries and enables us to hear the other and see different sides of all issues.... But this is a struggle, a thousand years struggle even."[84] The Anabaptist theologian John Howard Yoder began to revisit the Jewish-Christian schism in the early 1970s and continued to promote a new understanding in line with a dual covenant theology among Mennonites and the broader church until his death in 1997.[85] Similarly, discussions among Christians and Jews over the exegesis of portions of Old Testament pericopes are reminiscent of Jerome's talks with his Jewish teachers. Those who have participated in these events extol their value:

80. Leighton, Dawe, and Weinstein, "What Is the Meaning of 'Israel'?," 98.
81. http://www.icjs.org.
82. Jodock, "Christians and Jews."
83. Moore, *Christian Theology after the Shoah*, 135, 136.
84. Moore, *Toward a Dialogical Community*, 135.
85. Yoder, *Jewish-Christian Schism Revisited*.

> Ask any long-term participant of the dialogue, and they will tell you that interfaith text study works an intoxicating magic. It teaches Jews and Christians what they can learn in no other setting: that the other brings to the study of a particular text ways of seeing and hearing, ways of listening and learning that illumine portions of the textual terrain that otherwise remain in darkness.[86]

Across the spectrum of Protestant denominations, the seeds of change continue to produce expressions of dialogue and ongoing scenarios of shared cooperation based on a shared relationship of two covenants in parity with each other. Fresh proposals continue to critique earlier models while claiming a desire to remain faithful to the Christian message.[87]

Jewish theologians have also engaged in interreligious discussion with Christians, resulting in a spirit of rapprochement. For example, the work of Stuart Rosenberg, a rabbi actively involved in Jewish-Christian relations, is optimistic about the future. Hoping for the end of belligerence, Rosenberg proposes that reconciliation will happen when both realize that "the two religions are intended to function side by side," recalling Maimonides' words: "Christianity's success brings Judaism's end goals closer."[88] In a surprising turn on Christian supersessionism, he looks forward to the Christians as a new Israel, not in competition with its elder brother: "When Jacob and his brother become Israel, a moment of redemption is at hand."[89] A similar proposal constructs a Judaism that no longer shuns Christianity but sees it as universalizing the message of Torah to the Gentiles.[90] Further, the National Jewish Scholars Project produced a Jewish statement on Christianity entitled "Dabru Emet." The tone of mutuality is expressed in one of its eight pronouncements:

> The humanly irreconcilable difference between Jews and Christians will not be settled until God redeems the entire world as promised in Scripture. Christians know and serve God through Jesus Christ and the Christian tradition. Jews know and serve God through Torah and the Jewish tradition. That difference will not be

---

86. Catalona and Sandmel, "Speaking Theologically . . . Together," 5.

87. See Boesel, *Risking Proclamation, Respecting Difference*.

88. Rosenberg, *Christian Problem*, 99.

89. Ibid., 102. He adds elsewhere, "Only Christians (although possibly also Muslims) may be deemed to be members of the people of Israel, even as they practice different religions than Jewry does" (233).

90. Kogan, *Opening the Covenant*. See also Korn and Pawlikowski, *Two Faiths, One Covenant?*

settled by one community insisting that it has interpreted Scripture more accurately than the other; nor by exercising political power over the other. Jews can respect Christians" faithfulness to their revelation just as we expect Christians to respect our faithfulness to our revelation. Neither Jew nor Christian should be pressed into affirming the teaching of the other community.[91]

Another example of this reconciling tone comes from Jewish theologian Michael Wyschogrod, whose construction of a post-supersession Christianity envisions a Christian faith that validates God's ongoing covenant with the Jews and depreciates the uniqueness of the incarnation of God in Jesus Christ.[92] This desire for a tolerant Christianity is voiced by another scholar with desire to overturn classic Christian supersessionism: "Supersession theology no longer needs to be an insurmountable theological anchor. Only the embrace of multiple, separate, and equally valid tracks to the Divine will defuse the ever present danger of supersession theology."[93] These Jews in dialogue with Christians seem prepared not only to critique the past, but to forge an alliance of ecumenical cooperation for a better future.

In conclusion, Jerome's fourth-century association with Jews bears little resemblance to the accelerated trajectories of interfaith relations witnessed in the post-Holocaust era. Jerome's innovation embraced a shared textual and exegetical heritage with Jewish associates, but his Christian supersessionism did not allow him to cross over into a shared soteriological realm. His model resembles those who in the same way adhere to strong supersessionism. Other Christians have advanced theological and relational boundaries far beyond Jerome's fourth-century norms.

WHERE IS THE CHURCH'S LAND?

"The Hebrews hand on a tradition that this same place is named..."[94]

The fourth century witnessed the unimagined conversion of the Roman emperor to Christianity and the subsequent appropriation of Palestine to

---

91. http://www.jcrelations.net/Dabru_Emet_-_A_Jewish_Statement_on_Christians_and_Christianity.2395.0.html.

92. Wyschogrod, *Abraham's Promise*, 21.

93. Bibliowicz, *Jews and Gentiles in the Early Jesus Movement*, 113.

94. Jerome's comment about a location mentioned in Gen 14:2 (Hayward, *Saint*

Christianity's holy land. These events transpired so rapidly that some early Christian writers, such as Eusebius of Caesarea, witnessed both the Roman Empire's persecution of the church and its reversal after Constantine's conversion. Such was not the case with Jerome, for by the time he felt compelled to leave Rome, Christian pilgrimage to the holy land was a viable and thriving option, one that he chose and recommended for others. Jerome's beliefs about the sanctity of the land of the Bible formed an early element of his training in Christian exegesis and tradition. Although steeped in the Christian notion of Jerusalem's sanctity that emanated outward across Palestine, Jerome grew discontent with the tradition after events and personalities in the Origenist controversy redirected his conception of sacred space. His actions prove salutary for Christians who ponder the significance of the holy land in the twenty-first century. Political boundaries and populations have dramatically changed in sixteen hundred years, but the land remains along with the presence of Jewish, Muslim, and Christian people.

Jerome's Progressive Redefinition of Sacred Space

As discussed in chapter 4, and unlike the previous two components of Jerome's supersessionism, his preoccupation with the holy land was not a radical departure from standard Christian tradition. Jerome reflected that tradition quite consistently in his writings, namely, that the ancient territory of Israel had become the new land of the Christian church due to the sanctity of Christ's presence in Palestine. For Jews in biblical history, the land held honor as God's dwelling place, centered in the Jerusalem temple, where divine holiness radiated sanctity to its borders. For later Christians, the sanctity was centered in a church located in Jerusalem and regarded by them as God's temple. Just as significant was the strategic intersection of three nearby churches, all constructed in the early fourth century and all linked to three crucial events in the life of Jesus: Bethlehem as the place of his birth; Jerusalem as the place of his death, burial, and resurrection; and the Mount of Olives as the location of his ascension to heaven. Jerome chose Bethlehem as his home, and his letters recommend pilgrimage to Jerusalem and Bethlehem, the latter his preferred abode.

The triune camaraderie of churches was consistently maintained in harmony for roughly sixty years until the onslaught of the Origenist controversy disturbed that peace and shook Jerome's confidence in Jerusalem's

Jerome's Hebrew Questions on Genesis, 45).

sanctity. His writings thereafter display a disdain for pilgrimage to Jerusalem's holy sites coupled with an exaltation of Bethlehem as the supreme sacred space. In Jerome's characteristic fashion, he breathed life into an idea and sustained it with an arsenal of rhetoric. His favored technique to deflect veneration away from the earthly Jerusalem was to transfer its sanctity to the heavenly Jerusalem while redirecting its earthly sanctity to Bethlehem. Jerome therefore never rejected the concept of sacred space and pilgrimage; rather, he reformulated it by directing Christian devotion to the site of his own choosing. As he had unilaterally chosen the Hebrew text and Hebraic interpretations, so he authoritatively selected the new holy city. Bethlehem became Jerome's New Jerusalem on earth, jealously guarded and divinely blessed. As a dedicated monk, he claimed the right to live there, to establish a monastic community, and to invite pilgrims to worship at Jesus' birthplace. Jerome considered Palestine as God's land, and he fashioned himself as God's guardian of that sacred space.

The presence of Jewish land beneath the feet of Jerome informed his remapping of the land. It was not unoccupied space, thus Jerome needed to displace the previous occupants, the Jews, not by removing them physically but by replacing their Hebraic topography with Christian vocabulary: their geographic names were adopted, their holy spots were absorbed, and their soil was transferred to Christian ownership. Such rewriting produced a Christian kingdom, the new Israel, mediating its rule through the Byzantine governmental structures and, more importantly, through the church's spiritual authority.

Jerome's Trajectory

From the first century B.C.E. to the fourth century C.E., the land of Palestine had been successively ruled by the Jewish Hasmonean Empire, the pagan Roman Empire, and the Christian Byzantine Empire. Jerome was an immigrant to Palestine, a land shared by Christians, Samaritans, and Jews in the fourth century. His pilgrimage became a permanent settlement in Bethlehem, and his personal knowledge of the land is reflected in his writings. Christian presence and power dominated the land, inscribed its identity on its cities, utilized its peoples for its own purposes, and attempted for forge a Christian kingdom in the very place of the former Jewish kingdom. Aspirations were still alive within the Jewish people for a resurrected kingdom, even after their hopes for a rebuilt temple were dashed by Emperor Julian's sudden death.

Advancing to the nineteenth century and the present, Palestine's hegemony has passed from the hand of the Ottoman Turks to the British, and currently to the State of Israel. At present, the people living in Israel and the Palestinian territories represent the Jewish, Muslim, and Christian faiths.[95] Sadly, the "holy land" continues to experience unholy acts of conflict among the various religious communities, conflicts that are rooted in the distant and recent past.

Between Jerome's day and our own, the holy land has experienced a torn history of subjugation by rival powers and oppression of its native peoples by outside empires. Christian sovereignty over the land of Palestine ended suddenly with the Persian invasion in 614 and the Muslim invasion in 638. The brief reinstatement of Christian hegemony by the Crusaders some four hundred years later proved to be short-lived, and their kingdom fell to Muslim Saladin in 1187, whose victory was complete upon the Crusaders' abandonment of the holy land in 1291. After that time the Christian holy places that were not destroyed fell under the jurisdiction of successive kingdoms loyal to Islam. Palestine continued under Islamic rule until the defeat of the Ottoman Turkish Empire in World War I in 1917. Following thirty years of occupation under the British Mandate, the United Nations voted in 1947 to establish the State of Israel in Palestine after almost two thousand years, and the Jews in Palestine regained political sovereignty in their ancient lands. The day the State of Israel declared its independence, May 14, 1948, has become a defining moment in Jewish, Christian, and Muslim relations. On May 15, 1948, war broke out against the Jewish state by five Arab armies. The Israelis consider this their "War of Independence," while the Arabs name it "The Disaster."[96] Two responses to one event—this notion encapsulates the contemporary situation.

Since its inception in 1948, the Jewish state has endeavored to rewrite the map of Palestine into the homeland of the Jews, using biblical geography as its baseline. The borders of the State of Israel incorporate areas long inhabited by Arab Palestinians. The newly resurrected Hebrew language has inscribed Jewish geographical names over Arab ones, a metaphor for the presence of an emerging Israeli culture over an already existing Arab

---

95. Minority religious groups include the Druze, Samaritan, and Baha'i.
96. Kimmerling and Migdal, *Palestinian People*, 137.

"Ask the Jews!"

culture.[97] The Six Day War in 1967 expanded Israel's territory and led to the Jewish occupation of the Palestinian Arab West Bank and Gaza Strip as well as the Syrian Golan Heights. Since that time many religious Jews have settled inside those regions, claiming rights to that land on the basis of the covenant with Abraham. As in Jerome's time, the land's previous inhabitants were still present when the new occupants arrived to colonize their newly acquired territory. This situation is further complicated by the presence of both Christian and Muslim Arabs living in the Jewish state and the Palestinian territories, each group contending for rights to the land based on historical precedents, and each group remapping the State of Israel according to its own earlier image of pre-Israeli Palestine. In a fascinating case of déjà vu, this sort of rewriting of the geography of Palestine had been done by Christians about seventeen hundred years earlier.

In Jerome's time, Christian writers were divided into two factions: those who supported the Jewish hope of an earthly restoration of the Jewish kingdom (the Judaizing Christians) and those (like Jerome) who opposed any reinstatement of Jewish sovereignty. Jerome maligned his Christian brothers by castigating them as Judaizers. Rather than give a place to the historical Jewish interpretation of an eschatological hope for the Jews, Jerome's supersession allowed no future and no present for the rejected people. Into this matrix of competing claims for identity and geography, Jerome's example of rigid polarity becomes a starting point. His conflict with Rufinus and Melania, residents on the Mount of Olives in present-day Arab East Jerusalem, reveals the complexity of the intertwining of people and land. Jerome's castigation of Rufinus fractured relationships among Christian brothers within the same land and erected ecclesiastical barriers that separated Christians from each other.[98] Jerome's residence in Bethlehem, now part of the Palestinian Authority, raises another poignant reminder of contemporary struggles among the native Christians and Muslims whose city is separated from Jerusalem by a barrier of concrete and ideology. Jerome's appropriation of Palestine approximates the Zionist ideology adopted by some Jews and some Christians.

---

97. The intertwined nature of these events is noted by Krister Stendahl, who links Jewish exegesis with Jewish presence in the land: "The establishment of the State of Israel is changing all that [absence of Jewish presence] by giving the Jewish people a presence on the global scene, making Jewish invisibility obsolete also in hermeneutics" ("Qumran and Supersessionism," 403 n. 10).

98. Rebenich, *Jerome*, 41–51.

The contemporary Christian church, having lost its claim to the holy land a thousand years earlier when the Crusaders were defeated, still maintains the right of ownership over its holy places in the land. The presence of Orthodox and Roman Catholic priests in the State of Israel, representing a minute portion of the population, exerts minor influence on political realities outside of their own church's interests. However, the broader Christian church outside of the State of Israel does exercise some influence on the State whether defending the rights of Israelis for a divinely established nation in accord with perceived Christian eschatological aims, or seeking justice and peace for Arabs in conflict with the Israeli government. In order to more fully appreciate the tensions in the State of Israel between Jews, Arabs, and Christians, I will examine Christian concern for the State of Israel in three echelons according to the validation of the Jewish right to possess their ancient land.

Unqualified Support for the Jewish State

The Jewish commitment to the land of Israel lies deep in the religious traditions of the Torah, for the covenant is fundamentally tied to the occupation of the promised land,[99] and much of later rabbinic thought continues the dream of a return to the land after the Roman exile.[100] Jewish population in the land of Palestine was meager but continual until the numbers swelled during the late 1800s as persecution drove Jews from Russia and European countries. The long-held dream of diaspora Jewry for the ancient homeland gained impetus from the various expressions of Zionism. As a result, Jewish immigration into Turkish-occupied Palestine ballooned before the First World War.[101]

Christians also played a determinative role in early twentieth-century Zionism. In Great Britain, Christians who held to a Jewish restorationist doctrine had influence over governmental policy that resulted in the Balfour Declaration, committing British support for a Jewish homeland.[102]

---

99. See Brueggemann, *Land*. He makes this application in his conclusion: "If Christians could be clear that the gospel entrusted to Christians is also about land, perhaps a new conversation would emerge, but it will not as long as we misunderstand our faith in categories either existentialist or spiritual-transcendental" (203).

100. Suomala, "Jewish Concern for the Land."

101. For a comprehensive overview, see Sachar, *History of Israel*.

102. See Clark, *Allies for Armageddon*; and Tuchman, *Bible and Sword*.

This Christian support for a Jewish state received its impetus from an eschatology that included a restored Jewish nation, and such a motivation continues with those who "see in the building of a Jewish state a necessary vehicle for the advancement of the events of the end of the age."[103] Stephen Haynes discusses the role of dispensational premillennialism and its "witness-people" theology of the Jews. These Christians, often known as Christian Zionists, lend their support to the State of Israel because they view it as a sign of divine presence in the world. For example, Christians United for Israel is organized to "provide a national association through which every pro-Israel church, parachurch organization, ministry or individual in America can speak and act with one voice in support of Israel in matters related to Biblical issues."[104] The founder and national chairman is a Christian pastor, and the executive director is a Jew. This organization focuses full interfaith cooperation between Christians and Jews on the issue of Zionism. The foregoing example demonstrates that outright support for the State of Israel can generate strange bedfellows. Daniel Boyarin comments:

> The mind boggles and the imagination is beggared at the spectacle of right-wing Protestant presidents, Southern Baptist fundamentalist preachers . . . and the Jewish president of Harvard University . . . making common cause in demonizing those . . . who dissent radically from Israeli policy and practice toward the Palestinians.[105]

Christian Zionists are not alone in lending their support to the Zionist cause; so do certain "Holocaust theologians." Such writers are at the forefront of reconstructing Christian theology in line with post-Holocaust concerns, holding the very opposite theological posture as that of Christian Zionists. Haynes draws a striking number of parallels between the two groups that represent such divergent views. For example, each agrees on a non-spiritualized reading of the Old Testament, an opposition to the replacement of Israel by the church, and an equation of anti-Zionism with anti-Semitism.[106] The former is driven to an unqualified support of Israel

---

103. Ariel, *On Behalf of Israel*, 121.

104. http://www.cufi.org/site/PageServer?pagename=about_AboutCUFI.

105. Boyarin, *Border Lines*, xiii.

106. Haynes, *Reluctant Witnesses*, 168–70. Holocaust theologians "agree that the fundamental failure of Christendom in the past can be located in its conception and treatment of the Jews" (121) and include such writers as Franklin Littell, Alice and Roy Eckardt, James Moore, and Paul van Buren.

by an eschatological motivation, while the latter finds Christian ethics its driving force.[107]

Other Protestants have found common cause in embracing what they call a "New Christian Zionism" without the necessary presuppositions of dispensationalism or premillennialism, finding antecedents in church history from Justin Martyr to Karl Barth. Representing a wide spectrum of Protestant denominations around the world, they argue that "the people of Israel continue to be significant for the history of redemption, and that the land of Israel, which is at the heart of the covenantal promises, continues to be critical to God's providential purposes."[108] I find this broad coalition of Christians in line with my personal beliefs concerning the land promised to the Jews. The hermeneutic that "revises *so as to essentially discard* the national and territorial promises to Israel in the fulfillment of the plot line of Scripture is to call into question the integrity of God."[109] Without minimizing the difficult issues raised by the following positions on the Jewish state, Christian Zionism embraces the biblical assurance of God's covenant faithfulness and the recent expression of his providence in the history of the Middle East.

Qualified Support for the Jewish State

A complicating factor in this discussion is the reversal of roles between fourth-century Christians and Jews and their contemporary counterparts. In attempting to describe the difficulty, a Lutheran author says:

> We would need to consider the hermeneutical significance of the way that, through most of our synchronous history, Jews needed to apply texts born in a nation's life in a new context of exile and landlessness, while Christians were taking the texts of a powerless minority and applying them with force in the settled nations of dominant Christendom.[110]

The historical roles of Christians and Jews have been reversed since 1948 with the establishment of the Israeli state. Compared to the fourth century, the Christian church is now a minority in a majority Jewish nation.

107. See also Chafets, *Match Made in Heaven*.
108. McDermot, "New Christian Zionism," http://www.firstthings.com/webexclusives/2015/05/a-new-christian-zionism. He is the editor of *New Christian Zionism*.
109. Blaising, "Israel and Hermeneutics," 164–65.
110. Stendahl, "Jewish Concern for the Land," 112.

As precarious as the application of Christian ethics might be, the church continues to play a role in the holy land as it attempts to mediate between the parties in mutual contestation over the ownership of that land.

Some theologically and ethically minded Christians attempt to bridge the gulf between those who wholeheartedly endorse the Jewish state and those who reject its legitimacy. They see their Christian duty as lending support to the Jewish state only when it recognizes the rights of its Arab citizens and deals justly with those living in its occupied territories. In the evangelical community, those who embrace a strong supersessionist viewpoint ("one covenant people") reject a carte blanche approval of Zionism and favor justice for the Palestinians. Gary Burge defends this position and gathers support from "post-Zionist" scholars in Israel who "have revisited Israel's history and debunked the most 'sacred truths' of Zionism. . . . Novelists, filmmakers, musicians, journalists, and artists [have joined] the ranks of these critics who were challenging the moral underpinnings of the state."[111] He considers the land promise to be conditional upon the ethical conduct of the Israelis. Otherwise he suggests that God will expel the Jews again.[112] He raises Israel above its neighboring nations, elevating its Western-like democracy above neighboring Arab "tribal regimes," and places it even higher by comparing its ethical conduct "with the biblical model of nationhood because it claims that this heritage has empowered it to inherit the land."[113] With this lofty elevation of the State of Israel beyond any other nation, he seems to establish an unattainable standard. Other evangelicals continue to debate such qualified support within a framework of a non-Zionistic theological position.[114]

Roman Catholic relations with the State of Israel have lagged behind earlier theological discussions between Jews and Catholics. In 1993 the "Fundamental Agreement between the Holy See and the State of Israel" was published, a text expressing mutual respect for each party. It laid the groundwork for establishing full diplomatic relations between the Vatican and Israel.[115] Papal visits have sought to improve relations with the Israelis

---

111. Burge, *Whose Land? Whose Promise?*, 108. See also his *Jesus and the Land*, and the stinging critique of Christian Zionism by Sizer, *Zion's Christian Soldiers?*

112. Burge, *Whose Land? Whose Promise?*, 78–79.

113. Ibid., 133.

114. Johnston and Walker, *Land of Promise*.

115. Appendix 4 in Cunningham, Hofmann, and Sievers, eds., *Catholic Church and the Jewish People*, 233–39.

and Palestinians: Pope John Paul II in 2000, Pope Benedict XVI in 2009, and Pope Francis in 2014. These popes visited places significant to both Jews and Christians: the Western Wall and the Holocaust Memorial, where papal regrets for Christian anti-Semitism were expressed along with an affirmation of Israeli rights for a secure future, free from terrorism; and Christian holy places in Jerusalem and Nazareth as well as in the Palestinian territory of Bethlehem. There the popes affirmed the rights of the Palestinians to a state of their own. In spite of such high-profile events, the Roman Catholic Church is reticent about spiritually linking the Jews to the land of Israel. A Jewish critic observes the inconsistency: "It is not enough for the Catholic Church to take note of Jewish ties to the land 'that have deep biblical roots.' If they have deep biblical roots, then the Church must also take these ties seriously, not only as something that Jews have but as something the Church must struggle with. That decision was made when the Church decided to make the Hebrew Bible its own."[116] Once again, the integration of text and land cannot be ignored. The complexity of undoing the harmful effects of supersessionism must include an honest evaluation of entrenched consequences and a creative approach to solving such issues.

Dubious Support for the Jewish State

As in Jerome's day, where the possibility of a restored Jewish nation was never considered a possibility, some Christians refuse to lend their support to the Jewish state on theological grounds. They obviously cannot deny the possibility as their theological forebears had assumed before 1948. A group of Reformed evangelicals published a document in 2002 to combat Christian Zionism. Among the critiques, it dismisses Christian expectation for any concept of a holy land: "The people of God, whether the church of Israel in the wilderness in the Old Testament or the Israel of God among the Gentile Galatians in the New Testament, are one body who through Jesus will receive the promise of the heavenly city, the everlasting Zion." Further, it dismisses the concept of sacred space: "The entitlement of any one ethnic or religious group to territory in the Middle East called the 'Holy Land' cannot be supported by Scripture." It delegitimizes the State of Israel's existence based solely on religious grounds: "Lamentably, bad Christian theology is today attributing to secular Israel a divine mandate to conquer and hold Palestine." And finally, it condemns Christian Zionists whose "theology

116. Wyschogrod, "Bishops and the Middle East," 16.

puts those Christians who are urging the violent seizure and occupation of Palestinian land in moral jeopardy of their own bloodguiltiness."[117] The signatories are those whose theology of strong supersessionism aligns with the "one covenant people" view presented above.

From the broader Christian community, pleas for justice include calls by universities and mainline Protestant denominations for financial divestiture from Israel in light of injustice to the Palestinians. One particular book provides a blistering critique of Israel's treatment of its Palestinian citizens and those in the Occupied Territories. The authors' concern is to set the record straight by a "truthful historical accountability that must underlie the quest for justice."[118] The work retells the history of Zionism and Palestinian nationalism along with a critique of Holocaust theologians who justify the creation of the Jewish state. The authors plead for an understanding of both Jews and Arabs in light of Christian ethics: "Christian-Jewish solidarity today must include both a critique of Christian anti-Semitism and a concern to liberate the Jewish community to regain its prophetic voice toward its own system of power."[119] As an attempt to find the balance, the work leans more toward the Palestinian plight due to the supposedly oppressive nature of Israeli policy. In a similar way, Lutheran pastor and theologian Munther Isaac, a Palestinian from Bethlehem, argues against Zionism with a theological approach to the land.[120]

Most members of the Orthodox Christian communities in both Israel and the Palestinian territories hesitate or refuse to lend legitimacy to the State of Israel. In consequence, there is no dialogue between these groups and Jews nor with other Christian denominations, perhaps because their identity is based on national distinctives, such as Greek, Armenian, Syrian, or Coptic Orthodox. Thus, "for most indigenous Christians in the Middle East, their loyalty to the Arab identities precludes compromise with the State of Israel and with a Judaism involving the Return to Zion."[121] Theological tradition and political realities combine to produce friction, once

---

117. "Open Letter to Evangelicals and Other Interested Parties: The People of God, the Land of Israel, and the Impartiality of the Gospel." It was signed by twenty-six professors of Reformed Christian seminaries. The letter receives a point-by-point critique by Horner, *Future Israel*, 66–82.

118. Ruether and Ruether, *Wrath of Jonah*, xvi.

119. Ibid., 218.

120. Isaac, *From Land to Lands*.

121. Wigoder, *Jewish-Christian Relations*, 124.

again serving to reinforce the notion that sacred text and holy land cannot easily be separated.

CONCLUSION: REMAINING CHALLENGES FOR A SHARED IDENTITY

Jerome, full-fledged supersessionist and unconventional student of Hebrew truth, utilized alternative strategies for infiltrating traditional Christianity with newfound Jewish knowledge. Nowhere in those sacred texts did he find authorization to return to a Hebrew text, a Jewish exegesis, or the town of Bethlehem. No one in authority told this monk to pursue his distinctive agenda. Jerome's self-motivated intrusion into Hebraic culture becomes a paradigm for contemporary Christian and Jewish interaction. He embodies a bold yet ambivalent maneuver that lurched the Christian church sideways to its neighbor and propelled the church ahead with a slightly more Hebraized identity than it had possessed. Jerome's three moves taken individually seem reasonable. Taken together, they form a triad of patterned appropriation that exposes Christianity's indebtedness to Judaism. His endeavor to construct a literary legacy undergirded with text, exegesis, and land reduced the distance between Jerome and actual Jews in his day. Far from revising supersessionism, these achievements were modest and unwilling moves toward the Jews. Some of the seeds have taken root in the sharing of textual resources, but enormous challenges remain for contemporary efforts of Christian and Jewish relations concerning the soteriological and geographical dimensions of their religions.[122]

A twentieth-century Jewish rabbi entitled the epilogue of his book "If I Were a Christian." He writes: "I would go back to *the Jewish sources* to relearn my Christian history from the roots up.... I would seek to establish a *newer Christian mission* ... [that] would lead Christians back to their Jewish source."[123] A fourth-century Christian monk writes: "Therefore, it remains for us to return to the source, the Hebrew words, and see how they are written."[124] The yearning of a twentieth-century rabbi and the desire of a fourth-century monk continue to resonate with most Christians and Jews.

---

122. For a comprehensive discussion of the personalities and movements in Jewish and Christian relations, see Kessler, *Introduction to Jewish-Christian Relations*; and the companion, Kessler and Wenborn, eds., *Dictionary of Jewish–Christian Relations*.

123. Rosenberg, *Christian Problem*, 222–23.

124. *Ep.* 34.4 (CSEL 54:262).

"Ask the Jews!"

In the middle of the twentieth century, text, people, and land converged in the Middle East as they did in the fourth century. The conjunction of the discovery of Israel's ancient scrolls, the tragic event of the Holocaust, and the founding of the State of Israel is proving to be a remarkable catalyst for discussion in the twenty-first century. Jerome's texts suggest multiple possibilities for diminishing the distance between Jews and Christians. That gap has been reduced more in the last one hundred years than in the last fifteen hundred years, yet a host of difficulties remain. As theologians and historians grapple with ancient texts, two religious traditions, and a land far from holy, the space between Christians and Jews may yet continue to diminish. In this way Christians will demonstrate God's love for the Jews, who as the Jewish apostle Paul says, are "loved on account of the patriarchs, for God's gifts and his call are irrevocable" (Rom 11:28–29).

Bibliography

Adkin, Neil. *Jerome on Virginity: A Commentary on the Libellus de Virginitate Servanda (Letter 22)*. Cambridge: Francis Cairns, 2003.
Aitken, James K., ed. *T&T Clark Companion to the Septuagint*. New York: Bloomsbury T&T Clark, 2015.
Allison, Gregg R., *Sojourners and Strangers: The Doctrine of the Church*. Wheaton, IL: Crossway, 2012.
Ariel, Yaakov S. *On Behalf of Israel: American Fundamentalist Attitudes toward Jews, Judaism, and Zionism, 1865–1945*. Brooklyn: Carlson Pub., 1991.
———. *An Unusual Relationship: Evangelical Christians and Jews*. New York: New York University Press, 2013.
Augustine. *The City of God against the Pagans*. Edited and translated by R. W. Dyson. Cambridge: Cambridge University Press, 1998.
———. *On Christian Doctrine*. Translated by R. P. H Green. Oxford: Oxford University Press, 1997.
Avi-Yonah, Michael. *The Jews of Palestine: A Political History from the Bar Kokhba War to the Arab Conquest*. New York: Schocken, 1976.
Bader-Saye, Scott. *Church and Israel after Christendom: The Politics of Election*. Boulder, CO: Westview, 1999.
Baskin, Judith R. "Rabbinic-Patristic Exegetical Contacts in Late Antiquity: A Bibliographical Reappraisal." In *Approaches to Ancient Judaism: Studies in Judaism and Its Greco-Roman Context*, vol. 5, edited by W. S. Green, 53–80. Atlanta: Scholars, 1985.
Baumgarten, Albert I. "Marcel Simon's *Verus Israel* as a Contribution to Jewish History." *Harvard Theological Review* 92:4 (1999) 465–78.
Baum, Gregory. *Is the New Testament Anti-Semitic?* Rev. ed. Glen Rock, NJ: Paulist, 1965.
Becker, Adam H., and Annette Yoshiko Reed, eds. *The Ways that Never Parted: Jews and Christians in Late Antiquity and the Early Middle Ages*. 2003. Reprint, Minneapolis: Fortress, 2007.
Biblia Sacra: Iuxta Vulgatam Versionem. Edited by Roger Gryson and Robert Weber. 5th ed. Stuttgart: Deutsche Bibelgesellschaft, 2007.
Bibliowicz, Abel Mordechai. *Jews and Gentiles in the Early Jesus Movement: An Unintended Journey*. New York: Palgrave Macmillan, 2013.
Bitton-Ashkelony, Brouria. *Encountering the Sacred: The Debate on Christian Pilgrimage in Late Antiquity*. Berkeley: University of California Press, 2005.

Bibliography

Blaising, Craig. "The Future of Israel as a Theological Question." *Journal of the Evangelical Theological Society* 44:3 (2001) 435–50.

———. "Israel and Hermeneutics." In *The People, the Land, and the Future of Israel: Israel and the Jewish People in the Plan of God*, edited by Darrell L. Bock and Mitch Glaser, 151–67. Grand Rapids: Kregel, 2014.

Blaising, Craig, and Darrell L. Bock. *Progressive Dispensationalism*. Wheaton, IL: BridgePoint, 1993.

Bock, Darrell L., and Mitch Glaser. *To the Jew First: The Case for Jewish Evangelism in Scripture and History*. Grand Rapids: Kregel, 2008.

Bock, Darrell L., Walter C. Kaiser, and Craig A. Blaising, eds. *Dispensationalism, Israel and the Church: The Search for Definition*. Grand Rapids: Zondervan, 1992.

Boesel, Chris. *Risking Proclamation, Respecting Difference: Christian Faith, Imperialistic Discourse, and Abraham*. Eugene, OR: Cascade, 2008.

Boyarin, Daniel. *Border Lines: The Partition of Judaeo-Christianity*. Philadelphia: University of Pennsylvania Press, 2004.

———. *Carnal Israel: Reading Sex in Talmudic Culture*. Berkeley: University of California Press, 1993.

———. *Dying for God: Martyrdom and the Making of Christianity and Judaism*. Stanford: Stanford University Press, 1999.

———. "Justin Martyr Invents Judaism." *Church History* 70:3 (2001) 427–61.

———. "Semantic Differences; or 'Judaism'/'Christianity.'" In *The Ways that Never Parted: Jews and Christians in Late Antiquity and the Early Middle Ages*, edited by Adam H. Becker and Annette Yoshiko Reed, 65–86. 2003. Reprint, Minneapolis: Fortress, 2007.

Braaten, Carl E., and Robert W. Jenson. "Introduction." In *Jews and Christians: People of God*, edited by Carl E. Braaten and Robert W. Jenson, vii–xi. Grand Rapids: Eerdmans, 2003.

Braverman, Jay. *Jerome's Commentary on Daniel: A Study of Comparative Jewish and Christian Interpretations of the Hebrew Bible*. Washington, DC: Catholic Biblical Association of America, 1987.

Brockway, Allan R. *The Theology of the Churches and the Jewish People*. Geneva: WCC Publications, 1988.

Brown, Dennis. "Jerome and the Vulgate." In *A History of Biblical Interpretation*, edited by Alan J. Hauser and Duane F. Watson, 1: 355–79. Grand Rapids: Eerdmans, 2003.

———. *Vir Trilinguis: A Study in the Biblical Exegesis of Saint Jerome*. Kampen, Netherlands: Kok Pharos, 1992.

Brueggemann, Walter. *The Land: Place as Gift, Promise, and Challenge in Biblical Faith*. 2nd ed. Minneapolis: Fortress, 2002.

Buell, Denise Kimber. *Why This New Race: Ethnic Reasoning in Early Christianity*. New York: Columbia University Press, 2005.

Burge, Gary M. *Jesus and the Land: The New Testament Challenge to "Holy Land" Theology*. Grand Rapids: Baker, 2010.

———. *Whose Land? Whose Promise?: What Christians Are Not Being Told about Israel and the Palestinians*. Cleveland: Pilgrim, 2003.

Burrus, Virginia. "'In the Theater of This Life': The Performance of Orthodoxy in Late Antiquity." In *The Limits of Ancient Christianity: Essays on Late Antique Thought and Culture in Honor of R. A. Markus*, edited by William E. Klingshirn and Mark Vessey, 355–79. Ann Arbor: University of Michigan Press, 1999.

Bibliography

Burton, Philip. *The Old Latin Gospels: A Study of Their Texts and Language.* Oxford: Oxford University Press, 2000.

Cain, Andrew. *Jerome's Epitaph on Paula: A Commentary on the Epitaphium Sanctae Paulae.* Oxford: Oxford University Press, 2013.

———. "Jerome's *Epitaphium Paulae*: Hagiography, Pilgrimage, and the Cult of Saint Paula." *Journal of Early Christian Studies* 18:1 (2010) 105–39.

———. "Jerome's Pauline Commentaries between East and West: Tradition and Innovation in the Commentary on Galatians." In *Interpreting the Bible and Aristotle in Late Antiquity*, edited by Josef Lossl and John W. Watt, 91–110. Burlington, VT: Ashgate, 2011.

———. *The Letters of Jerome: Asceticism, Biblical Exegesis, and the Construction of Christian Authority in Late Antiquity.* Oxford: Oxford University Press, 2009.

Cameron, John. "The Rabbinic Vulgate?" In *Jerome of Stridon: His Life, Writings and Legacy*, edited by Andrew Cain and Josef Lossl, 117–29. Burlington, VT: Ashgate, 2009.

Catalona, Rosann M., and David Fox Sandmel. "Speaking Theologically . . . Together." In *Irreconcilable Differences: A Learning Resource for Jews and Christians*, edited by David Sandmel, Rosann Catalano, and Christopher Leighton, 1–10. Boulder, CO: Westview, 2001.

Cavallera, Ferdinand. *Saint Jérôme; Sa Vie et Son Oeuvre.* 2 vols. Paris: Louvain, 1922.

Chafets, Ze'ev. *A Match Made in Heaven: American Jews, Christian Zionists, and One Man's Exploration of the Weird and Wonderful Judeo-Evangelical Alliance.* New York: HarperCollins, 2007.

Charlesworth, James H., ed. *Jews and Christians: Exploring the Past, Present, and Future.* New York: Crossroad, 1990.

Chestnut, Glenn F. "A Century of Patristic Studies, 1888–1988." In *A Century of Church History: The Legacy of Philip Schaff*, edited by Henry W. Bowden, 36–73. Carbondale: Southern Illinois University Press, 1988.

Chin, Catherine M. *Grammar and Christianity in the Late Roman World.* Philadelphia: University of Pennsylvania Press, 2008.

Clark, Elizabeth A. *The Origenist Controversy: The Cultural Construction of an Early Christian Debate.* Princeton: Princeton University Press, 1992.

———. *Reading Renunciation: Asceticism and Scripture in Early Christianity.* Princeton: Princeton University Press, 1999.

Clark, Victoria. *Allies for Armageddon: The Rise of Christian Zionism.* New Haven, CT: Yale University Press, 2007.

Clement of Alexandria. *The Stromata.* In *The Ante-Nicene Fathers*, edited by A. Roberts and J. Donaldson, 2:299–568. Grand Rapids: Eerdmans, 1885. Reprint, 1994.

Cohen, Shaye J. D. "Adolph Harnack's 'The Mission and Expansion of Judaism': Christianity Succeeds Where Judaism Fails." In *The Future of Early Christianity: Essays in Honor of Helmut Koester*, edited by Birger A. Pearson, A. T. Kraabel, G. W. E. Nickelsburg, and N. R. Petersen, 163–69. Minneapolis: Fortress, 1991.

———. *From the Maccabees to the Mishnah.* 2nd ed. Louisville: Westminster John Knox, 2006.

Corpus Christianorum, Series Latina. Turnhout: Brepols, 1953–.

Corpus Scriptorum Ecclesiasticorum Latinorum. Edited by Isidorus Hilberg. Vienna: Verlag der Osterreichischen Akademie der Wissenschaften, 1996.

Cranfield, C. E. B. *A Critical and Exegetical Commentary on the Epistle to the Romans.* Vol. 2. Edinburgh: T. & T. Clark, 1979.

Bibliography

Cunningham, Philip A., Norbert J. Hofmann, and Joseph Sievers, eds. *The Catholic Church and the Jewish People: Recent Reflections from Rome*. New York: Fordham University Press, 2007.

———. *Seeking Shalom: The Journey to Right Relationship between Catholics and Jews*. Grand Rapids: Eerdmans, 2015.

De Lange, Nicholas R. M. *Origen and the Jews: Studies in Jewish-Christian Relations in Third-Century Palestine*. Cambridge: Cambridge University Press, 1976.

Demsky, Aaron. "Holy City and Holy Land as Viewed by Jews and Christians in the Byzantine Period: A Conceptual Approach to Sacred Space." In *Sanctity of Time and Space in Tradition and Modernity*, edited by A. Houtman, M. Poorthuis, and J. Schwartz, 285–96. Leiden: Brill, 1998.

Dietz, Maribel. "Itinerant Spirituality and the Late Antique Origins of Christian Pilgrimage." In *Travel, Communication, and Geography in Late Antiquity: Sacred and Profane*, edited by Linda Ellis and Frank L. Kidner, 125–34. Burlington, VT: Ashgate, 2004.

Dillon, Matthew. *Pilgrims and Pilgrimage in Ancient Greece*. London: Routledge, 1997.

Dunn, James D. G. "From the Crucifixion to the End of the First Century." In *Partings: How Judaism and Christian Became Two*, edited by Hershel Shanks, 27–53. Washington, DC: Biblical Archaeology Society, 2013.

———, ed. *Jews and Christians: The Parting of the Ways A.D. 70 to 135*. Tubingen: Mohr, 1992.

———. *The Partings of the Ways: Between Christianity and Judaism and Their Significance for the Character of Christianity*. London: SCM, 1991.

———. *The Partings of the Ways: Between Christianity and Judaism and Their Significance for the Character of Chrisitianty*. 2nd ed. London: SCM, 2006.

Egeria's Travels. Translated by John Wilkinson. Oxford: Oxbow, 2006.

Ellis, E. Earle. "The Old Testament Canon in the Early Church." In *Hebrew Bible / Old Testament: The History of Its Interpretation*, vol. 1, *From the Beginnings to the Middle Ages*, pt. 1, *Antiquity*, edited by Magne Saebo. Gottingen: Vandenhoeck & Ruprecht, 1996.

Erickson, Millard J. *Christian Theology*. 3rd ed. Grand Rapids: Baker, 2013.

Eusebius of Caesarea. *Church History*. Translated by Arthur C. McGiffert. In *A Select Library of the Nicene and Post-Nicene Fathers*, 2nd ser., vol. 1. 1890. Reprint, Grand Rapids: Eerdmans, 1991.

———. *The Onomasticon*. Translated by G. S. P. Freeman-Grenville. Jerusalem: Carta, 2003.

———. *The Proof of the Gospel, Being the Demonstratio Evangelica*. Translated by William J. Ferrar. London: SPCK, 1920.

Flannery, Edward H. *The Anguish of the Jews: Twenty-Three Centuries of Antisemitism*. Mahwah, NJ: Paulist, 1999.

Frank, Georgia. *The Memory of the Eyes: Pilgrims to Living Saints in Christian Late Antiquity*. Berkeley: University of California Press, 2000.

———. "The Pilgrim's Gaze in the Age before Icons." In *Visuality Before and After the Renaissance*, edited by Robert S. Nelson, 98–115. Cambridge: Cambridge University Press, 2000.

Fredriksen, Paula. *Augustine and the Jews: A Christian Defense of Jews and Judaism*. New York: Doubleday, 2008.

———. "What 'Parting of the Ways'? Jews, Gentiles, and the Ancient Mediterranean City." In *The Ways that Never Parted: Jews and Christians in Late Antiquity and the*

Bibliography

Early Middle Ages, edited by Adam H. Becker and Annette Yoshiko Reed, 35–64. 2003. Reprint, Minneapolis: Fortress, 2007.

Fredriksen, Paula, and Adele Reinhartz. "Introduction." In *Jesus, Judaism, and Christian Anti-Judaism*, edited by Paula Fredriksen and Adele Reinhartz, 1–7. Louisville: Westminster John Knox, 2002.

Fredriksen, Paula, and Judith Lieu. "Christian Theology and Judaism." In *The First Christian Theologians: An Introduction to Theology in the Early Church*, edited by G. R. Evans, 85–101. Malden, MA: Blackwell, 2004.

Fredriksen, Paula, and Oded Irshai. "Christian Anti-Judaism: Polemics and Policies." In *The Cambridge History of Judaism*, vol. 4, *The Late Roman-Rabbinic Period*, edited by Steven T. Katz, 977–1034. Cambridge: Cambridge University Press, 2006.

Furst, Alfons. *Augustins Briefwechsel mit Hieronymus*. Munster: Aschendorff, 1999.

Gager, John G. *The Origins of Anti-Semitism: Attitudes toward Judaism in Pagan and Christian Antiquity*. Oxford: Oxford University Press, 1983.

———. "The Parting of the Ways: A View from the Perspective of Early Christianity: 'A Christian Perspective.'" In *Interwoven Destinies: Jews and Christians Through the Ages*, edited by Eugene J. Fisher, 62–76. Mahwah, NJ: Paulist, 1993.

———. *Reinventing Paul*. Oxford: Oxford University Press, 2000.

Gallager, Edmon L. "The Old Testament 'Apocrypha' in Jerome's Canonical Theory." *Journal of Early Christian Studies* 20:2 (2012) 213–33.

Goodman, Martin. "Modeling the 'Parting of the Ways.'" In *The Ways that Never Parted: Jews and Christians in Late Antiquity and the Early Middle Ages*, edited by Adam H. Becker and Annette Yoshiko Reed, 119–30. 2003. Reprint, Minneapolis: Fortress, 2007.

Graves, Michael. "The Biblical Scholarship of a Fourth-Century Woman Marcella of Rome." *Ephemerides Theologicae Lovanienses* 87:4 (2011) 375–91.

———. *The Inspiration and Interpretation of Scripture: What the Early Church Can Teach Us*. Grand Rapids: Eerdmans, 2014.

———. *Jerome's Hebrew Philology: A Study Based on His Commentary on Jeremiah*. Leiden: Brill, 2007.

———. "'Judaizing' Christian Interpretations of the Prophets as Seen by Saint Jerome." *Vigiliae Christianae* 61 (2007) 142–56.

Grudem, Wayne A. *Systematic Theology: An Introduction to Biblical Doctrine*. Grand Rapids: Zondervan, 1994.

Hall, Sidney G., III. *Christian Anti-Semitism and Paul's Theology*. Minneapolis: Fortress, 1993.

Harnack, Adolph. *History of Dogma*. Vol. 1. Translated by Neil Buchanan. London: Williams & Norgate, 1905.

Hasselhoff, Görge K. "Revising the Vulgate: Jerome and His Jewish Interlocutors." *Zeitschrift für Religions und Geistesgeschichte* 64:3 (2012) 209–21.

Haynes, Steven R. *Prospects for Post-Holocaust Theology*. Atlanta: Scholars, 1991.

———. *Reluctant Witnesses: Jews and the Christian Imagination*. Louisville: Westminster John Knox, 1995.

Hayward, C. T. R. "Jewish Traditions in Jerome's Commentary on Jeremiah and the Targum of Jeremiah." *Proceedings of the Irish Biblical Association* 9 (1985) 100–120.

———. *Saint Jerome's Hebrew Questions on Genesis: Translated with Introduction and Commentary*. Oxford: Clarendon, 1995.

Bibliography

Hayward, Robert. "Saint Jerome, Jewish Learning, and the Symbolism of the Number Eight." In *Meditations of the Heart: The Psalms in Early Christian Thought and Practice*, edited by Andreas Andreopoulos, Augustine Casiday, and Carol Harrson, 141–59. Turnhout, Belgium: Brepols, 2011.

Hengel, Martin. *The Septuagint as Christian Scripture: Its Prehistory and the Problem of Its Cannon*. Grand Rapids: Baker, 2004.

Himmelfarb, Martha. "The Parting of the Ways Reconsidered: Diversity in Judaism and Jewish-Christian Relations in the Roman Empire: 'A Jewish Perspective.'" In *Interwoven Destinies: Jews and Christians Through the Ages*, edited by Eugene J. Fisher, 47–61. Mahwah, NJ: Paulist, 1993.

Hirshman, Marc. *A Rivalry of Genius: Jewish and Christian Biblical Interpretation in Late Antiquity*. Translated by Batya Stein. Albany: State University of New York Press, 1996.

Hockendos Matthew D. "The German Protestant Church and Its Judenmission, 1945–1950." In *Antisemitism, Christian Ambivalence, and the Holocaust*, edited by Kevin P. Spicer, 189–95. Bloomington: Indiana University Press, 2007.

Holm, Jean, and John Bowker. *Sacred Place*. London: Pinter, 1994.

Holwerda, David E. *Jesus and Israel: One Covenant or Two?* Grand Rapids: Eerdmans, 1995.

Horbury, William. *Jews and Christians in Contact and Controversy*. Edinburgh: T. & T. Clarke, 1998.

———. "Old Testament Interpretation in the Writings of the Church Fathers." In *Mikra: Text, Translation, Reading and Interpretation of the Hebrew Bible in Ancient Judaism and Early Christianity*, edited by M. J. Mulder and H. Sysling, 727–87. Minneapolis: Fortress, 1990.

Horner, Barry E. *Future Israel: Why Christian Anti-Judaism Must Be Challenged*. Nashville: B & H Academic, 2007.

Horton, Michael. *The Christian Faith: A Systematic Theology for Pilgrims on the Way*. Grand Rapids: Zondervan, 2011.

Hosmer, Robert. "The Epistles of St. Jerome: A Study of Attitudes toward Jews and Hebrew Studies." MA thesis, Smith College, 1975.

Howorth, H. H. "The Influence of St. Jerome on the Canon of the Western Church." Parts 1–3. *Journal of Theological Studies* 10:40 (July 1909) 481–96; 11:3 (April 1910) 321–47; 13:49 (October 1911) 1–18.

Hunt, E. D. *Holy Land Pilgrimage in the Later Roman Empire, AD 312–460*. Oxford: Clarendon, 1982.

———. "The Itinerary of Egeria: Reliving the Bible in Fourth-Century Palestine." In *The Holy Land, Holy Lands, and Christian History*, edited by R. N. Swanson, 34–54. Suffolk: Ecclesiastical History Society, 2000.

———. "Were There Christian Pilgrims before Constantine?" In *Pilgrimage Explored*, edited by J. Stopford, 25–40. Woodbridge, Suffolk: York Medieval, 1999.

Irenaeus. *Against Heresies*. In *The Ante-Nicene Fathers*, edited by A. Roberts and J. Donaldson, vol. 1. 1885. Reprint, Grand Rapids: Eerdmans, 1993.

Isaac, Jules. *Jesus and Israel*. Edited by Claire H. Bishop, translated by Sally Gran. New York: Holt, Rinehart and Winston, 1971.

Isaac, Munther. *From Land to Lands, from Eden to the Renewed Earth: A Christ-Centred Biblical Theology of the Promised Land*. Carlisle: Langham Partnership, 2015.

Jacobs, Andrew. "The Lion and the Lamb: Reconsidering Jewish–Christian Relations in Antiquity." In *The Ways that Never Parted: Jews and Christians in Late Antiquity and*

Bibliography

the Early Middle Ages, edited by Adam H. Becker and Annette Yoshiko Reed, 95–118. 2003. Reprint, Minneapolis: Fortress, 2007.

———. *Remains of the Jews: The Holy Land and Christian Empire in Late Antiquity.* Stanford: Stanford University Press, 2004.

Jaffee, Martin S. *Early Judaism.* Upper Saddle River, NJ: Prentice-Hall, 1997.

Jellicoe, Sidney. *The Septuagint and Modern Study.* Oxford: Clarendon, 1968.

Jerome. *Against Vigilantius.* Translated by W. H. Freemantle. In *A Select Library of the Nicene and Post-Nicene Fathers*, 2nd ser., vol. 6. 1892. Reprint, Grand Rapids: Eerdmans, 1989.

———. *Apology against the Books of Rufinus.* Translated by John N. Hritzu. Washington, DC: Catholic University of America Press, 1965.

———. *Commentaries of Origen and Jerome on St. Paul's Epistle to the Ephesians.* Translated by Ronald E. Heine. Oxford: Oxford University Press, 2002.

———. *Commentary on Galatians.* Translated by Andrew Cain. Washington, DC: Catholic University of America Press, 2010.

———. *Commentary on Isaiah.* Translated by Thomas P. Scheck. Mahwah, NJ: Newman, 2015.

———. *Commentary on Jeremiah.* Translated by Michael Graves, edited by Christopher A. Hall. Downers Grove, IL: IVP Academic, 2011.

———. *Commentary on Matthew.* Translated by Thomas P. Scheck. Washington, DC: Catholic University of America Press, 2008.

———. *Dogmatic and Polemical Works.* Translated by John N. Hritzu. Washington, DC: Catholic University of America Press, 1965.

———. *Letters and Select Works.* Translated by W. H. Freemantle. In *A Select Library of the Nicene and Post-Nicene Fathers*, 2nd ser., vol. 6. 1892. Reprint, Grand Rapids: Eerdmans, 1989.

———. *The Letters of St. Jerome.* Translated by C. C. Mierow. Vol. 1. New York: Newman, 1963.

———. *On Illustrious Men.* Translated by Thomas P. Halton. Washington, DC: Catholic University of America Press, 1999.

———. *St. Jerome's Commentaries on Galatians, Titus, and Philemon.* Translated by Thomas P. Scheck. Notre Dame, IN: University of Notre Dame Press, 2010.

Jobes, Karen H., and Moises Silva. *Invitation to the Septuagint.* 2nd ed. Grand Rapids: Baker, 2015.

Jodock, Darrell. "Christians and Jews in the Context of World Religions." In *Covenantal Conversations*, edited by Darrell Jodock, 135–38. Minneapolis: Fortress, 2008.

Justin Martyr. *Dialogue with Trypho.* Translated by Thomas B. Falls, revised by Thomas P. Halton, edited by Michael Slusser. Washington, DC: Catholic University of America, 2003.

Johnston, Philip, and Peter Walker, eds. *The Land of Promise: Biblical, Theological and Contemporary Perspectives.* Downers Grove, IL: InterVarsity, 2000.

Kamesar, Adam. "The Church Fathers and Rabbinic Midrash: A Supplementary Bibliography, 1985–2005. *Review of Rabbinic Judaism* 9 (2006) 190–96.

———. *Jerome, Greek Scholarship, and the Hebrew Bible: A Study of the Quaestiones Hebraicae in Genesim.* Oxford: Clarendon, 1993.

Kamin, Sarah. "The Theological Significance of the Hebraica Veritas in Jerome's Thought." In *Sha`arei Talmon: Studies in the Bible, Qumran, and the Ancient Near East Presented*

BIBLIOGRAPHY

to *Shemaryahu Talmon*, edited by Michael Fishbane and Emanuel Tov, 243–53. Winona Lake, IN: Eisenbrauns, 1992.

Kaminsky, Joel S. Review of *Anti-Judaism and Early Christian Identity: A Critique of the Scholarly Consensus*, by Miriam S. Taylor. *Church History* 66 (1997) 304.

Kato Teppei. "Jerome's Understanding of Old Testament Quotations in the New Testament." *Vigiliae Christianae* 67 (2013), 289–315.

Kedar, Benjamin. "Jewish Traditions in the Writings of Jerome." In *The Aramaic Bible: Targums in the Historical Context*, edited by D. R. G. Beattie and M. J. McNamara, 420–30. Sheffield: JSOT, 1994.

———. "The Latin Translations." In *Mikra: Text, Translation, Reading, and Interpretation of the Hebrew Bible in Ancient Judaism and Early Christianity*, edited by M. J. Mulder and H. Sysling, 331–34. Philadelphia: Fortress, 1988.

Kelly, J. N. D. "The Bible and the Latin Fathers." In *The Church's Use of the Bible: Past and Present*, edited by D. E. Nineham. London: SPCK, 1963.

———. *Jerome: His Life, Writings, and Controversies*. London: Duckworth, 1975.

Kessler, Edward. *An Introduction to Jewish-Christian Relations*. Cambridge: Cambridge University Press, 2010.

Kessler, Edward, and Neil Wenborn, eds. *A Dictionary of Jewish–Christian Relations*. Cambridge: Cambridge University Press, 2008.

Kieffer, Rene. "Jerome: His Exegesis and Hermeneutics." In *Hebrew Bible / Old Testament: The History of Its Interpretation*, vol. 1, *From the Beginnings to the Middle Age*, pt. 1, *Antiquity*, edited by Magne Saebo, 663–81. Gottingen: Vandenhoeck & Ruprecht, 1996.

Kimmerling, Baruch, Joel S. Migdal. *The Palestinian People: A History*. Cambridge, MA: Harvard University Press, 2003.

Kinzer, Mark S. *Postmissionary Messianic Judaism: Redefining Christian Engagement with the Jewish People*. Grand Rapids: Brazos, 2005.

Kinzig, Wolfram. "Jewish and 'Judaizing' Eschatologies in Jerome." In *Jewish Culture and Society under the Christian Roman Empire*, edited by Richard Kalmin and Seth Schwartz, 409–29. Leuven: Peeters, 2003.

———. "'Non-Separation': Closeness and Co-operation between Jews and Christians in the Fourth Century." *Vigiliae Christianae* 45 (1991) 27–53.

———. Review of *Anti-Judaism and Early Christian Identity: A Critique of the Scholarly Consensus*, by Miriam S. Taylor. *Journal of Theological Studies* 48 (1997) 643–49.

Kogan, Michael S. *Opening the Covenant: A Jewish Theology of Christianity*. New York: Oxford University Press, 2007.

Korn, Eugene, and John Pawlikowski, eds. *Two Faiths, One Covenant?: Jewish and Christian Identity in the Presence of the Other*. Lanham, MD: Rowman & Littlefield, 2005.

Kraus, Matthew. "Christian, Jews, and Pagans in Dialogue: Jerome on Ecclesiastes 12:1–7." *Hebrew Union College Annual* 70/71 (1999–2000) 183–231.

Krauss, S. "The Jews in the Works of the Church Fathers." *Jewish Quarterly Review* 6 (1894) 225–61.

Kreuzer, Siegfried. "From 'Old Greek' to the Recensions: Who and What Caused the Change of the Hebrew Reference Text of the Septuagint?" In *Septuagint Research: Issues and Challenges in the Study of the Greek Jewish Scriptures*, edited by Wolfgang Kraus and R. Glenn Wooden, 225–38. Atlanta: Society of Biblical Literature, 2006.

Kuehnel, Bianca. "Jewish Symbolism of the Temple and the Tabernacle and Christian Symbolism of the Holy Sepulchre and the Heavenly Tabernacle." *Jewish Art* (1987) 147–68.

BIBLIOGRAPHY

Kugel, James L. *How to Read the Bible: A Guide to Scripture, Then and Now.* New York: Free Press, 2007.
Kunin, Seth. "Judaism." In *Sacred Place,* edited by Jean Holm, with John Bowker, 115–48. London: Pinter, 1994.
La Bonnardière, Anne-Marie. "Did Augustine Use Jerome's Vulgate?" In *Augustine and the Bible,* translated and edited by Pamela Bright, 42–51. Notre Dame, IN: University of Notre Dame Press, 1986.
Lardet, Pierre. *L'Apologie de Jerome contre Rufin: Un commentaire.* Vigiliae Christianae Supplement 15. Leiden: Brill, 1993.
Law, Timothy Michael. *When God Spoke Greek: The Septuagint and the Making of the Christian Bible.* New York: Oxford University Press, 2013.
Leighton, Christopher M., Donald G. Dawe, and Avi Weinstein. "What Is the Meaning of 'Israel' for Jews and Christians?" In *Irreconcilable Differences: A Learning Resource for Jews and Christians,* edited by David Fox Sandmel, Rosann M. Catalano, and Christopher M. Leighton, 91–111. Boulder, CO: Westview, 2001.
Levinson, Joshua. "There Is No Place Like Home: Rabbinic Responses to the Christianization of Palestine." In *Jews, Christians, and the Roman Empire: The Poetics of Power in Late Antiquity,* edited by Natalie B. Dohrmann and Annette Yoshiko Reed, 99–120. Philadelphia: University of Pennsylvania Press, 2013.
Lieu, Judith. *Christian Identity in the Jewish and Graeco-Roman World.* Oxford: Oxford University Press, 2004.
———. *Image and Reality: The Jews in the World of the Christians in the Second Century.* London: T. & T. Clark, 1996.
———. "'The Parting of the Ways': Theological Construct or Historical Reality?" *Journal for the Study of the New Testament* 56 (1994) 101–19.
Limor, Ora. "Christian Sacred Space and the Jew." In *From Witness to Witchcraft: Jews and Judaism in Medieval Christian Thought,* edited by Jeremy Cohen, 55–77. Wiesbaden: Harrassowitz, 1996.
———. "'Holy Journey': Pilgrimage and Christian Sacred Landscape." In *Christians and Christianity in the Holy Land: From the Origins to the Latin Kingdoms,* edited by Ora Limor and Guy G. Stroumsa, 321–53. Turnhout: Bropols, 2006.
———. "Reading Sacred Space: Egeria, Paula, and the Christian Holy Land." In *De Sion exibit lex et verbum domini de Hierusalem,* edited by Yitzhak Hen, 1–15. Turnhout: Brepols, 2001.
Lindbeck, George. "What of the Future?: A Christian Response." In *Christianity in Jewish Terms,* edited by Tikva Frymer-Kensky, David Novak, Peter Ochs, David Fox Sandmel, and Michael A. Signer. Boulder, CO: Westview, 2000.
Lossl, Josef. "A Shift in Patristic Exegesis: Hebrew Clarity and Historical Verity in Augustine, Jerome, Julian of Aeclanum, and Theodore of Mopsuestia." *Augustinian Studies* 32:2 (2001) 157–75.
MacCormack, Sabine. "Loca Sancta: The Organization of Sacred Topography." In *The Blessing of Pilgrimage,* edited by Robert Ousterhout, 7–40. Chicago: University of Illinois Press, 1990.
Manuel, Frank E. *The Broken Staff: Judaism through Christian Eyes.* Cambridge, MA: Harvard University Press, 1992.
Maraval, Pierre. "The Bible as a Guide for Early Christian Pilgrim to the Holy Land." In *The Bible in Greek Christian Antiquity,* ed. and trans. Paul M. Blowers, 375–88. Notre Dame: University of Notre Dame Press, 1997.

Bibliography

Marcos, Natalio Fernandez. *The Septuagint in Context: Introduction to the Greek Version of the Bible*. Translated by Wilfred G. E. Watson. Leiden: Brill, 2000.

Markschies, Christoph. "Hieronymus und die *Hebraica Veritas*: Ein Beitrag zur Archaologie des protestantischen Schriftvertandnisses." In *Die Septuaginta zwischen Judentum und Christentum*, edited by Martin Hengel and Anna Maria Schwemer, 131–81. Tubingen: Mohr, 1994.

Markus, Robert A. *The End of Ancient Christianity*. Cambridge: Cambridge University Press, 1990.

———. "How on Earth Could Places Become Holy?" *Journal of Early Christian Studies* 2 (1994) 257–71.

Margerie, Bertrand de. *An Introduction to the History of Exegesis*. Vol. 2, *The Latin Fathers*. Translated by P. de Fontnouvelle. Petersham, MA: Saint Bede's, 1994.

McDermot, Gerald R. "A New Christian Zionism." *First Things*, May 13, 2015. http://www.firstthings.com/web-exclusives/2015/05/a-new-christian-zionism.

———. *The New Christian Zionism: Fresh Perspectives on Israel and the Land*. Downers Grove, IL: InterVarsity, 2016.

McKane, William. *Selected Christian Hebraists*. Cambridge: Cambridge University Press, 1989.

Metlen, Michael, "Letter of St. Jerome to the Gothic Clergymen Sunnia and Frithila Concerning Places in Their Copy of the Psalter Which Had Been Corrupted from the Septuagint." *Journal of English and German Philology* 36 (1937) 515–42.

Moore, James F. *Christian Theology after the Shoah*. Studies in the Shoah 7. Lanham, MD: University Press of America, 1993.

———. *Toward a Dialogical Community: A Post-Shoah Christian Theology*. Lanham, MD: University Press of America, 2004.

Muller, Mogens. *The First Bible of the Church: A Plea for the Septuagint*. Journal for the Study of the Old Testament Supplement Series 206. Sheffield: Sheffield Academic, 1996.

Musurillo, Herbert. *The Acts of the Christian Martyrs*. Oxford: Oxford University Press, 1972.

Newman, Hillel I. "Between Jerusalem and Bethlehem: Jerome and the Holy Places of Palestine." In *Sanctity of Time and Space in Tradition and Modernity*, edited by Alberdina Houtman, Marcel Poorthuis, and Joshua Schwartz, 215–30. Leiden: Brill, 1998.

———. "How Should We Measure Jerome's Hebrew Competence?" In *Jerome of Stridon: His Life, Writings and Legacy*, edited by Andrew Cain and Josef Lossl, 131–40. Burlington, VT: Ashgate, 2009.

———. "Jerome and the Jews." PhD diss., Hebrew University, January 1997.

———. "Jerome's Judaizers." *Journal of Early Christian Studies* 9 (2001) 421–52.

Novak, David. "From Supersessionism to Parallelism in Jewish-Christian Dialogue." In *Jews and Christians: People of God*, edited by Carl E. Braaten and Robert W. Jenson, 95–113. Grand Rapids: Eerdmans, 2003.

Nugent, Pauline. "Prefaces for Profit–Without Prophets." *Studia Patristica* 33 (1997) 352–57.

O'Connell, John P. *The Eschatology of Saint Jerome*. Mundelein, IL: Seminarii Sanctae Mariae ad Lacum, 1943.

Oden, Thomas C. *Classic Christianity: A Systematic Theology*. New York: HarperCollins, 1992.

———. *The Rebirth of Orthodoxy: Signs of New Life in Christianity*. San Francisco: HarperCollins, 2003.

BIBLIOGRAPHY

Oden, Thomas C., and J. I. Packer. *One Faith: The Evangelical Consensus*. Downers Grove, IL: InterVarsity, 2004.

"An Open Letter to Evangelicals and Other Interested Parties: The People of God, the Land of Israel, and the Impartiality of the Gospel." Submitted by the faculty of Knox Theological Seminary, Ft. Lauderdale, FL, 2002. http://www.bible-researcher.com/openletter.html.

Orthodox Study Bible. Edited by Jack Norman Sparks. Nashville: T. Nelson, 2008.

Paget, James Carlton. Review of *Anti-Judaism and Early Christian Identity*, by Miriam S. Taylor. *Zeitschrift für antikes Christentum* 1 (1997) 195-225.

Parker, David, editor. *Jesus, Salvation and the Jewish People: Papers on the Uniqueness of Jesus and Jewish Evangelism*. Milton Keynes: Paternoster, 2011.

Parkes, James. *The Conflict of the Church and the Synagogue: A Study in the Origins of Antisemitism*. London: Soncino, 1934.

Patrologiae Latina, edited by J. P. Migne. Paris: Migne, 1844.

Penna, Angelo. *San Gerolamo*. Turin: Marietti, 1949.

Perrone, Lorenzo. "'The Mystery of Judaea' (Jerome, *Ep*. 46): The Holy City of Jerusalem between History and Symbol in Early Christian Thought." *Jerusalem: Its Sanctity and Centrality to Judaism, Christianity, and Islam*, edited by Lee I. Levine, 221–39. New York: Continuum, 1999.

Porter, Stanley E., and Brook W. R. Pearson, "Why the Split? Christians and Jews by the Fourth Century." *Journal of Greco-Roman Christianity and Judaism* 1 (2000) 82–119.

Rausch, David A. *Fundamentalist-Evangelicals and Anti-Semitism*. Valley Forge, PA: Trinity, 1993.

Reaburn, Mary. "St. Jerome and Porphyry Interpret the Book of Daniel." *Austrailian Biblical Review* 52 (2004) 1–18.

Rebenich, Stefan. *Jerome*. New York: Routledge, 2002.

———. "Jerome: The 'Vir Trilinguis' and the 'Hebraica Veritas.'" *Vigiliae Christianae* 47 (1993) 50–77.

Reed, Annette Yoshiko, and Adam H. Becker. "Introduction: Traditional Models and New Directions." In *The Ways that Never Parted: Jews and Christians in Late Antiquity and the Early Middle Ages*, edited by Adam H. Becker and Annette Yoshiko Reed, 1–34. 2003. Reprint, Minneapolis: Fortress, 2007.

Reinhartz, Adele. "A Fork in the Road or a Multi-Lane Highway?: New Perspectives on the 'Parting of the Ways' Between Judaism and Christianity." In *The Changing Face of Judaism, Christianity, and Other Greco-Roman Religions in Antiquity*, edited by Ian H. Henderson and Gerbern S. Oegema, 280–95. Gottingen: Gutersloher Verlagshaus, 2006.

Richardson, Peter. *Israel in the Apostolic Church*. Cambridge: Cambridge University Press, 1969.

Ridderbos, Herman. *Paul: An Outline of His Theology*. Translated by John Richard DeWitt. Grand Rapids: Eerdmans, 1975.

Robertson, O. Palmer. *The Israel of God: Yesterday, Today, and Tomorrow*. Phillipsburg, NJ: Presbyterian and Reformed, 2000.

Rokeah, David. *Jews, Pagans, and Christians in Conflict*. Leiden: Brill, 1982.

Rosenberg, Stuart E. *The Christian Problem: A Jewish View*. New York: Hippocrene, 1986.

Rousseau, Philip. *Ascetics, Authority, and the Church: In the Age of Jerome and Cassian*. Oxford: Oxford University Press, 1978.

Bibliography

Rubenstein, Richard L. *After Auschwitz: History, Theology, and Contemporary Judaism.* 2nd ed. Baltimore: Johns Hopkins University Press, 1992.

Rudin, A. James. "Current Evangelical-Jewish Relations: A Jewish View." In *Evangelicals and Jews in an Age of Pluralism*, edited by Marc H. Tanenbaum, Marvin R. Wilson, and A. James Rudin, 29–43. Grand Rapids: Baker, 1984.

Rudolph, David J., and Joel Willitts, eds. *Introduction to Messianic Judaism: Its Ecclesial Context and Biblical Foundations.* Grand Rapids: Zondervan, 2013.

Ruether, Herman J., and Rosemary Radford Ruether. *The Wrath of Jonah: The Crisis of Religious Nationalism in the Israeli-Palestinian Conflict.* 2nd ed. Minneapolis: Fortress, 2002.

Ruether, Rosemary. *Faith and Fratricide: The Theological Roots of Anti-Semitism.* New York: Seabury, 1974.

Sachar, Howard M. *A History of Israel: From the Rise of Zionism to Our Time.* 3rd ed. New York: Knopf, 2007.

Salvesen, Alison. "A Convergence of the Ways?: The Judaizing of Christian Scripture by Origen and Jerome." In *The Ways that Never Parted: Jews and Christians in Late Antiquity and the Early Middle Ages*, edited by Adam H. Becker and Annette Yoshiko Reed, 233–58. 2003. Reprint, Minneapolis: Fortress, 2007.

Schreckenberg, Heinz. *Die christlichen Adversus-Judaeos-Texte und ihr literarisches und historisches Umfeld (1.-11. Jh.).* Frankfurt am Main: P. Lang, 1990.

Schremer, Adiel. *Brothers Estranged: Heresy, Christianity, and Jewish Identity in Late Antiquity.* Oxford: Oxford University Press, 2010.

Schulz-Flugel, Eva. "The Latin Old Testament Tradition." In *Hebrew Bible / Old Testament: The History of Its Interpretation*, vol. 1, *From the Beginnings to the Middle Ages*, pt. 1, *Antiquity*, edited by Magne Saebo, 645–50. Gottingen: Vandenhoeck & Ruprecht, 1996.

Schwartz, Seth. "Memory in Josephus and the Culture of the Jews in the First Century." In *Common Judaism: Explorations in Second-Temple Judaism*, edited by Wayne O. McCready and Adele Reinhartz, 185–94. Minneapolis: Fortress, 2006.

Schwarz, Werner. *Principles and Problems of Biblical Translation: Some Reformation Controversies and Their Background.* Cambridge: Cambridge University Press, 1955.

Segal, Alan F. *Rebecca's Children: Judaism and Christianity in the Roman World.* Cambridge, MA: Harvard University Press, 1986.

Segal, Eliezer. "*Aristeas* or Haggadah: Talmudic Legend and the Greek Bible in Palestinian Judaism." In *Common Judaism: Explorations in Second-Temple Judaism*, edited by Wayne O. McCready and Adele Reinhartz, 159–72. Minneapolis: Fortress, 2006.

Seidman, Naomi. *Faithful Renderings: Jewish-Christian Difference and the Politics of Translation.* Chicago: University of Chicago Press, 2006.

Shutt, R. J. H., trans. *Letter of Aristeas.* In *The Old Testament Pseudepigrapha*, edited by James H. Charlesworth, vol. 2. Garden City, NY: Doubleday, 1985.

Simon, Marcel. *Verus Israel: A Study of the Relations between Christians and Jews in the Roman Empire, AD 135-425.* Translated by H. McKeating. London: Vallentine Mitchell, 1986.

Sivan, Hagith. *Palestine in Late Antiquity.* Oxford: Oxford University Press, 2008.

———. "Pilgrimage, Monasticism, and the Emergence of Christian Palestine in the 4th Century." In *Blessings of Pilgrimage*, edited by Robert G. Ousterhout, 54–65. Chicago: University of Illinois Press, 1990.

Bibliography

Sizer, Stephen. *Zion's Christian Soldiers?: The Bible, Israel and the Church*. Downers Grove, IL: InterVarsity, 2008.

Skarsaune, Oskar, and Reidar Hvalvik, eds. *Jewish Believers in Jesus: The Early Centuries*. Peabody, MA: Hendrickson, 2007.

Skehan, Patrick W. "St. Jerome and the Canon of the Holy Scriptures." In *A Monument to Saint Jerome*, edited by Francis X. Murphy, 259-87. New York: Sheed & Ward, 1952.

Smith, Julie Ann. "'My Lord's Native Land': Mapping the Christian Holy Land." *Church History* 76:1 (March 2007) 1-31.

Soulen, R. Kendall. *The God of Israel and Christian Theology*. Minneapolis: Fortress, 1996.

Sparks, H. F. D. "Jerome as Biblical Scholar." In *The Cambridge History of the Bible*, vol. 1, edited by P. R Ackroy and C. F. Evans, 510-41. Cambridge: Cambridge University Press, 1970.

Spence, Stephen. *The Parting of the Ways: The Roman Church as a Case Study*. Leuven: Peeters, 2004.

Stamper, John W. *The Architecture of Roman Temples: The Republic to the Middle Empire*. Cambridge: Cambridge University Press, 2005.

Stemberger, Gunter. "Christians and Jews in Byzantine Palestine." In *Christians and Christianity in the Holy Land: From the Origins to the Latin Kingdoms*, edited by Ora Limor and Guy G. Stroumsa, 293-319. Turnhout: Bropols, 2006.

———. "Exegetical Contacts between Christians and Jews in the Roman Empire." In *Hebrew Bible / Old Testament: The History of Its Interpretation*, vol. 1, *From the Beginnings to the Middle Ages*, pt. 1, *Antiquity*, edited by Magne Saebo, 569-86. Gottingen: Vandenhoeck & Ruprecht, 1996.

———. *Jews and Christians in the Holy Land*. Translated by Ruth Tuschling. Edinburgh: T. & T. Clark, 2000.

Stendahl, John. "Jewish Concern for the Land," pt. 2. In *Covenantal Conversations: Christians in Dialogue with Jews and Judaism*, edited by Darrell Jodock, 99-113. Minneapolis: Fortress, 2008.

Stendahl, Krister. "Qumran and Supersessionism—and the Road Not Taken." In *The Bible and the Dead Sea Scrolls*, edited by James H. Charlesworth, vol. 3, 397-406. Waco, TX: Baylor University Press, 2006.

Stern, David H. *Messianic Judaism: A Modern Movement with an Ancient Past*. Clarksville, MD: Messianic Jewish, 2007.

Suomala, Karla. "Jewish Concern for the Land," pt. 1. In *Covenantal Conversations: Christians in Dialogue with Jews and Judaism*, edited by Darrell Jodock, 92-99. Minneapolis: Fortress, 2008.

Sutcliffe, E. F. "Jerome." In *The West from the Fathers to the Reformation*, edited by G. W. H. Lampe, 80-101. Cambridge University Press, 1969.

Swete, H. B. *An Introduction to the Old Testament in Greek*. Cambridge: Cambridge University Press, 1914.

Tanenbaum, Marc H., Marvin R. Wilson, and A. James Rudin, eds. *Evangelicals and Jews in Conversation on Scripture, Theology, and History*. Grand Rapids: Baker, 1978.

Taylor, Joan E. *Christians and the Holy Places: The Myth of Jewish-Christian Origins*. Oxford: Clarendon, 1993.

———. "Introduction." In Eusebius of Caesarea, *The Onomasticon*, translated by G. S. P. Freeman-Grenville. Jerusalem: Carta, 2003.

Taylor, Miriam S. *Anti-Judaism and Early Christian Identity: A Critique of the Scholarly Consensus*. Studia Post-Biblica 46. Leiden: Brill, 1995.

Bibliography

Tkacz, Catherine Brown. "Labor Tam Utilis: The Creation of the Vulgate." *Vigiliae Christianae* 50 (1996) 42–72.

Torjesen, Karen J. "The Rhetoric of the Literal Sense: Changing Strategies of Persuasion from Origen to Jerome." In *Origeniana Septima*, edited by W. A. Bienert and U. Kuhneweg, 633–44. Leuven: Leuven University Press, 1999.

Tsafrir, Yoram. "Jewish Pilgrimage in the Roman and Byzantine Periods." *Akten des XII. Internationalen Kongresses für christliche Archäologie (Jahrbuch fur Antike und Christentum* 20.1) (1995) 369–76.

Tuchman, Barbara W. *Bible and Sword: England and Palestine from the Bronze Age to Balfour.* New York: Random House, 1984.

Van Buren, Paul M. *A Theology of the Jewish Christian Reality.* 3 vols. New York: Seabury, 1980–88.

Vanhoozer, Kevin J. *The Drama of Doctrine: A Canonical-Linguistic Approach to Christian Theology.* Louisville: Westminster John Knox, 2005.

VanderKam, James, and Peter Flint. *The Meaning of the Dead Sea Scrolls.* San Francisco: HarperCollins, 2002.

Vanlaningham, Michael G. *Christ, the Savior of Israel: An Evaluation of the Dual Covenant and Sonderweg Interpretations of Paul's Letters.* Frankfurt: P. Lang, 2012.

Vermes, Geza. *An Introduction to the Complete Dead Sea Scrolls.* Minneapolis: Fortress, 1999.

Vessey, Mark. "Jerome and the *Jeromanesque*." In *Jerome of Stridon: His Life, Writings, and Legacy*, edited by Andrew Cain and Josef Lossl, 225–35. Burlington, VT: Ashgate, 2009.

———. "Jerome's Origen: The Making of a Christian Literary Persona." *Studia Patristica* 28 (1993a) 135–45.

Walker, P. W. L. *Holy City, Holy Places: Christian Attitudes to Jerusalem and the Holy Land in the Fourth Century.* Oxford: Clarendon, 1990.

Ware, Timothy. *The Orthodox Church.* New York: Penguin, 1993.

Wasserstein, Abraham, and David J. Wasserstein. *The Legend of the Septuagint: From Classical Antiquity to Today.* Cambridge: Cambridge University Press, 2006.

Weingarten, Susan. *The Saint's Saints: Hagiography and Geography in Jerome.* Leiden: Brill, 2005.

White, Carolinne. *The Correspondence (394–419) between Jerome and Augustine of Hippo.* Lewiston, NY: Edwin Mellen, 1990.

White, L. Michael. "Adolph Harnack and the 'Expansion' of Early Christianity: A Reappraisal of Social History." *The Second Century* 5:2 (1985/1986) 97–127.

Wiesen, David S. *St. Jerome as a Satirist. A Study in Christian Latin Thought and Letters.* Ithica, NY: Cornell University Press, 1964.

Wigoder, Geoffrey. *Jewish-Christian Relations since the Second World War.* Manchester: Manchester University Press, 1988.

Willebrands, Johannes. *Church and Jewish People: New Considerations.* New York: Paulist, 1992.

Wilken, Robert L. "*In Novissimis Diebus*: Biblical Promises, Jewish Hopes, and Early Christian Exegesis." *Journal of Early Christian Studies* 1 (1993) 1–19.

———. *John Chrysostom and the Jews: Rhetoric and Reality in the Late 4th Century.* Berkeley: University of California Press, 1983.

———. *The Land Called Holy: Palestine in Christian History and Thought.* New Haven, CT: Yale University Press, 1992.

Bibliography

Wilkinson, John. *Jerusalem Pilgrims before the Crusades*. 2nd ed. Warminster: Aris & Phillips, 2002.

———. "Jewish Holy Places and the Origins of Christian Pilgrimage." In *The Blessings of Pilgrimage*, edited by Robert Ousterhout, 41–53. Chicago: University of Illinois Press, 1990.

———. "Visits to Jewish Tombs by Early Christians." *Akten des XII. Internationalen Kongresses für christliche Archäologie (Jahrbuch fur Antike und Christentum 20.1)* (1995) 452–65.

Willebrands, Johannes Cardinal. *Church and Jewish People: New Considerations*. New York: Paulist, 1992.

Williams, A. Lukyn. *Adversus Judaeos: A Bird's-Eye View of Christian Apologiae until the Renaissance*. Cambridge: Cambridge University Press, 1935.

Williams, Megan Hale. "Lessons from Jerome's Jewish Teachers: Exegesis and Cultural Interaction in Late Antique Palestine." In *Jewish Biblical Interpretation and Cultural Exchange Comparative Exegesis in Context*, edited by Natalie B. Dohrmann and David Stern, 66–86. Philadelphia: University of Pennsylvania Press, 2007.

———. *The Monk and the Book: Jerome and the Making of Christian Scholarship*. Chicago: University of Chicago Press, 2006.

Williamson, Clark M. *A Guest in the House of Israel: Post-Holocaust Church Theology*. Louisville: Westminster John Knox, 1993.

Wilson, Stephen G. *Related Strangers: Jews and Christians, 70–170 C.E.* Minneapolis: Fortress, 1995.

Worship and Service Hymnal. Carol Stream: Hope, 1974.

Wurthwein, Ernst. *The Text of the Old Testament: An Introduction to the Biblia Hebraica*. 3rd ed. Revised and expanded by Alexander Achilles Fischer, translated by Erroll F. Rhoads. Grand Rapids: Eerdmans, 2014.

Wyschogrod, Michael. *Abraham's Promise: Judaism and Jewish-Christian Relations*. Edited by R. Kendall Soulen. Grand Rapids: Eerdmans, 2004.

———. "The Bishops and the Middle East." *First Things*, April 1990, 15–16.

Yoder, John Howard. *The Jewish-Christian Schism Revisited*. Edited by Michael G. Cartwright and Peter Ochs. Grand Rapids: Eerdmans, 2003.

Young, Frances M. *Biblical Exegesis in the Formation of Christian Culture*. Cambridge: Cambridge University Press, 1997.

———. "The Interpretation of Scripture." In *The First Christian Theologians: An Introduction to Theology in the Early Church*, edited by G. R. Evans, 24–38. Malden, MA: Blackwell, 2004.

Zenger, Erich. "The Covenant That Was Never Revoked: The Foundations of a Christian Theology of Judaism." In *The Catholic Church and the Jewish People: Recent Reflections from Rome*, edited by Philip A. Cunningham, Norbert J. Hofmann, and Joseph Sievers, 92–112. New York: Fordham University Press, 2007

Subject Index

Abigaum, Jerome's letter to, 120
acrostic poems, 45
Adam
    burial place, 106, 126–27
    and Church of the Holy Sepulcher, 116
Adversus Judaeos tradition, 3, 4, 31, 51n90, 84, 138, 150
Aelia Capitolina, 99, 122, 124
Aelius Donatus, 1, 89
aggada, hidden Christian meaning in, 79
Aitken, James A., 145
Akiba (Rabbi), 79
Alexander of Cappadocia, 101
Alexandria, library in, 37
"All Hail the Power of Jesus' Name," 149
allegorical and spiritual senses, 6–7, 77–78, 87
Allison, Gregg, 153
alms, 97
Ambrose, 4, 31, 55n108, 133n157
American Jewish Committee, 151, 155
American Schools of Oriental Research, 144, 144n14
Antioch, 1, 39, 100, 111
Antipatris, 112
antiquity, authority of, 66
apocryphal texts, 44–47, 55, 59, 61–62
    danger of, 47
    incorporation into Latin canon, 68
    Jerome citing as "Scripture," 63
    Jerome's attitude toward, 46, 76
Apollinaris, 74, 94

Aquila, 34, 65, 82, 85
Aquilea, 100
Arabs and Israel, 166–68, 171, 173
Aristeas, 36, 37n29, 37n33, 38
Athanasius, 43–44
    Jerome sanctioning of writings, 47
Augustine, 5
    City of God, 31
    on Christian converts from Judaism, 83n70
    On Christian Doctrine, 30
    correspondence with Jerome, 83
    Jerome defense to, 59, 74
    Jerome's conflict with, 48–53
    on Jerome's translation skills, 31
    Questions on the Heptateuch, 53
    request for Jerome's translation of the Septuagint, 52–53
    and Western church's councils, 68
authority, Jews as, 123

Bader-Saye, Scott, 159n74
Balfour Declaration, 168
Barabbas. *See* Baranina (Barabbas)
Baranina (Barabbas), 55–57, 74, 90
Barnabas, 3n5, 17
Barth, Karl, 170
Bartholomew (patriarch), 151
Baruch, 61, 69
Baum, Gregory, 19
Becker, Adam H., "The Ways that Never Parted," 22
Benedict XVI (pope), 172

Subject Index

"The Berlin Declaration on the Uniqueness of Christ and Jewish Evangelism in Europe Today," 156
Bethlehem, 2, 8, 33, 89, 99, 107–37, 139, 164–65, 167, 172–74
   Church of the Nativity, 7
   historical roots in David, 137
   as holier than Jerusalem, 119–20
   as Jerome's center of earthly sanctity, 130
   Jerome's description of fields, 114
   Jerome's relocation to, 100–111, 167
   Jerome's views on, 136
   Jerome's writings vs. Eusebius, 122
   monastery, 7, 131, 139
   Paula's arrival, 113–14
   promoting over Jerusalem, 124–35
   as supreme sacred space, 165
biblical literalism, 154
Birkat Ha Minim (Curse on the Heretics), 11, 23, 86
Bitton-Ashkelony, Brouria, 118
Boyarin, Daniel, 22, 169
Braverman, Jay, analysis of Jerome's commentary on Daniel, 80
Burge, Gary, 171

Cain, Andrew, 28, 43, 67, 130, 143
Calvary, 106, 126
canon, 43–49, 55, 58–59, 61–63, 67–68, 141
Carthage (397), canon of, 44
Castrutius, Jerome's letter to, 120
cataloguing the holy land, 121–23
Chalcis, 88, 100, 110n53
chiliasts, 132
chosen people, Jews as, 152–53
Chosen People Ministries, 155
Christ. *See* Jesus Christ
Christian Apocrypha, 55. *See also* apocryphal texts
   defending, 61–62
Christian canon, Greek vs. Jewish sacred text in Hebrew, 43
Christian church
   claim to holy land, 99
   as Israel's replacement, 139
   and Jewish Scriptures, 103
Christian concerns for the Jewish state
   dubious support for, 172–74
   qualified support, 170–72
   unqualified support, 168–70
Christian exclusivity, Jerome's perception of, 93
Christian holy land, Israel as, 7
Christian identity
   new course of, 88
   rooted in opposition to the Jews, 138
Christian land theology, Madaba Map and, 109
Christian Old Testament scripture, 140–46
Christian pilgrimage, 101–9
   first detailed itinerary for Palestine, 102
   origin of, 103
Christian pilgrims, claims on tombs of Old Testament personalities, 107–8
Christian supersessionism
   absence of, 157–63
   contradictions necessitated by, 63–64
   defining, 2–4
   economic, 2
   essence of, 138
   Jerome's reshaping of, 71
   mild, 152–57
   punitive, 2–3
   strong, 149–51
   structural, 3
   temple's desolation as proof, 133
Christian writers, in Jerome's time, 167
Christian Zionism, 168–70, 172
   Reformed evangelicals document to combat, 172–74
Christianity
   conversion of Roman emperor to, 163
   equal legitimacy with Judaism, 157
   Harnack on superiority, 11
   Jerome's loyalty to tradition, 92
   vs. Judaism in the fourth century, 148
   as only true religion, 10
   post-supersession, 163

Subject Index

Christians/Jews interaction
  borders, 6–8
  Christian supersessionism of
    Judaism, 10–13
  continuity and interchange, 20–25
  separation proposal in 4th c., 23
  separation with continuity, 13–14
  separation with equal legitimacy,
    14–20
Christians United for Israel, 169
Church of Eleona, 7
Church of the Holy Sepulcher, 7, 105–
    06, 109, 130, 131
  and Adam, 116
  Jerome on, 113
churches, construction near holy places,
    102
Clark, Elizabeth, 77
Clement of Alexandria, 38, 91
Cohen, Shaye, 11
Commission for Religious Relations
    with the Jews (1974), 158
Constantine, 7, 9, 31, 101–02, 103n19,
    104–05, 125, 132, 136, 164
  and memorialization of sacred
    space, 125–26
Constantinople, 1, 31, 39, 81, 100, 151
Constantius, 31
contempt
  language evolution into doctrine,
    148
  theology of, 31
  undoing the notion of, 161
Council of Jamnia (Yavneh), 11, 23
Council of Rome, canonical list, 44, 69
Council of Trent, 67
Council of Yavneh (Jamnia), 23
covenants
  God with Israel, 6, 158–59, 161–62c
  simultaneously two, 152
Cranfield, C.E.B., 152
Crusaders, 166, 168
Curse on the Heretics (Birkat Ha
    Minim), 11, 23, 86
Cyprian, 3n5, 47
Cyril of Jerusalem, 38, 106n34, 130

Damasus (pope), 2, 34, 65, 101
  Jerome's defense for delaying
    response to, 147
  Jerome's letters to, 72–73
  and Jerome's translations, 32
Daniel
  confusion from copying errors, 40
  Jerome's commentary on, 80
  prologue, 58
David, 99, 122, 137, 140
  desire to see the goodness of the
    Lord, 134
  tomb of, 107, 123n117
Dead Sea Scrolls, 35, 143–44
  Institute, 144
"Declaration on the Relation of the
    Church to Non-Christian
    Religions" (Roman Catholic
    church), 157
Desiderius, Jerome's invitation to visit
    Bethlehem, 120
dialogue, continual, 161–62
diaspora Jewry, and ancient homeland,
    168
The Disaster, Arabs and, 166
dispensational premillennialism, 169–70
dispensationalism, 154
divine blessing, Israel forfeiture of, 12
divine truth, in Hebrew sources, 42–43,
    66, 138, 140, 147
divinity of Jesus, 17
Donatus, 89
Dor, 112
dual covenant theology, 156, 159, 161
Dunn, James, 16–17, 21, 24
Durham-Tubingen Research
    Symposium on Earliest
    Christianity and Judaism, 16–17

Eastern council of Laodecia (364), 44
Ecclesiastes, Jerome's commentary on,
    34, 65, 77
ecclesiastical texts, 44
economic supersessionism, 2
Ecumenical Patriarchate of
    Constantinople, 151
Egeria (nun from Spain), 102

Subject Index

Eleazar (son of Aaron), 108
Elijah, 112, 114
Emmaus, 112
Ephrem, 133
Epiphanius, 31n5, 38, 129
Erasmus, 27
ethnic differences, Christians vs. Jews, 17
Eucaenia (annual ceremony to commemorate dedication of church), 105
Eusebius of Caesarea, 31n5, 38, 40, 72, 91, 105, 122, 125, 130n144, 132, 164
    on Christian holy land, 125
    Onomasticon (travel guide), 7, 102, 108, 121–23
Eusebius of Cremona, 57
Eusebius of Emesa, 71
Eustochium, 85, 111, 116
evangelical Christians, 149–50, 152–57, 171–73
    and exclusivity of Christianity, 156
    and Messianic Jews, 155
    opposition to anti-Semitism, 154
Evangelical Lutheran Church, in America, 161
Evangelical Theological Society, 156

Firmilianus (bishop in Cappadocia), 102
Francis (pope), 172
Fredriksen, Paula, 23–24
Friends of Israel Gospel Ministry, 156
"Fundamental Agreement between the Holy See and the State of Israel" (1993), 171
fundamentalists in America, 154

Gager, John, 20, 159–60
Galatians, commentaries on, 47
garden of Eden, vs. garden near Jesus' tomb, 106
Gentile Christian church, as the true Israel, 31
German Protestant Church, complicity in Holocaust, 160
Gibeah, 112

Graves, Michael, 29, 42, 89, 94, 145
    on Hebrew tutors, 79
Great Britain, Jewish restorationist doctrine, 168–69
Greek manuscripts. *See also* Septuagint
    textual criticism of, 143
Gregory of Nazianzus, 1, 100, 132, 133
Gregory of Nyssa, 128
Grudem, Wayne, 150

Habakkuk, commentaries on, 47
Haggai, commentaries on, 47
Hanukkah (Feast of Lights), 105
Harnack, Adolf von, *Die Mission und Ausbreitung des Christentums in den Ersten Drei Jahrhunderten*, 10–11
Haynes, Stephen, 169
Hayward, T.R., 27, 81
heavenly Jerusalem, 100, 110, 113, 121, 124–28, 132, 134, 137, 139, 165, 172
Hebraica veritas. *See* Hebrew truth (*Hebraica veritas*)
Hebrew alphabet, significance of number of letters in, 45
Hebrew canon
    double books, 45
    Jerome's preference for, 43–48
Hebrew language, 98, 141, 166
    Jerome on learning, 75, 85
    Jerome's reason for translating from, 57
    Jerome's study of, 1, 5, 8, 29, 30, 72, 79, 141–42
    Jerome's view of, 53, 73–74, 78
    mystical truth embedded in, 53
    as original tongue before Babel, 72, 78
Hebrew Old Testament, 5
    canonical list, 69
    Jerome's elevation of authority of, 30
    Jerome's preference for, 33–43, 58, 72, 75, 142
    Jerome's translation from, 35
    Orthodox churches and, 145
    textual criticism of, 143

Subject Index

ultimate authority, 42
Hebrew truth (*Hebraica veritas*), 4, 33, 34n18, 35, 45, 48, 49, 53, 59–61, 70, 73, 86, 88, 123, 137, 139, 140, 141, 143, 146, 147
    Christian church and, 70–98
    Jerome's ambivalent approach, 86–88
    Jerome's discourse about, 71–82
    Jerome's gradual conversion to, 91
    Jerome's move towards, 146–47
    resolution of Jerome's approach to, 88–98
    vs. Septuagint, 65–66
Hebrew tutors, 5, 72, 74, 76, 79, 82. *See also* Jewish teachers
Hebrews, vs. Jews, Jerome's use, 96–97
Helena (queen), 7, 102
heretics, Jerome on Christian, 94
Herod the Great, 104
Hesychius, 39
Hilarion, 129
Hillary, Jerome sanctioning of writings, 47
Himmelfarb, Martha, 21
Hippo (393), canon of, 44
Hirshman, Marc, 80
Holocaust, 14, 15, 20, 139–40, 148–50, 154, 156–57, 160, 172, 175
Holocaust theologians, 160, 169, 173
holy city, Jerome remapping, 124–35
holy land, 1, 7–8, 99, 100–01, 106, 110, 125, 128, 131, 132, 135–39, 164, 171–74
    cataloguing, 121–23
    Christian maps of, 108–09, 137
    Christian monasticism in, 108
    history of subjugation, 166–68
    Jerome's remapping from Jewish to Christian, 111–23
Holy of Holies, 106
holy places, churches associated with, 102
Holy Sepulcher, Church of the, 7, 105–06, 109, 130, 131
    and Adam, 116
    Jerome on, 113
holy space
    creation by Jesus' presence, 115
    Jerome's understanding of, 117
Holy Spirit, and Septuagint changes, 145
Horbury, William, 18–19
hosanna, 73
Hunt, E.D., 131, 133

Ibn Ezra, 80
idolatry, 99, 129, 131, 132, 135
Ignatius, 17
Innocent I (pope), 68
Institute for Christian and Jewish Studies, 161
Institute for Jewish-Catholic Relations, 159
Institute of Holy Land Studies, 155
interfaith text study, 162
International Catholic-Jewish Liaison Committe (1970), 158
International Organization for Septuagint and Cognate Studies (IOSCS), 144–45
Isaac, Jules, 13–14
Isaac's sacrifice at Golgotha, 106
Isaiah, Jerome's commentary on, 62
Israel, State of
    calls for financial divestiture, 173
    Christian concerns for, 168–70
    conflict over borders, 167
    criticism of, 171–73
    establishment of, 166, 175
    Orthodox and Roman Catholic priests in, 168
    Orthodox Christian communities and, 173
    Roman Catholic relations with, 171–72
    support for, 155, 169
Issac, Munther, 173

Jacobs, Andrew, 29, 41, 92, 114, 130
Jacob's well, 115
Jeremiah, Jerome's commentary on, 80, 145

Subject Index

Jerome
  attendance of Jewish synagogue services, 74, 80–81
  authoritarian spirit, 66, 118
  authority as mediator of truth, 96
  canonical list, 69
  desiring to be inspired by Spirit, 64
  excommunication of, 129–30
  first journey to Palestine, 111–15
  form of self-promotion, 96
  as gatekeeper, 95–98
  Hebrew as source text for Latin translations, 143
  historical consequences of influence, 67
  as iconoclast, 88–92
  letters with derogatory comments about Jews, 82–84
  mission to return to the source, 32
  on Old Testament scriptures, 43–48, 142
  ordination as priest, 100
  personal contact with Jewish teachers, 148
  pilgrimage and settlement in Bethlehem, 100–111
  on pilgrimage to holy land, 100, 127–29
  as prophet, 64
  purposes for writings, 81
  reactions to Latin translations of, 67
  recent scholarship on, 26–29
  reputation from relationship with female friends, 109–10
  research on textual-critical import, 145
  responses to Augustine, 50–52
  as scholar and monk, 28
  self-description as 4th-century author, 27
  self-motivated intrusion into Hebraic culture, 174
  self-portrait, 65
  Septuagint vs. Hebrew truth, 65–66
  Stridon as birthplace, 1
  textual shift from Greek Septuagint to Hebrew text, 141–43
  translation skills, Augustine on, 31
  views
    ambivalent hermeneutical shift, 147–48
    argument against divine inspiration of Septuagint, 5
    on benefits of the earthly Jerusalem, 126
    as innovative supersessionist, 4–8
    insults against Judaizers, 93–94
    on Jewish aspirations for regaining holy land, 1
    on Old Testament scriptures, 143–46
    rejection of Christian tradition in favor of Jewish, 92
    theory of language, 53
    as traditionalist, 92–95
Jerome's authority, vs. church's authority, 52
Jerome's trajectory on Old Testament, 148–63
  one covenant people (strong supersessionism), 149–51
  two covenant peoples (mild supersessionism), 152–57
  two covenant peoples (no supersessionism), 157–63
Jerome's trajectory on sacred space, 165–74
Jerome's writings
  Against John of Jerusalem, 130
  Book of Hebrew Names, 121
  Book of Hebrew Places, 121, 122
  commentaries, 77–82, 85–86, 145
    on Daniel, 80
    on Ecclesiastes, 34, 65, 77
    on Ephesians, 47
    on Galatians, 47
    on Habakkuk, 47
    on Haggai, 47
    on Isaiah, 62, 125
    on Jeremiah, 80, 145
    on Micah, 47
    on Nahum, 47
    on Obadiah, 91, 92

Subject Index

on Philemon, 47
on Titus, 47
on Zephaniah, 47
Hebrew Questions on Genesis, 6, 26–27, 81, 121
On Illustrious Men, 64, 98
Jerusalem, 113, 164
   charity for the poor, 97
   Church of the Resurrection, 7
   featured on the Madaba Map, 109
   Jerome's shifts in interpretation of scripture, 126
   Jerome's views on, 136
   Jerome's writings vs. Eusebius, 122
   as Jewish capital of restored Israel, 154
   replacement of eschatological sanctity, 131–35
   replacement of present sanctity, 124–31
   souvenirs, 105
   spiritual virtues, 116–17
Jesus Christ, 104, 152
   divinity of, 17
   faith in, 153n45
   fulfillment in, 2
   Jewish rejection as messiah, 3
   Jews as killers of, 31, 135
   Jews cursed for rejection of, 147
   salvation through, 158
Jewish customs, 81, 83, 84, 95, 108
Jewish exegesis, absence in Christian writings, 89
Jewish fables, vs. Jewish midrashic traditions, 80
Jewish guilt for Christ's death, Roman Catholic revocation of tradition, 157–58
Jewish pilgrimage, background to, 104
Jewish prayers, 86
Jewish religion, vitality of, 15
Jewish revolts (70, 135 CE), 11, 16, 17, 23, 140
Jewish sacred text in Hebrew, vs. Christian sacred text in Greek, 43
Jewish State. *See* Israel, State of

Jewish teachers, 4, 26–29, 39, 70, 72, 76, 79, 83, 85, 86–89, 91, 141, 142, 146, 148, 161
   Hebrew study from, 76–77
   justification for hiring, 74
   referred to as "my Hebrews," 96
Jewish temple, 17, 99, 103–11, 115, 122, 164
   destruction, 11, 12, 117, 135
   proposal to rebuild, 132–33, 166
Jewish theologians, interreligious discussion with Christians, 162
Jews. *See also* Christians/Jews interaction
   attitude towards Jerome, 142
   authority of, 76
   Christian church's indebtedness to, 139
   Christianity's stereotypes vs. Jerome's view, 67
   church as replacement for, 150
   claims on Palestine, 99
   emphasis on legitimacy, 154
   vs. Hebrews, Jerome's use, 96–97
   holding the key to truth, 123
   Jerome's derogatory discourse against, 82–86
   as Jerome's tutors, 5
   Jerome's views as a rejected people, 93
   land as God's dwelling place, 164
   in North Africa, 83
   as pejorative description, 147
   relevance in Bible's storyline, 3
   Rufinus' attack on, 56
   "witness-people" theology of, 169
Jews for Jesus, 156
John (bishop in Jerusalem), 129–30
John Cassian, 131
John Chrysostom, 3n5, 4, 81, 84, 133
   sermons against Jews, 31
John Paul II (pope), 172
Jordan River, 101, 107, 114, 121
Josephus, 37, 38, 80, 104n25
Joshua, 7, 109, 110, 127
   tomb of, 108
Judaizers, 6, 22, 29, 58, 93–95, 132, 167

Subject Index

Judaizing, accusation by Jerome, 93, 94, 95, 132, 143, 153
Judith, Jerome's reference to, 46, 47, 61, 62
Julian (emperor), attempt to revive Judaism's sacrificial cult, 105, 132–33, 135, 166
Julian of Aeclanum, 67
Jupiter, temple of, 119
Justin Martyr, 3n5, 17, 37, 140, 170
  the church as the "true Israel," 31n4, 141n8

Kamesar, Adam, 26–27, 35, 78, 81
Kedar, Benjamin, 79–80, 87–88
kingdom of heaven, 1, 110n53, 135
Kinzig, Wolfram, 18, 94
Kirjath-Sepher, 114–15

Laeta (daughter-in-law of Paula), 47
Laodecia, Eastern council of (364), 44
Late Judaism, 12
Latin translations, confusion from multiple, 32
Letter of Aristeas, 36, 37n29, 37n33, 38
Levites, mystical number of, 45
Lieu, Judith, 16, 20–21, 25
Limor, Ora, 103
literal and historical senses, Hebrew traditions preservation of, 77
Lucian, 35, 39, 40
Lucinius, Jerome's letter to, 120
Lydda, 77, 112

Maccabees, 105
MacCormack, Sabine, 106
Madaba Map, 108–9
Mamre, Constantinian church, 107
Marcella, Jerome's letters to, 30, 73, 116–20, 130
Markus, Robert, 108
marriage, between Jews and Christians forbidden, 31
Matthew, Jerome on, 66
Matthias, Jerome mention of, 46
Megiddo, 112
Melania the Elder, 129–31, 167

Melchizedek, 116
Melito (bishop of Sardis), 101
Mennonites, 161
Messianic Jews, 154–55
Micah, tomb of the prophet, 114
Micah, commentaries on, 47
Midrash, 16, 73, 80, 81
mild supersessionism, 152–57
Minim, 11, 22, 23, 86
Die Mission und Ausbreitung des Christentums in den Ersten Drei Jahrhunderten (Harnack), 10–11
monastery in Bethlehem, 101, 131
  Jerome's establishment of, 111
monasticism, 1, 4, 66, 73, 87, 95, 108, 111, 115, 130, 131, 139, 146, 165
Moore, James, 161
Moresheth, 114
Mount of Olives, 89, 102, 104–5, 107, 115, 129, 142, 164, 167
  Church of Eleona on, 7
  monastery, 54
Muslim invasion, 166

Nahum, commentaries on, 47
National Jewish Scholars Project, "Dabru Emet," 162
Nazareans, 154
Nazi Germany, 13, 14, 148, 149, 160
New Covenant, 150, 156, 159
New International Version of Bible, revision, 155
new Israel, church as, 7, 54, 138, 150, 152, 162, 165
New Testament texts
  and Christian anti-Judaism, 159
  commentaries on, 47
  sources quoted in, 42, 73–74
Newman, Hillel, 28–29, 78, 93, 95
Nicene Council, 62
Nicopolis (Emmaus), 112
north Africa, churches in, 44
Nostra Aetate ("In Our Times"), 157

Obadiah
  first commentary on, 91
  Jerome's late commentary on, 92

200

Subject Index

Oden, Thomas, 153
Oea, church of, 50, 51
"Old Latin" (*Vetus Latina*), 32, 32n8, 36n25, 44, 50, 67
Old Testament canon
    Jerome's list, 59
    Jerome's views on, 44–45
Old Testament text. *See also* Hebrew Old Testament; Septuagint
    church interpretation of, 146–63
    Jerome's suggestion on Jewish tampering, 85
    justification of translations, 48
    Septuagint vs. Hebrew text, 139
Origen, 3n5, 5, 26, 33, 35, 38, 40, 51, 57, 72, 74, 88, 95, 96, 98, 106
    argument against hopes for rebuilt Jerusalem, 132
    conflict over theology of, 127, 129–30, 131, 136, 164
    construct of supernatural authority, 96
    Hexapla, 33, 40, 71, 143
    Jerome on, 91
    movement to ostracize followers, 54
    response to restoration of the Jews to homeland, 124, 125
    on visits to sacred sites in Palestine, 101
Orthodox Christian communities, and State of Israel, 173
Orthodox church, ecumenical relations with Jews, 151
Ottoman Turkish Empire, defeat in World War I, 166

Palestine, 1, 2, 11, 31, 40, 41, 49, 83, 96, 97, 99, 100, 101, 102, 106, 108, 109, 111, 115, 120, 121, 122, 125, 129, 136, 164, 168. *See also* holy land
    Christian churches first established, 7
    as Christian holy land, 163
    Christian presence in, 165
    Christianizing map, 7
    history of external control over, 166–67
    Jewish claims on, 99
Palladius, 131
Parkes, James, 14, 15, 19
    The Conflict of the Church and the Synagogue, 13, 31n5
parting model, 19, 20
    alternatives, 20–25
    problems with, 23
patrons of Jerome, 2, 30, 43, 47, 72, 73, 74, 85, 101, 110, 111
Paula, 2, 43, 47, 74, 85, 101, 108, 116, 130
    preference for living in Bethlehem, 110–11
    sainthood, 131
    travel with Jerome to Palestine, 111–15
Paulinus, 99, 128, 129, 130
Pearson, Brook R. W., 17
Pella, 11, 23
Perronet, Edward, 149
Persian invasion, 166
Philemon, commentaries on, 47
Philo, 36, 37, 38
philo-Semitism, 14, 72, 82, 92, 94, 153–54
Philostorius, 133
pilgrimage
    background of Jewish, 104
    to holy land, 100, 164
    of Jerome, 100–111
    Jerome's invitations, 116–21
    Jerome's reversal of position on, 127–29
    Jerome's vision with Jerusalem as goal, 136
    as mandatory, 118
    temple-based, 104
Pionus, 102
Porter, Stanley K., 17
premillennialism, 154, 169, 170
promised land, 7, 116, 168
    Jerome on, 134–35
prophet, vs. translator, 39
Protestants, 11, 68, 149, 157, 170, 173
    theologians' inter-faith discussion, 159
Psalter, Septuagint-based vs. Jerome's Gallican, 70

Subject Index

Pseudo-Justin, 38
Ptolemy II Philadelphus (king of Egypt), 37
   hidden christological prophecies from, 41
punitive supersessionism, 2–3

rabbinic Judaism, 8, 11, 21, 23, 25, 27, 37, 39, 50, 77, 78, 79, 81*n*64, 100, 106, 109, 139, 144, 148, 168
rabbis, as teachers, 8. *See also* Jewish teachers
Rausch, David, 154
Rebenich, Stefan, 26
reconciliation, in Jewish-Christian relations, 162
Reed, Annette Yoshiko, 22, 23
Reformed Protestants, and Christian supersessionism, 149–50
Reinhartz, Adele, 24
relics, treasuring of, 108
res et signa (reality and signs), 53
returning to the source, Jerome's mission to, 32
rhetoric vs. reality debate, 18
rhetorical language, Jerome vs. Origen, 96
Rokeah, David, 18
Roman Catholic Church, 67, 158, 168
   authority, vs. Jerome's authority, 52
   "Declaration on the Relation of the Church to Non-Christian Religions," 157
   relations with Israel, 171–72
Rome, 100
   Jerome's association with, 136
   Jerome's letters in, 65
   Jews expelled from Jerusalem by, 124
Rosenberg, Stuart, 162
Ruether, Rosemary, 19–20
Rufinus, 5, 54–58, 60, 74, 89–91, 95, 129, 130, 131, 133, 142, 167

sacred space, 7, 8, 99–100, 103, 105, 123, 124, 165, 172
   Christian relocation of center, 106
   Constantine and memorialization of, 125
   Jerome's progressive redefinition of, 124–65
   Jerome's removal of geographical markers, 128
   rabbinic conception of, 106
sacred text, three-tiered approach to, 44
Saladin, 166
Salvesen, Alison, 88
sarcasm, in Roman society, 93
satire, 93
Schremer, Adiel, 25
Schulz-Flugel, Eva, 53
2 Chronicles, Jerome on corruption, 39–40
Second Temple Judaism, 104, 107, 144
Segal, Alan, 16
Seidman, Naomi, 39
Septuagint, 5–6, 26–27, 141, 143
   4th c. Christian world view of Greek, 36–43
   absence of uniform, 44
   Augustine's questions and, 52
   Augustine's request for, 49
   vs. Hebrew text, for Jerome's translation, 32
   vs. Hebrew truth, 65–66
   Jerome's argument against divine inspiration of, 5, 38–39, 127
   Jerome's contradictory statements against, 5–6
   Jerome's defense of, 59–61
   Jerome's letters to Marcella on, 30
   Jerome's personal rejection, 33
   Jerome's positive statements, 34
   rabbinic tradition, 39
   Rufinus on Jerome's use, 54–55
   source of, 144–45
Septuagint canon
   approval of, 68
   Jerome's opposition to, 68
the Seventy (translators), 34, 41, 141
   divine inspiration, 37–38, 55
   hidden Trinitarian doctrine, 59
Shoah, 139*n*5. *See* Holocaust.
Simon, Marcel, 15
Sivan, Hagith, 109
Six Day War (1967), 166
Society for Biblical Literature, 144*n*14

Subject Index

Socrates, 133
Solomon, 112
    ring, 106
    temple, 105, 122
    tomb, 107
Soulen, R. Kendall, 2, 3, 138, 159*n*74
Sozomen, 133
Spence, Stephen, 19
spiritual meaning, of Jerusalem, 117
Stendahl, Krister, 167*n*97
Stridon, 1
strong supersessionism, 149–51
structural supersessionism, 3
Strugnell, John, 144*n*13
supersessionism. *See* Christian supersessionism
Symmachus, 34, 65, 85
synagogues, 4, 11, 12, 13, 19, 30, 31, 55, 56, 73, 74, 78, 60, 82, 83, 84, 86, 89, 90, 97, 135, 147
    expansion in Roman Empire, 10
    services, 80–81

Talmud, 12, 17, 80, 81
    canonical list, 69
    and mistranslations of Septuagint, 39
Targum Pseudo-Jonathan, 80
Targums, 81
Taylor, Miriam, 18
temple, second built by Herod the Great, 11, 12, 17, 99, 107, 109, 111, 115, 117, 132, 135, 137, 164
    desolation as proof of Christian supersession, 133
    pilgrimage to, 103–05
temple mount, 105, 106, 107, 108, 133
Tertullian, 3*n*5, 38, 94*n*124, 118
    response to restoration of the Jews to homeland, 124
text and canon
    Jerome's arguments over, 48–58
    Jerome's inconsistency regarding, 58–63
textual supersessionism, resolution of Jerome's approach to, 63–68
Theodora, 120–21
Theodoret, 133

Theodosius, Emperor, 31
Theodotion, 34, 40, 50, 58, 65
    Jerome's views on Greek translations, 85
Titus, commentaries on, 47
tomb of Christ, discovery of, 125
tombs of righteous men and women, Jewish tradition of visiting, 107
Torah, 37, 155
    Christianity as universalizing the message of, 162
    and festivals of Passover, Weeks, and Booths, 104
    and promised land, 168
Torjesen, Karen, 92–93, 96
tower of Ader, 122
traditionalist, Jerome as, 92–95
translator, vs. prophet, 39
triumphalism, 4, 12–13, 154

unity of the church, Augustine on, 49–50

Vanhoozer, Kevin, 153
Vessey, Mark, 27, 95
Vetus Latina ("Old Latin"), 32*n*8
Vulgate, 35*n*21, 67, 84, 127*n*125

War of Independence of Israel, 166
Weingarten, Susan, 123
Wiesen, David, 93
Wilken, Robert, 134
Wilkinson, John, 102
Williams, Megan Hale, 27–28, 71–72, 73, 79, 87
Wilson, Stephen, 17–18
World Council of Churches, 160
World Evangelical Alliance, "The Berlin Declaration on the Uniqueness of Christ and Jewish Evangelism in Europe Today," 156
World Jewish Congress, 151
Wyschogrod, Michael, 163

Yoder, John Howard, 161

Zephaniah, commentaries on, 47
Zionism, 155, 167–73

Scripture Index

OLD TESTAMENT

Genesis
12:4	146n23
14:2	163n94
19:14–15	140n6

Exodus
12:40	37n33
23:14–17	104n23
29:25	139n5

Numbers
3:39	45
9:2	80

Deuteronomy
16:16	104n23
27:26	85

Joshua
14:15	127n125

Judges
59

Ruth
59, 137

1–2 Samuel
45

1–2 Kings
45

1–2 Chronicles
33, 45

Ezra
45, 46

Nehemiah
45, 46

Esther
44

Job
33, 49

Psalms
30, 33, 45, 51, 57, 60, 61, 74, 111, 117, 119, 120, 130

27:13	134
71	59
85:9	99n2
87:2	113
95	132n149
132:6	43
132:7	118
132:14	110

Proverbs
18:4	33, 42, 45

Scripture Index

Ecclesiastes — 33, 34
1:14	79n46, 96n132
4:13–16	79n49

Song of Songs — 33

Isaiah — 40, 62, 94n122, 94n124, 125, 140
2:1–4	104n24
3:12	62n142
5:19	86n88
8:14	79n49
11:1	42
11:10	117
13:10	96n132
15:4	86n85
28:20	80
49:7	86n88
50:4–7	86n86
56:6–8	104n24
58:2	80n57
64:4	42
66:13	105n27
66:14	105n27
66:18–24	104n24

Jeremiah — 45, 62, 80, 145
18:18	62n142
19:10	135n167

Ezekiel — 61, 94n124, 107
5:5	109n51; 116n87
10:33	139n4
11:22–23	107n39
34:31	80n57
38:12	109n51

Daniel — 40, 58, 59, 80
2:2	137n177

Hosea
3:4	86n84
11:1	42

Amos
1:11	86n88
4:13	92
5:23	86n83

Obadiah — 91, 92

Jonah — 50
4:6	36n25, 56

Micah — 47
1:10	65n151
2:5	86n85
4:1–4	104n24
4:11–13	132n151
5:2	137n175
5:5–6	99n2
5:7–14	132n151
7:8–13	132n151

Nahum — 47

Habakkuk — 47

Zephaniah — 47
1:15–16	105n26
2:12–15	132n151
3:18	78n40

Haggai — 47

Zechariah — 66, 140
2:8	85n82
2:10	135n165
2:12	99n3
6:9–15	78n39
8:19	78
8:20–23	104n24
12:10	42
14:16–21	104n24

Malachi — 97n135

Scripture Index

NEW TESTAMENT

Matthew 66

2:15	42
2:23	42
23:29	104
24:2	133
27:32–33	106n32
27:33	127n125
27:48	86n87
27:52–53	127n128
27:53	127

Luke

11:47–48	104

John

19:37	42
7:38	42

Acts 17

2	104n23

Romans

11:28–29	175
11:29	14, 158n70
9–11	152–53

1 Corinthians

2:9	42
10:31	ix

Galatians 143

4:26	124n118
6:16	149

Ephesians 47

5:14	126n124

Titus 47

1:14	80n52

Philemon 47

Hebrews

11	134
12:22	124n118

Revelation 83

4:4	45

APOCRYPHA

Tobit 46, 47, 62

Judith 46, 47, 61, 62

Wisdom of Solomon 46, 46n74

1:4	62
12:3	99n3

Ecclesiasticus 46

13:2	62
22:6	62

Baruch

5:5	61

1–2 Esdras 46

Scripture Index

Hymn of the Three Hebrew Children	46, 55
Susanna	46, 55, 85
Bel and the Dragon	46
1 Maccabees	47
2:26–27	46
5:48	99n2
2 Maccabees	46, 47
1:7	99n3

PSEUDEPIGRAPHA

1 Enoch	26:1, 109n51
Jubilees	8:19, 109n51

DEAD SEA SCROLLS   35, 143–44

TALMUD   12, 17, 80, 81

b. Yoma

54a–b	109n51

www.ingramcontent.com/pod-product-compliance
Lightning Source LLC
Chambersburg PA
CBHW070323230426
43663CB00011B/2198